The Blac
Career C

REVISED EDITIO

Beatryce Nivens

The Black Woman's Career Guide

REVISED EDITION

DOUBLEDAY
NEW YORK LONDON TORONTO SYDNEY AUCKLAND

PUBLISHED BY DOUBLEDAY
a division of Bantam Doubleday Dell Publishing Group, Inc.
666 Fifth Avenue, New York, New York 10103

DOUBLEDAY and the portrayal of an anchor with a dolphin
are trademarks of Doubleday, a division of Bantam Doubleday Dell
Publishing Group, Inc.

The Black Woman's Career Guide is published simultaneously in hardcover and
paperback editions.

"A Job Is Not Forever" first appeared in *Essence,* September 1977.
"Allied Health Needs You" first appeared in *Essence,* August 1977.
"Computer Technology: Careers with a Future" first appeared in *Essence,*
February 1982.
"Women in Banking" first appeared in *Essence,* November 1977.
"Home Grown Businesses" first appeared in *Essence,* November 1978.
"Working for Uncle Sam" first appeared in *Essence,* September 1978.
"The Ad World" first appeared in *Élan,* February 1982.

Library of Congress Cataloging-in-Publication Data
Nivens, Beatryce.
    The Black women's career guide.

    Includes bibliographical references and index.
    1. Vocational guidance for women—United States.
2. Afro-American women—Employment. I. Title.
HF5382.5.U5N5 1987   650.1'4'088042   87-1193
ISBN 0-385-24160-7
ISBN 0-385-24161-5 (pbk.)

For my parents,

Surluta Nivens and the late Thomas J. Nivens, who gave me all the opportunities that have enabled me to write this book

Sources and
Acknowledgments

Many hundreds of people from all walks of life took an active interest in this book. Black men and women from all over the country wanted its success. Friends, neighbors, colleagues, and strangers volunteered their time to ensure its completion. To all of them I am deeply appreciative. Special thanks go to the network of people who referred me to the interviewees: Brent Johnson; Birdell and Edyth Jackson; the staff at the National Association of Black Accountants; Estelle Wallach; Doris Wilkinson; Robert MacDonald; Craig Polite; Valjeanne Jones; Carolyn Hughes; Rose Harris; Irene Soloway; Henry Roberts; Gail Dunbar; Patricia Roberts; Ruth Clark; Joyce Johnson; Susan Taylor; La Verne Powlis; Juliette McGinnis. Special thanks go to Barbara DuMetz, who provided most West Coast names.

There are friends who gave encouragement, made phone calls, loaned typewriters, or helped in other ways: Yvonne Brinson; Frank Ennix; Johnnie Jones; Claudette Furlonge; Joyce Dudley; Valerie Register; Mr. and Mrs. Edward Hunter; Gloria Young; Roy Roberts; Jonathon Jones; Julie Cherry. Special thanks go to R. Joyce Whitley and Georgia Perkins, who opened their homes to me and my manuscript; they provided me with a quiet place to write and get away from daily pressures. My sincere thanks to all those who helped. Space does not permit me to mention all of your names, but I thank you deeply. Two special friends have been a tremendous influence on the development of this book. My deepest thanks to Ewart Bertete and Joseph Lyle. My deepest thanks to Joseph for helping me complete the book.

Rarely do we have the opportunity to meet people who will volunteer their time and effort. I am indebted to two workers: Jénee Gaskin and Rosie Rizzo. Jénee believed in the book and became my research assistant. She interviewed women, transcribed tapes, and spent many hours slaving over the book. I thank her for being there. Rosie Rizzo typed a great portion of the first draft. Her professionalism and promptness speeded the book's completion. I thank her for this service.

During the course of completing the book, several typists plodded along with typing. Many of them felt especially proud of the book and performed "above and beyond the call of duty." My gratitude to Vilar Orse, Mary McAllister, Susan Rushmore, and Fay Burrell. Maria Romero and Angela Kinamore were special workers. Special thanks to Josephine Standish, who spent many hard and long hours typing the final draft.

I am truly grateful to my agent, Carol Mann, who encouraged me to write the book, offered suggestions, and made sure it was given a publishing audience. She has been particularly helpful to many struggling Black writers and I thank her for it.

Marie Brown was the acquiring editor for this book. Her expertise and support helped me complete it. After moving to a new position, she still gave her support and comments. I am forever grateful to her for this help. Loretta Barrett took over the project. I thank her for being there and taking an active interest in the book. Her former assistant Paul Aron spent many hours on the book. His perceptions, comments, and care for detail are greatly appreciated.

Many thanks to Janet Byrne, my new editor, who believed that *The Black Woman's Career Guide* should be updated and reissued. I thank her for her wonderful support.

My sincere thanks to Elza Dinwiddie. Her professional support has added to the book's worth. Thank you for being there.

My writing has been shaped and developed by many. My deepest appreciation to John Oliver Killens, the late Donald Graham, Frankie Walker, Hattie Gossett, present and past editors of *Essence*, Henry Glover and Joseph Okpaku.

Without the training of Richard Nelson Bolles, the first part of this book could not have been written. His career-planning insights have helped countless numbers of career writers. I thank him for his aggressive research in this area.

I would also like to thank the many of professional organizations which promptly sent career information. Without this valuable information much of Part Two would have been difficult to write. The Department of Labor's Occupational Outlook Handbook was also a valuable source of information for researching Part Two.

Catalyst Library was extremely helpful in providing career information and a quiet place to do research. I would like to thank Gurley Turner and her staff for their two years of help.

Over two hundred women were interviewed for this book. Space does not allow for the inclusion of some of their interviews, but I sincerely thank all the participants for their time, cooperation, and efforts. Each one contributed to the book, and I am sincerely grateful.

Contents

Introduction

In the five years since publication of the original edition of *The Black Woman's Career Guide*, many things have happened to the Black career woman. We are now slightly more than five million strong in the labor force. Of that number, nearly 50 percent are in white-collar jobs. Although we have had twenty or more years of turmoil and drastic change, we are still better off careerwise than our mothers. We have broken through career barriers, gotten off our knees as household workers (nearly 60 percent of us *were* once domestic workers), and become physicists, corporate executives, engineers, accountants, pilots, public relations executives, computer programmers, and entered a host of other careers.

In this new edition of *The Black Woman's Career Guide*, women who are profiled represent many different professional pioneers. Donna Mendes is one of the few Black vascular surgeons in the country. Norrene Johnson-Duffy and Lilia Abron-Robinson are engineers, and Abron-Robinson is one of the few Black women with a doctorate in the field of engineering. Judith Cummings has scaled the corporate ladder to become a bureau chief at the New York *Times*. Susan Taylor is the editor-in-chief of *Essence,* a major women's magazine. Jessie Maple is the first Black woman to gain entrance into the camera persons' union, and she has also opened a movie theater. Lydia Hammond is one of the few Black women fashion photographers. Paula Chomondcley has become chief financial officer for a large health insurance organization. Rose TenEyck has maneuvered her way up to the top of radio sales. After a banking career, Mary Kate Bush has achieved a coveted directorship of the International Monetary Fund. Sherry Suttles continues to make history as a Black woman in city management. And Joyce Whitley is still one of the best-known Black urban planners.

Yes, in many ways we are better off than even our sisters a generation ago. Nineteen eighty-five statistics show that educationally, our college enrollment is nearly four times that of even our sisters in the 1960s. In the new edition of *The Black Woman's Career Guide*, *fifteen* women have bachelor's degrees, *two* have associate's degrees, *eight* have master's degrees, *three* have M.B.A.s, *two* have J.D.s, *five* have health professional degrees (M.D., D.D.S., D.P.M., O.D.), *one* has an M.S.W., and *one* has an M.S.W. and a Ph.D., and *fourteen* have no college degrees (though a few have done some college work).

Since 1982, many Black women in traditional jobs such as teaching, social work, library science, and counseling have "burned out," or been laid off or frozen out of these fields. I have counseled and spoken to many of these women. Some of them have been successful in moving into the profit sector; others have started their own businesses. Others still feel stuck in not-for-profit jobs.

For many who have moved into the corporate arena, some are now beginning to bump their heads against "the invisible glass ceiling." Of those who have become frustrated in climbing the corporate ladder, some have retreated to the not-for-profit area or opened their own businesses. And I predict that many more Black women will abandon or be forced from corporate America, and will start their own businesses or return to the not-for-profit sector. This, in fact, will be the trend of 1990s.

As we monitor the directions in which Black career women are going, it is interesting to note the various career paths and movements of the women originally profiled in *The Black Woman's Career Guide*. Most have made considerable career moves. When I began writing the update, I was startled at the number who had changed jobs or careers or started their own businesses. Unlike our mothers, who remained for fifteen, twenty, thirty, or forty years at one job, today's Black career woman has the power to change. Discomfort level on the job, job dissatisfaction, salaries, and career immobility are all reasons for job changes.

And although our parents chided us about the perils of job hopping, many of us seek to take risks and move on.

But still, in this era of career change and "reaching for the top," there are many Black women locked into poverty or known as the working poor or the unemployed. Recent unemployment statistics show that Black women have a very high unemployment rate of 14.9 percent. The majority of us are still relegated to "female ghetto" positions with low pay and status.

The U.S. Department of Labor, Women's Bureau reports: "Black women made advances in many socioeconomic areas over the past decade. However, despite their strong and continued labor force experience and their increased years of schooling, Black women still are more likely than white women to be unemployed, to be in low-paying jobs, and to account for a large proportion of those living in poverty."

To further illustrate this, the Women's Bureau also reports that "the growth of Black female headed families has been especially dramatic; nearly 50% of all Black families were headed by Black women. And these women heads of households 'had lower median earnings, lower median ages, lower labor force participation rates and higher unemployment rates than white women.' "

And we are still at the bottom of the economic ladder. Black women working full time earn an average salary of $13,000; white women, $14,677. The average Black family's income is $14,506 as compared to that of whites, which is $25,757, according to the Women's Bureau.

The majority of us are still locked into low-paying and low-status jobs, and it is my hope that the new edition of *The Black Woman's Career Guide* will help meet the career needs of those Black women who want to move ahead. It has been written to help the Black woman career changer move successfully to a new career in more marketable areas. It is also for the recent college graduate seeking employment in this tight job market, the woman who is reentering the job market, and the unemployed Black woman who is looking for a job. The guide emphasizes movement into viable careers of the eighties and nineties.

Part One of the guide is about job hunting methods. It explores traditional and nontraditional job hunting procedures, has career planning exercises, and examines résumé planning and writing and interviewing techniques. The nontraditional job hunting approach is emphasized because of its successful use for job seekers. But in today's competitive job market, the astute job seeker uses a combination of the traditional and the nontraditional job seeking methods.

Part Two explores the following careers: law; social work; health services; psychology; engineering; science; computers; communications; advertising; fashion and beauty; accounting; banking; starting your own business; sales; insurance; real estate; retailing; personnel; federal, state, and local government positions; and nontraditional careers. Each chapter contains general information about the career, educational and training requirements, salaries, and career resources.

Most important, Part Two contains profiles of about sixty Black women. These women cover a wide range of careers and represent a cross section of Black careerists. Each woman could be a neighbor, friend, or colleague. Most of the women are strugglers; some have started at the bottom; some have started as secretaries; others have changed careers or built on existing ones.

All have experienced racism and sexism, but have made career movement despite this double burden. They know that if they were white males, their careers would be further along. They still, however, continue to struggle against the odds. They know that they will probably never be a corporation's chief executive officer, but they hope to build satisfying and profitable careers.

The Black Woman's Career Guide does not want to project these women as proof that Black women have "made it." But we have had too few role models. Traditionally, we have limited our career horizons because role models were not readily available to us. These women are deeply concerned about their communities and the career options that are available to Black women. And it is their hope that the book will stimulate your interest in many careers.

I hope that the guide will provide you with valuable information to make good career selections. Today's tight and competitive job market is limiting, but with the book's help you can possibly beat the odds.

Beatryce Nivens
New York City

The Black Woman's Career Guide

REVISED EDITION

Part One

Steering Your Own Ship

1

Planning Your Career

Many of you are unhappy with your jobs, but it's no wonder. Look at how you "happened" into them. Some of you relied on parents' or a do-gooder's advice. Some of you took the lesser of two evils view: it's this job or a worse one. Still others of you didn't care so long as you gained employment. Many of you still feel work is a "twenty-five to life sentence." You say, "Why worry about something you have no control over?" or "Let's just hope for the best."

Hoping for the best isn't the best approach to finding a job. It says you have little or no control over your life. You are a victim of circumstance. But you do take control over other aspects of your life: taking a vacation, getting married, having a dinner party. All require planning. You wouldn't think of taking a trip to Jamaica without knowing the travel arrangements: transportation mode, accommodations, length of stay, time of departure and return, anticipated activities while there, and cost. You wouldn't get married without plans: location, guests, expenses. You couldn't have a dinner party without knowing the number of guests, time, place, and menu. But you plunge into jobs and careers without giving much thought, direction, or planning to it. It's not surprising that so many workers dislike their jobs.

When you consider that the average woman spends twenty-three years of her life in the work force and a Black woman probably spends more (from age eighteen to sixty-five), shouldn't you begin taking more control over something you'll be doing for about fifty years? Think about the time you spend at work on an hourly, weekly, and yearly basis: 8 hours a day; 40 hours a week; 160 hours per month; 2,000 hours per year (based on 50 weeks a year); almost 100,000 hours per work lifetime (based on working from age eighteen to sixty-five).

Beginning Your Journey Up a Good Career Path

One way to begin planning for a better life's work is to discover what you really want to do, the career that fits your life-style and makes you happier. You'll be more satisfied spending a hundred thousand hours at fulfilling work. But you must plan for it. It takes time, effort, and determination.

Today's competitive job market is another good reason to consider career planning. In the current market, job slots are at a premium and only well-prepared, astute applicants land jobs. You can no longer approach job hunting casually.

Today's job seeker is expected to know herself, her skills, and her five- and ten-year goals, the company where she wants to work, the position she seeks, and the answers to other soul-searching questions. She can no longer just rely on traditional job hunting methods: want ads, private, federal, or state employment agencies, school or college placement offices, civil service examinations, friends, teachers, or relatives. In the current job market, these methods are not as successful as launching your own job hunting campaign, taking control of your destiny, and securing a position based primarily on your own resources.

Let's look at the statistics. In a Department of Labor study of ten million job seekers, traditional job hunting methods were not very effective for Black and other minority job seekers (see Table 1). The study shows the percentage of Black and other minority race people using a particular method who found jobs that way. In all occupations only 14 percent found jobs through local want ads; 15 percent through private employment agencies; 20 percent of seekers found jobs through state employment services; 14 percent through school or college placement offices; 12 percent through teachers; and 13 percent through civil service examinations.

Given these low percentages, let's see why these traditional methods are not effective. First, let's explore the method used by many job hunters: the daily ritual of answering want ads. Take the case of Mary (not her real name), an unemployed college counselor who believed in the "résumé system." Every Sunday, she would look in the newspaper, scan it for counseling positions, prepare cover letters and résumés, and rush them to the post office. After several weeks, she received one or two responses that didn't lead to interviews because the jobs were already taken.

A friend told her that getting the Sunday newspaper on Saturday night was better because employers pick up résumés from mail boxes on Monday. The friend explained that employers usually post jobs in newspapers one week in advance. Then they wait until the ad appears and, if a post office box number is used, they usually go to pick up the applications on Monday. By Tuesday employers are too overwhelmed by the number of responses to go through another hundred or so résumés.

Mary picked up the newspaper on Saturdays and repeated her ritual. The response rate got better, but there were no firm job offers. She became depressed and doubted her credentials.

One day it occurred to her to apply directly to the colleges and universities in the area. She made a list of them, called each director of counseling, uncovered several unposted positions, arranged interviews, successfully passed them, and received two job offers. She found a job after she ceased answering want ads.

There are other problems associated with want ads. Although many are legitimate, some are not. Some employment agencies have staffs which write ads to lure you to their offices. For example, an agency may place an ad stating: "Interesting position with travel agency. Opportunity to travel the world. $329 a week. No experience necessary. Must have good communications skills." The ad doesn't say that this fantastic opportunity does not exist or was filled months ago. Once you go to the employment agency, you are told the job has been filled. Then you are offered a secretarial job paying $170 a week.

TABLE 1

EFFECTIVENESS RATES[1] OF SELECTED
JOB SEEKING METHODS

METHOD	ALL OCCUPATIONS	BLACK AND OTHER MINORITY RACES		
		WHITE-COLLAR	BLUE-COLLAR	SERVICE, EXCEPT PRIVATE HOUSEHOLD
Applied directly to employer	38.1	33.1	40.3	42.2
Asked friends:				
About jobs where they work	23.4	23.1	23.6	24.6
About jobs elsewhere	7.7	11.4	4.6	3.1
Asked relatives:				
About jobs where they work	21.3	15.5	22.2	27.8
About jobs elsewhere	5.1	3.8	6.9	(²)
Answered newspaper ads:				
Local	13.6	15.9	8.4	14.1
Nonlocal	5.9	(²)	(²)	(²)
Private employment agency	15.2	21.3	(²)	(²)
State employment service	20.1	16.9	22.5	21.3
School placement office	13.5	12.1	(²)	(²)
Civil Service test	13.0	16.3	(²)	(²)
Asked teacher or professor	12.4	17.7	(²)	(²)
Union hiring hall	18.9	(²)	(²)	(²)
Contacted local organization	17.6	12.3	11.8	(²)

[1]Percent obtained by dividing number of persons reporting method used to get job by total number of persons who used the method to look for work.
[2]Rate not shown where base is less than 75,000.

Source: U. S. Department of Labor, Bureau of Labor Statistics, *Job Seeking Methods Used By Workers.*

In other cases, employment agencies place ads for nonexistent jobs to collect résumés for further use. It's a great way to get a diverse group of people on file with a wide variety of experience. It's a good rule of thumb to remember that most plum jobs are not advertised through want ads.

Federal or state employment agencies are limited in the types of job opportunities they have. Even if they find a job for you, it's probably one you don't want. Or you may be told of one which requires taking a civil service examination. Then, you must pass the test with a high score and wait your turn in a line of thousands to become employed.

Finding jobs through your school or college placement office means relying on the recruiters who come to your campus. You must have top-notch, marketable skills and be prepared for stiff competition. Some of you may get jobs this way, but many college students, particularly liberal arts majors, can't rely on this method.

Another favorite way of finding a job is relying on your friends, relatives, or teachers. Many of you have found jobs this way, but you probably approached it in a haphazard way. You limited your search by only telling some people. Or you casually mentioned your out of work status, which may not have given people the idea you were seriously seeking employment.

According to the Department of Labor study, the most successful method of job hunting for Blacks and other minority job seekers is applying directly to the employer; that means going straight to the people who can hire you. This can be done in several ways. A popular one is applying to personnel departments, but personnel often does not hear about the best jobs. One of the best job search methods is the nontraditional approach to the job market: isolating the person who can hire you and convincing him or her that you're qualified for the position.

Finding a Job and Plotting a Career by Using the Nontraditional Approach to the Job Market

In today's competitive job market, you will need a combination of job seeking methods including traditional ones. The nontraditional approach[1] offers you more control over job hunting. This approach is not an easy one. It takes time, motivation, and self-discipline, but its results will help put you in a job within a career that you will be happy in. It requires looking deep within yourself to uncover your secret occupational desires, exploring those career desires, talking to people in those careers, isolating an organization which best suits your career aspirations, and locating the person who can hire you.

The nontraditional approach works for students, housewives returning to the job market, career changers, and other job seekers too.

Discovering Your Occupational Desires

Let's begin your journey to a better career by uncovering your secret occupational desires.[2] Everyone has them, but some are afraid to explore them. They feel that their secret occupational desires will take too much time to fulfill; others find their desires silly or unobtainable. Still others feel that the security of their present job isn't worth risking. But indulge yourself. Discover your real occupational desires.

On a sheet of paper, label the top, "The Top Five Jobs I Would Like to Have in the Future." In Table 2, a job seeker we'll call Linda has selected doctor, saleswoman, public relations representative, actress, and business owner. In the future, she would like to explore these fields. What are your choices?

After selecting your top five jobs, choose two that you like best.

TABLE 2

LINDA'S CHOICES
THE TOP FIVE JOBS I WOULD LIKE
TO HAVE IN THE FUTURE

---

1. Doctor
2. Saleswoman
3. Public Relations Representative
4. Actress
5. Business Owner

TABLE 3

LINDA'S PRIORITY CAREERS

---

1. Doctor
2. Saleswoman—Priority Number Two
3. Public Relations Representative—Priority Number One
4. Actress
5. Business Owner

Which one will give you the most enjoyment? Label it "Priority Number One." Choose the next best and label it "Priority Number Two."

In Table 3, Linda best likes public relations representative and has made it "Priority Number One." She has selected saleswoman as "Priority Number Two." What are your priority careers?

Discovering your priority careers is the first step to finding a better job/career. Our initial positive feelings about careers are sometimes the best indicators of those careers that will make us happiest.

Career Exploration

You now have some idea of the careers that will make you happiest. In Part Two of the book, you will learn more about your selected careers. You will learn about the nature of them, educational and training requirements, salaries, and you will read profiles of women who work in the fields. For now, let's explore other ways to learn about your chosen careers.

A source of career information is the Occupational Outlook Handbook (OOH). The OOH is published by the Department of Labor, Bureau of Labor Statistics, and can be used to find career information on careers: the nature of a career; educational and training requirements; employment outlook; earnings. Its price is $23.00 (hardcover); $20.00 (paper) and it is available from The Bureau of Labor Statistics, Publications Sales Center, P.O. Box 2145, Chicago, Ill. 60690.

Another source, professional and trade associations, can provide a wealth of career information. Most career areas have national professional or trade associations that attempt to provide interested people with information on the field.

Career articles can also be helpful. *Essence, Black Enterprise,* and *The Black Collegian* have informative career articles. Career books are excellent sources, too (see Appendix A).

Going to the Source: Talking to People in the Field

Talking to people in your selected career can also be invaluable and one of the best sources of information. Who knows careers better than the people working in them? But how will you talk to people in these fields? Generally, most people are afraid to approach others for advice. You may think people will become offended by your inquiries, but most will welcome them. Even the busiest executive has time to talk about herself and her work.

Gaining access to people is easier than you may think. You must, however, plan your approach carefully. If your objective is to find information and *not a job,* most people will give you fifteen or twenty minutes of their time.

There are several ways to get informational interviews. Think of yourself as a reporter who must write a story on a particular career. First you must do the preliminary research: exploring the career. To make the story well-rounded, you'll want to interview people in the field. You'll need to see several people because you do not want a biased article. One interview can lead you to another until you've uncovered all the necessary facts. In fact, some people who have conducted informational interviews have ended up talking to fifty or more people. Imagine the wealth of career information they now have.

To locate people to interview, start in your own backyard. Do you have friends, teachers, relatives, fellow employees, business acquaintances who are in your field of interest or know of people who are? Size up where you work. If you are interested in accounting, is there an accountant on your job? One woman who is interested in respiratory therapy overlooked the respiratory therapy department in the hospital where she worked. She had a large pool of respiratory therapists right down the hall.

Another source is your church or Black women's organizations that you may belong to. If you are interested in teaching, perhaps the pastor's wife is a teacher and will talk about her field. Or, if you're interested in advertising, maybe one of your club members works in the field. If you don't belong to any organizations, join. (For a list of Black women's organizations, see Appendix B.)

The number of resources is unlimited and you should not be afraid of approaching others for career information. Sharon White had no problems asking a complete stranger for career information. While she was taking a career planning seminar in another city, the seminar's leader requested that each participant approach a person in a field of interest. Sharon, a stranger in town, wanted to talk to someone in advertising sales at a large magazine. She selected a magazine with headquarters in that city and called for an appointment.

She sought the advertising sales manager and made her pitch. She explained that she was only in town for the day, wanted *information* about advertising sales, and would only use fifteen or twenty minutes of the manager's time. The advertising manager was delighted and invited her to the office. There, the manager gave Sharon a wealth of information about the field, showed her how to give a sales presentation, and convinced her to consider the field seriously.

Or take the case of Harriet (not her real name), a city worker who took an eight-week career-planning seminar which was sponsored by her employer. One assignment was to talk to people in her chosen field. In the future, she wanted to open a business, but she had no contacts with business owners. She asked a counselor at the school she attends at night who gave her five names.

Without using the counselor as a reference, she prepared a "rap sheet" of things to say and called two Black women business owners. One invited her to the office; the other, whose busy schedule prevented a personal visit, agreed to a phone interview. Both women gave Harriet a wealth of information and the experience has encouraged her to pursue business ownership.

In an informational interview, you should gather the following information: 1) the skills, educational qualifications, and work experience needed to gain entry-level positions; 2) salary ranges; 3) the way that the interviewee gained entrance; 4) advantages and disadvantages Black women have in gaining access to the field; 5) skills most used in entry-level positions.

Deciding Where You Want to Work

Now you must take your career planning homework one step further: decide where you want to work. To best determine where you want to work, you should look at your work likes and dislikes. What makes you like or dislike your work. For example, if time clocks drive you crazy, working for an organization that uses them will make you unhappy. Or if you are concerned about the welfare of people and your company isn't, you will have conflicting values with your organization, which can cause great unhappiness.

Too many people overlook the fact that they must select organizations, as well as have organizations select them. Too many workers are frustrated because they did not take the time to determine what makes them happy at work. You have the right to select work environments that will make you happy. You have control of selecting one organization over another by looking for certain qualities in each.

Other factors to consider about future work are the city where you want to work, the organization's goals, people that you want to work with (research oriented, extroverted, or quiet people), and the salary and position you want.

Another thing which may be important in considering a prospective organization is how working there will affect your personal life. For example, if you are a mother, or a person who wants more leisure time, you should consider an organization with flexible working hour arrangements, such as four-day or three-day work weeks, or paired or shared job positions.

Today, many companies are concerned with workers' productivity and have instituted flexible work programs for their employees. With these programs, you can build a career without sacrificing having children and/or more leisure time. At the same time, employers have found that flexible work programs motivate employees to do better work because they are happier. Flexible work programs also help employees by taking away rush-hour blues. They can choose their time to come in and to leave.

Employers who have flexible work programs may have several arrangements including four-day or three-day work weeks, or flexible work schedules. With the four-day work week, employees must work forty hours, but in fewer days. This requires that an employee work an additional two hours each of the four days.[3] A few employers, like higher education institutions, allow employees to work thirty-two hours in a four-day work week. With the three-day work week, employees are allowed to work twelve hours each day.[4]

In the flexible work schedule, employees must work eight hours but can choose hours within a specified time frame. For example, an employee can come in between 7 A.M. and 1 P.M., put in eight hours, and leave between 3 P.M. and 9 P.M. With this system, early risers can come to work and leave early. Late risers can come and leave late. Arrangements can also be made to credit those who work more hours by allowing them to take off that number of hours in the future.[5] Or if an employee works less than eight hours, she won't be penalized but can make up the additional time at a later date.

Job pairing allows you and another person to split work hours in one full-time job with both of you having responsibility for the completion of the work.[6] For example, two college counselors can job pair a counseling job, a forty-hour-a-week job. Each one works twenty hours. If one is out, the other takes over. In this system, the employer gets two part-timers doing the work of one full-timer. The employees get to have more time to take for other aspects of their lives.

Job sharing allows two employees to work half-time, "but each is responsible for their designated half of the work."[7] In this situation, employees usually get more work done because they are there for a shorter time and must complete work within that time frame.

After giving some thought to the qualities you want in the organization where you will work, start locating the organizations that best qualify. Some of you may decide to work in the most prestigious organization in the field. Others may look for a company with the best training and advancement opportunities. Still others may prefer an organization in their hometowns. But regardless of your reasons, you should learn as much about your prospective employer as possible.

If you are interested in working for private industry, you can find information about your prospective company by looking in directories like *Dun and Bradstreet's Reference Book,* or by reading magazine articles in *Fortune, Business Week, The Wall Street Journal,* and the New York *Times.*

Annual reports and recruiting brochures are also good sources of information about companies. Annual reports usually outline the financial and overall performance of the company, including new developments, services, and systems. Recruitment brochures generally describe the type of employees companies want. Annual reports and recruiting brochures are available by contacting personnel and public relations departments.

Finding the Woman or Man Who Can Give You the Job

Once you've selected the organization, you must find out who can hire you: manager, supervisor, director, department chairperson, or agency head. To help locate corporate presidents, directors, and vice-presidents, use the *Dun and Bradstreet's Book of Corporate Managements*. To find presidents or directors in other organizations, look in annual reports, brochures, catalogues, or call the companies and ask for their names.

If possible, bypass personnel departments and go directly to the person in charge. Since personnel will have to get approval from the person who will hire, bypassing them will eliminate the middle person. Armed with information about yourself, the career area and position you want, the organization and its needs, future trends, and financial solvency, you are ready to call, write to, or meet the person who can hire you.

Dazzling the Person Who Can Hire You with Your Skills

Employers want to know that you can do the job; they want to know that you have the right skills. Skills are simply tasks that we do well. They can be God-given talents, like the ability to sing, or things you've learned, such as operating machines, typing, writing, or communicating.

There are several ways to uncover skills. One way is to size up the tasks that you have performed on your job. Table 4 lists job-related skills. Check off the skills that you have acquired at your present or last

TABLE 4

LIST OF SELECTED JOB-RELATED SKILLS

—administering	—dispensing	—locating	—questioning
—advising	—distributing	—making	—record keeping
—analyzing	—dramatizing	layouts	—recruiting
—appraising	—editing	—managing	—rehabilitating
—arranging	—entertaining	—mediating	—remembering
—assembling	—estimating	—monitoring	—repairing
—auditing	—evaluating	—motivating	—reporting
—budgeting	—examining	—negotiating	—representing
—calculating	—exhibiting	—observing	—reviewing
—classifying	—explaining	—obtaining	—screening
—coaching	—finding	information	—selling
—collecting	—fund raising	—operating	—serving
—compiling	—group	—organizing	—sketching
—conceptualizing	facilitating	—persuading	—speaking
—confronting	—handling	—planning	—summarizing
—constructing	complaints	—preparing	—supervising
—controlling	—handling	—printing	—talking
—coordinating	detail work	—prioritizing	—teaching
—corresponding	—imagining	—problem	—training
—counseling	—initiating	solving	—translating
—creating	—inspecting	—processing	—trouble-
—dealing with	—interpreting	information	shooting
pressure	—interviewing	—programming	—updating
—deciding	—investigating	—promoting	—writing
—delegating	—judging	—proposal	
—designing	—listening	writing	

job. Go back and check off the skills that you have mastered at other jobs.

Look at the skills that you have checked off. Think again. Do you have more? Go back to the list and think about your job duties. What other things do you do on the job? Think about the accomplishments you have made at work. For example, did you develop an office management system which saved workers 25 percent in time? Did you write a proposal for your school district that netted $250,000 in federal funds? Did you revise forms that saved time for your colleagues and the accounting department? Think back and determine things you did to improve the well-being of others, yourself, and the organization. Check off the skills learned in those activities.

Another way to uncover skills is to think about your different roles: mother; wife; volunteer worker; community organizer; student. Do not look narrowly at these roles. Think of what you have accomplished in them. For example, many women serve in responsible positions like treasurer, president, or fund raiser in civic or community groups but do not think they've gained marketable skills. Many feel skills gained in these extracurricular activities are worthless because they were not paid. Think about the woman who raised $35,000 for a local women's group. These marketable skills can be transferred to a paid position.

If you are having trouble uncovering your skills, use the Dictionary of Occupational Titles (DOT), another book published by the Department of Labor, Bureau of Labor Statistics, which is available in many libraries (ask your librarian). DOT lists the skills used in many jobs. Locate your job and write down the skills.

To dazzle an employer with your skills, you must determine the skills he or she is looking for. To help convince the employer that you have these skills, you must write an effective résumé.

Writing an Effective Résumé

Before meeting the top person, you should have an essential job hunting tool: the résumé. The résumé is an important document and can be used to sell you in the best possible light.

Some of you may be unnerved at the thought of writing résumés. But when you have a thorough knowledge of how to write them, your fears should be allayed. First, a résumé is not an autobiography. It is a brief summary of your educational and work history and skills. Along with a well-written cover letter, it is the forerunner, your entry into an employer's office for an interview.

Writing an effective résumé requires planning. Do not approach your résumé in a haphazard way. Neat and well-organized résumés convey that you have good work habits. Poorly prepared and sloppy ones convey sloppy work habits. Overdetailed, long, and difficult to read résumés are hardships for employers and may end up in the file-for-future-reference box or wastebasket.

Résumé planning requires looking at yourself again. This time, you will look at yourself in specific terms regarding your educational background and work history (see Table 5).

Résumés should be tailored for each job and you can have as many as ten different types. Résumé tailoring means showing your prospective employer that you can do the particular job that he or she is hiring for. To tailor your résumé, you should know something about the qualifications for the job. For example, if you want a public relations position and know that public relations specialists carry out planning, writing, editing, and research duties, you must gear your résumé to reflect your skills in these areas.

To find the skills that are used in various jobs, turn again to the Dictionary of Occupational Titles (DOT). For example, DOT lists the following skills for a public relations representative:

Plans and conducts public relations program designed to create and maintain favorable public image for employer or client. Plans and directs development and communication of information designed to keep public informed of employer's programs, accomplishments, or point of view. Arranges for public relations efforts in order to meet needs, objectives, and policies of individual, special interest group, business concern, nonprofit organization, or governmental agency, serving as in-house staff member or as outside consultant. Prepares and distributes fact sheets, news releases, photographs, scripts, motion pictures, or tape recordings to media representatives and other persons who may be interested in learning about or publicizing employer's activities or message. Purchases advertising space and time as required. Arranges for and conducts public-contact programs designed to meet employer's objectives, utilizing knowledge of changing attitudes and opinions of consumers, clients, employees, or other interest groups. Promotes goodwill through such publicity efforts as speeches, exhibits, films, tours, and question/answer sessions. Represents employer during community projects and at public, social, and business gatherings. May specialize in researching data, creating ideas, writing copy, laying out artwork, contacting media

TABLE 5

RÉSUMÉ CHRONOLOGY

EDUCATION

1. What high school did you attend (name and address)? Dates of attendance?
2. What were your best subjects in high school?
3. Which subjects didn't you like in high school?
4. Did you win any awards, scholarships, or honors in high school?
5. What extracurricular activities were you involved in during high school?
6. What were your top three achievements in high school?
7. What community or civic activities were you involved in during high school?
8. Is there anything special about your high school years?
9. What vocational or trade school did you attend (name and address)? Dates of attendance?
10. What subjects did you take in vocational or trade school? Which did you like best? Which did you like least?
11. What certificate or diploma did you receive in vocational or trade school?
12. What was your date of graduation?
13. What college did you attend (name and address)? Dates of attendance? Degree?
14. What was your major/minor?
15. Look at your transcript. Are there any subject areas in which you have 20 or more credits that can be used as a minor or to show proficiency in the area?
16. What were your college extracurricular activities?
17. What were your top three achievements in college?
18. Is there anything special about your college years that you would like to note?
19. What graduate school did you attend (name and address)? Dates of attendance? Degree?
20. Did you receive any special training?

MAJOR WORK EXPERIENCE

1. List all your employers (names, addresses, type of organizations, dates of employment, titles).
2. List all summer jobs, unpaid or volunteer work, internships, and part-time work.
3. Next to each position, list job duties and skills.
4. Think of five things that you did beyond each job description.
5. Think of three things that you did on each job which makes you proud.
6. What were the results of the tasks you did on the job? What happened as a result?
7. What are your strengths on the job? Your weaknesses?
8. What other jobs or careers will your skills transfer to?

PROFESSIONAL ASSOCIATIONS, GROUPS, CLUBS

1. List the associations, groups, and clubs to which you belong.
2. Are any of them relevant to the job you are seeking?

representatives, or representing employer directly before general pub-
lic. May specialize in one type of public-relations effort, such as
fund-raising campaigns or political issues. May specialize in dissemi-
nating facts and information about organization's activities or gov-
ernment agency's programs to the general public and be also known
as PUBLIC INFORMATION OFFICER.

You can also find required job skills in some of the career material
that is published by professional and trade associations. For example,
the Public Relations Society of America (PRSA) publishes *Careers in
Public Relations,* a booklet that lists skills required for public relations
work. Table 6 shows the skills that are listed.

On a piece of paper, list the skills needed in your career. Now look
again at your list of job-related skills (go back to Table 4). Locate your
transferable skills and cross match them with the skills required for
your career as shown in Table 6.

Be sure to relate your job-related skills to a job function. Do not write
down "planning," but "planned a new curriculum campaign." For example, let's say you are a teacher who would like to go into public
relations. Maybe you planned a new curriculum campaign for your
school district. In order to execute the project, you did extensive planning: You analyzed problems and opportunities; defined goals; recommended and planned activities; budgeted; assigned responsibilities to
others; personally gathered information from administrators and colleagues and from external sources and so forth. Although no one told
you public relations work was involved, you used many of the skills
public relations workers employ to launch campaigns. Can you use
these skills in the area of public relations? Perhaps you have more
public relations experience than you imagined. Now you are ready to
tailor your résumé to your selected career.

In tailoring your résumé, be imaginative. Develop a résumé that will
immediately show employers your worth to their organizations. Design
a résumé that says you're "tailor-made" for the job.

Your résumé also should be results oriented. It is not enough to say
"was responsible for sales territory in Northeast." What were the results? What was your sales volume? Was it an increase over that of
previous salespeople? Did you win a commendation for it? Think of the
results achieved by the work you did. Did you make suggestions that
increased office efficiency? Did your proposal bring $200,000 into the

TABLE 6

PUBLIC RELATIONS SPECIALIST*

SKILLS NEEDED FOR PUBLIC RELATIONS WORK	MATCHING SKILLS I HAVE
1. Analyzing problems and opportunities.	1.
2. Defining goals.	2.
3. Recommending and planning activities.	3.
4. Budgeting.	4.
5. Assigning responsibilities to others including non-public relations personnel.	5.
6. Ability to personally gather information from management, colleagues in organization, and external sources.	6.
7. Ability to continually evaluate what has been learned.	7.
8. Formulating recommendations and gaining approval for them from their managements.	8.
9. Ability to work with and sometimes through other functions, including personnel, legal, and marketing staffs.	9.
10. Ability to be persuasive with others.	10.
11. Ability to represent organization.	11.
12. Ability to write with a sound, clear style to pro-	12.

SKILLS NEEDED FOR PUBLIC
RELATIONS WORK   MATCHING SKILLS I HAVE

duce reports, news re-
leases, booklets, speeches,
film scripts, trade maga-
zine articles, product information and technical material, employee publications,
newsletters, shareholder
reports.

13. Ability to set up channels   13.
of dissemination of mate-
rial to appropriate newspaper, broadcast, general and
trade publication editors.
Ability to enlist their interest in publishing an organization's news and features.

14. Knowledge of how news-   14.
papers and other media op-
erate, the areas of specialization of publications, and
interests of individual editors.

15. Ability to grab attention of   15.
editors and broadcasters in
spite of competition.

16. Ability to develop mutual   16.
respect and cooperation
with the press.

17. Background knowledge of   17.
the techniques of prepara-
tion of brochures, special
reports, films, and multi-
media programs.

18. Ability to plan and coordi-   18.
nate special events like
news conferences, conven-
tion conferences, conven-

tion exhibits, special show-
ings, new facility and
anniversary celebrations,
contest and reward pro-
grams, tours, and special
meetings. Ability to pay attention to detail, prepare
special booklets, publicity,
and reports for special
events.

19. Ability to prepare speeches   19.
    for others and deliver
    speeches. Ability to effec-
    tively address individuals
    and groups.

20. Ability to gather facts   20.
    through interviews, review
    of library materials, infor-
    mal conversations, survey
    techniques.

21. Ability to study results af-   21.
    ter program is completed
    and evaluate its implemen-
    tation and effectiveness.

* Source: *Careers in Public Relations,* Public Relations Society of America (an adaptation).

school district? Did your company institute a training program as a result of your ideas? Be generous by putting your best foot forward and "blowing your own horn" in your résumé.

There are three types of résumés: chronological, functional, and combination. One of the most familiar is the chronological, which lists your educational and work history in reverse chronological order starting with your present or last position or educational institution. Most employers know and like this type of résumé. If your work history has been consistent and you want to stay in the same field, it is probably the best to use. Even career changers can effectively use it if you have marketable skills which indicate you can handle the job. For example, a manager in one career can usually transfer her management skills to another (see Table 7). (The names in the résumés have been changed.)

The functional résumé is used best when there are gaps in your work history or for the career changer. It can be tailored to particular jobs and you can highlight appropriate skill areas. Refer to the case of the teacher wanting a public relations job. With a functional résumé, she can emphasize the appropriate categories of skills (planning, writing, editing, and research), and play down her teaching background. However, many employers will not settle for your list of skills categories along with your educational background. They may want more. To avoid any problems when using the functional résumé, you can adapt it by including places of employment (see Table 8). Or you can use the combination résumé, which combines areas of skills as well as employment dates and places (see Table 9).

Most people have trouble assessing which résumé to use and then how to properly write it. Let's look at a few examples of before and after résumés. In the first example, Jean Brown wants a trainer's job in personnel (see Table 10). She has been a teacher in several adult education programs. In the fall after graduation from college, she worked as a clerk-typist and, between teaching and working for the state, she worked as a secretary for a bank. In the "before" résumé, Jean has mistakenly included all her jobs. She should only emphasize jobs which are most relevant to the one she wants. Secondly, she has mistakenly listed her positions in the wrong order. Present or last jobs come first in chronological résumés.

Now let's analyze the best method for Jean to use in getting a personnel position. In her present job, she is a field coordinator and training specialist with the Arizona State Department of Civil Service. In the

TABLE 7

THE CHRONOLOGICAL RÉSUMÉ

Linda Jones
345 West 18th Street
New York, New York 10016

BUSINESS EXPERIENCE:

1978–Present

Aberbrooks, Hill and Jourdaine
New York, New York

Senior Buyer
Head of junior sportswear department. Supervisor of staff of 40. Increased department sales volume from 6 million to 8½ million dollars by devising "Creative Marketing Model," which is used by all branch stores.

1970–1978

Lyles Hollywood Department Store
Detroit, Michigan

Buyer
Responsible for buying and selling of junior sportswear, a $400,000 volume department.

Instituted new buyer's reporting system, which improved overall accountability procedures.

Created "disco" environment (jukebox music, sales staff in disco attire, and strobe lighting effects) and changed department's name to "This Generation," put in soda fountain; this increased sales by 50%.

Was promoted from Assistant Buyer in six months after recommending, designing and establishing new store policy on customer relations.

EDUCATION:

1968–1970   Wilson Institute of Technology
                               Detroit, Michigan

                               Received A.A. degree in fashion merchandis-
                               ing. Was on the Dean's List for four semes-
                               ters. Received "The Helen Lewis Walker
                               Award For Most Promising Senior." Was
                               President of Future Retailers of America.

TABLE 8

THE FUNCTIONAL RÉSUMÉ (An adaptation)

Karen MaGee
80 Locust Lane
Valley Stream, New York 11574
(516) 555-0377

MAJOR WORK EXPERIENCE: WRITING/JOURNALISM

Author of two best-selling children's books, *The Swan* (sold 20,000 copies) and *Come Little Children* (sold 50,000 copies), with a total revenue of $280,000. Have written over 25 articles as contributing editor to *Seventeen, Cosmopolitan, Black Enterprise, Ms.,* and *Ebony.*

Was stringer for *Newsday.* Developed "What's Happening in Long Island" column, which received average of 100 letters per week. Assisted Fashion Editor of *Newsday* in marketing project.

Have published over 50 poems in 35 literary magazines. Won the Cameron Award for Distinguished Poetry.

BROADCAST WRITING

Writer for news program on WJNH, Cable TV. Helped gather and write the news. Established new format for reporting the news, which increased listening audience by 40%.

PUBLIC RELATIONS

Writing consultant for L. J. Lee Public Relations Firm. Prepared proposals, press releases and press conferences for clients. Awarded "Public Relations Society

Award" for placing news items with over 200 newspapers and UPI.

RESEARCH

Was writer for research project. Worked closely with marketing specialist in gathering and interpreting statistics. Marketing and research analysis resulted in $600,000 grant.

EDUCATION: University of Maryland, B.A., 1974. New York University, M.A., Journalism, 1976.

TABLE 9

THE COMBINATION RÉSUMÉ

Mary Carter
800 West End Avenue #8
New York, New York 10024
(212) 555-6576 Home
(212) 555-3331 Office

TRAINING: Hired and trained paraprofessionals. Developed training program and manual now used as a model for training more than 600,000 paraprofessionals. Have designed training materials for more than 800 individuals under my charge.

MANAGEMENT AND SUPERVISION: Responsible for planning and directing program for several areas. Instituted new policy, which increased retention and performance rate for more than 3,000 individuals on national examinations. Immediate supervisor for 160 individuals.

RESEARCH: Devised computer software program for entire system to measure accountability and analyze work flow, which helped bring additional $1 million to organization.

1983–Present Avery Fisher High School—
Training specialist for district. Administrator of paraprofessional program.

1980–1983 Hampton Peters Educational Institute—
Trainer/teacher for more than 1,200 individuals. Increased productivity for these individuals by 40%, based on city-wide and national test results.

EDUCATION: B.A., Brooklyn College, 1979.
On Dean's List for eight semesters. President of the Student Government Association.

M.A.T., Smith College, 1980.
Awarded the Mary Katherine Holmes Fellowship ($6,000). Sent to London School of Economics on exchange for 3 months and awarded Certificate.

TABLE 10

"BEFORE"

Jean Brown
84 Main Street
Phoenix, Arizona
Home: (602) 555-1140
Bus.: (602) 555-1136

EDUCATION: University of Arizona, Tucson, Arizona, B.B.A., 1973

WORK
EXPERIENCE:

Sept. 1973–Nov. 1973 *Clanden's Boutique,* Phoenix, Arizona.

Clerk-Typist—Handles typing and clerical duties for boutique's owner.

Dec. 1973–Aug. 1975 *City of Phoenix Municipal Department,* Phoenix, Arizona.

Teacher— Teaches Adult Education in G.E.D. Program to municipal employees.

Aug. 1975–Jan. 1976 *Board of Education, Adult Training Program,* Phoenix, Arizona.

Teacher— Teaches Adult Education courses.

Feb. 1976–June 1977 *Carter National Bank,* Phoenix, Arizona.

Secretary— Handles secretarial duties for loan officers.

July 1977–Present *Arizona State Department of Civil Service,* Phoenix, Arizona.

Field Coordinator— Coordinates special education programs.

"before" résumé (see Table 10), this position is hidden at the end. In her "after" résumé, Jean selects the combination résumé, which emphasizes her personnel skills and also lists places of employment and dates (see Table 11). She decides to take out the clerk-typist position at Clanden's Boutique because it has little relevance to her occupational objective and was only a stepping stone to a professional job.

In the "after" résumé, Jean listed skills needed for personnel: training and administration. Since she has training experience at her present job, she emphasized skills learned there. Where she listed places of employment and dates, she changed "teacher" to "training specialist" because she realized training was her primary duty in these positions. As a result of her present job, she joined the International Association of Personnel Women and the American Society for Training and Development, but she left this important information out of her "before" résumé.

Next, let's look at Renée Brown, who wants to become a journalist. In her "before" résumé, she mistakenly put her educational background first. (See Table 12.) In some cases, this is understandable, but in Renée's it's not. Let's examine her résumé more closely. She has three work experiences which are applicable to journalism: intern, American Society of Magazine Editors; reporting apprentice, Trans-Urban News Service; research assistant for author Rhonda Smith *(Careers of the 80's)*. However, by the time an employer reads through her extracurricular activities, he or she may get tired of reading and overlook these important items.

To put her most marketable skills and work history in the best light in the "after" résumé, she puts her journalism experience first. Afterwards, she groups "other work experience" together and puts "education" last (see Table 13).

Mary Lee has no full-time paid work experience but has gained valuable skills working for her uncle's construction company. She wants a sales position, but she had trouble in preparing a résumé. To help her write one, a counselor had her determine the skills needed for sales and uncover her related experience. The counselor suggested the functional résumé because Mary does not have a steady work history.

Mary then isolated "market research," "administration and management," and "sales" as areas of expertise. She had previously overlooked her "sales experience" in real estate and for a distributor company because they were part-time positions. Yet the counselor pointed out

TABLE 11

"AFTER"

Jean Brown
84 Main Street
Phoenix, Arizona
Home: (602) 555-1140
Bus.: (602) 555-1136

**WORK
EXPERIENCE**

Training: Assist in the design and implementation of academic and skills components of training. Coordinate activities of Saturation Approach to Learning Academic Skills Program. Make performance appraisals to establish participants' readiness for employment. Conduct workshop sessions on résumé writing, job interviewing techniques, and job-hunting strategies.

Design criteria for validation of SAL effectiveness. Designed training manual used as a model for training participants. Initiated workshop session with regional office to develop a more effective approach to the utilization of SAL.

Administration: Interview, screen, and select applicants. Make analysis of diagnostic qualifying test, and make recommendations for appropriate programs for participants.

Participated in the selection of trainers by interviewing and recommending candidates for hire. Also, trained and supervised new trainers.

Participated in efforts to establish academic credit for training. Program granted six college credits by the State of Arizona.

**EMPLOYMENT
HISTORY**

1977–Present *Arizona State Department of Civil Service,* Phoenix, Arizona.

Training Specialist.

1976–1977	*Carter National Bank,* Phoenix, Arizona.
	Administrative Assistant.
1975–1976	*Board of Education Adult Training Program,* Phoenix, Arizona.
	Training Specialist.
1973–1975	*City of Phoenix Municipal Department,* Phoenix, Arizona.
	Training Specialist.
EDUCATION	University of Arizona, B.B.A., Business Education, 1973.
AFFILIATIONS	International Association of Personnel Women; American Society for Training and Development.
REFERENCES	Furnished Upon Request.

TABLE 12

"BEFORE"

Renée Brown
346 Lyndenhurst Blvd.
Newark, New Jersey
(201) 555-2420

EDUCATION:

A.B., Mount Holyoke College,
South Hadley, Massachusetts,
1983. Major: English.

College Extracurricular Activities:
—Education and Cultural
  Committee Chairperson
—Afro-American Association
—Director of Third World
  Programs, WMHC
—Disc Jockey, WMHC
—Student Advisor
—Diana Ramos Dance Workshop
—English Club, member
—Debating Club, member
—Promotional Assistant—Sweet
  Earth Records
—Intern, American Society of
  Magazine Editors *(Working
  Woman Magazine, Sales &
  Marketing Management*
  magazine)

WORK EXPERIENCE:

Aug. 1985–Present

Membership Director, Girl
Scout Council of New York,
New York, New York.
Developed and organized
promotional and recruitment
campaign for an assigned
geographical area. Supervised
volunteer staff.

Jan. 1985–June 1985   *Tutor and Career Orientation*
                                   Coordinator, The College of
                                   Staten Island, Staten Island,
                                   New York.
                                   Tutored high school students in
                                   academic advisory program.
                                   Coordinated career development
                                   program.

OTHER WORK EXPERIENCE:

June 1985–Nov. 1985   *Reporting Apprentice,* Trans-
                                   Urban News Service, Brooklyn,
                                   New York.
                                   Wrote and published articles
                                   based on basic reporting, beat
                                   reporting, research and investi-
                                   gative reporting. Did layout and
                                   editing for in-house publication
                                   Metro News-Review.

Sept.1986–Present   *Research Assistant,* Rhonda Smith,
                                   author of *Careers of the 80's,* New
                                   York, New York.
                                   Responsible for interviewing women
                                   in traditional and non-traditional
                                   careers. Also edited interview drafts.

PROFESSIONAL
ORGANIZATIONS: National Council of Negro Women.

TABLE 13

"AFTER"

Renée Brown
346 Lyndenhurst Blvd.
Newark, New Jersey
(201) 555-2420

MAJOR WORK EXPERIENCE: WRITING, EDITING, REPORTING

June 1985–Nov. 1985

Reporting Apprentice—
Worked as a reporting apprentice for Trans-Urban News Service. Wrote and published articles based on basic reporting, beat reporting, research and investigative reporting. Did layout and editing for in-house publication *Metro News-Review.*

Sept. 1984–Apr. 1985

Research Assistant—
Worked for author Rhonda Smith on new book *Careers of the 80's* (Windom Books). Interviewed 50 women in traditional and non-traditional careers. Also transcribed and edited interview drafts.

Summer 1984

Intern—
Was intern in the American Society of Magazine Editors program. Worked on staff of *Working Woman Magazine.* Researched information for two major columns (September and October issues). Also represented publication at several press conferences.
Also worked as intern for *Sales & Marketing Management* magazine. Researched, wrote and published three major articles in the September issue of the publication.

OTHER WORK EXPERIENCE:

Aug. 1985–Present

Membership Director—
Developed and organized promotional and
recruitment campaign for Girl Scout Council of New York. Also supervised staff.

Jan. 1985–June 1985

*Tutor and Career Orientation
    Coordinator*—
Tutored high school students in academic
advisory program at The College of Staten
Island. Also coordinated career development program.

Jan. 1985

Intern—
Researched programs in consumer affairs
for WNET-TV's *Help Yourself.*

Oct. 1981–Oct. 1982

Promotional Assistant—
Promoted album, wrote press releases, ar-
ranged concert and lecture series for Sweet
Earth Records.

EDUCATION:

A.B., Mount Holyoke College, 1985.
Major: English.
Academic Honors—
1st Prize, City University of New York
First Annual Spring Poetry Contest
(1984); Richmond Masonic Scholarship
Award (1985); Journalism Award (1985);
English Honors in Poetry (1985).
Extracurricular Activities—
Education and Cultural Committee
Chairperson; Afro-American Association;
Director of Third World Programs,
WMHC; Disc Jockey, WMHC; Student
Advisor; Diana Ramos Dance Workshop;
English Club; Debating Club.

PROFESSIONAL
ORGANIZATIONS:

National Council of Negro Women.

REFERENCES:

Furnished upon request.

that she had built up impressive sales records with both companies. Before counseling, Mary thought she had little or no sales experience, but she discovered she has a substantial amount (see Table 14).

Regardless of the type of résumé you choose, it should be neat, attractive, and no longer than one or two pages. A résumé's wording should be succinct, crisp, and have impact. It shouldn't read: "I looked up material and organized it," but *"Researched, compiled, and organized data."* Or, "I decided policy for the staff," should be changed to *"Designed, implemented, and evaluated staff policy."* Use action words where possible and leave out the word "I." You should also be careful to put positions other than your present one in the past tense. For example, if three years ago you worked as a teacher, do not put "Teach emotionally disturbed children," but "Taught emotionally disturbed children."

You should leave out extraneous information such as health, birth date, weight, marital status, number and ages of children, hobbies, and references. These items will make your résumé lengthy and could open up illegal questions that employers may ask, like "I see you're fifty-four years old. Do you really think you should be changing careers at this age?"

Your résumé should be professionally typed. After you have it typed, you can take it to a printer to have a hundred or more copies offset. You should request that white or ivory bond or linen weave paper be used.

If you are contacting your prospective employer by mail, a cover letter should accompany your résumé. The letter should give the position you desire, your qualifications, and ways you feel you can be of benefit to the company. It should always be addressed to a specific person and each letter should be individually typed by a professional.

A cover letter should have impact and be able to grab the employer's attention. (See Table 15.) You should remember that employers receive many résumés and cover letters each week and yours should make a lasting impression. It should be professional and thought provoking. For example, if you have read about a new program or are aware of a pressing problem of a prospective employer, point out how you can help in the cover letter. This will not only be impressive but will probably get you an immediate interview.

TABLE 14

Mary Lee
490 Broad Street
Chicago, Illinois
(312) 533-8001 (Business)
(312) 689-0340 (Home)

MAJOR WORK EXPERIENCE

1972–Present

Market Research—
Established market identification procedures resulting in increased sales of 35% as Assistant to President of Ramstead Construction Company. Implemented a research program utilizing technical resources to complete a census of Cook and surrounding counties, which served as a source of market identification for the sales department. Assisted in developing sales forecasting methods, which proved 99% correct eight months in advance. Assisted in the preparation of proposals for demonstration contract from Housing and Urban Development (HUD), resulting in approximately $200,000 worth of construction contracts.

ADMINISTRATION AND MANAGEMENT

Managed Ramstead's office with staff of 50 people. Established uniform policy for employees, resulting in increased employee morale and efficiency and decrease in employee turnover.

SALES

Took and passed state real estate examination and am licensed agent. Worked for a year selling real estate at Ulbright Realtors. First year, sales amounted to $370,000 in real estate.

Was distributor for Lee Products. In first month, sales volume was $2,000 of the moderately priced products. Awarded "Royal Saleswoman of the Year" (1975), and awarded 4 Sales Gold Certificates for best recruiting record.

EDUCATION   Morgan State University
                               B.A. in History, 1972

TABLE 15

SAMPLE COVER LETTER

1933 Game Street
Los Angeles, California
September 8, 1987

Ms. Linda Gooding
Director of Personnel
Lindenhouse Company
840 West Street
Los Angeles, California

Dear Ms. Gooding:

While reading the latest issue of *Women In Personnel,* I came across an article "Women Being Moved into Industrial Counseling at Lindenhouse Company." I immediately became interested in your company's new and vital work and thought my background might be of help in launching your new program.

I have worked for eighteen years as a rehabilitation counselor at various state agencies. Last year, I developed and implemented an industrial counseling program for Morris Aircraft in conjunction with the state's alcohol and drug abuse program. This successful program had over 100 participants who were treated and counseled, and, as a result, Morris reports work productivity is at an all-time high.

I have a master's degree in rehabilitation counseling and have completed requirements for the professional certificate in the field. I have also taken and passed the Civil Service Examination for Rehabilitation Vocational counselors.

I would like to explore career possibilities with you. In a few days, I will contact your secretary to arrange a time when we can meet.

Sincerely,
Marilyn Douglass

Interviews*

If your résumé and cover letter can grab your prospective employer's interest and get you an interview, you must prepare for it. Your objective in interviewing should be to get the job. By now, you should know yourself, your goals, the position you want, and something about the company, and the interview should be easier to tackle than if you were unprepared.

You should practice for the interview by getting the help of a friend. You and she should go over possible interview questions. A list of most frequently asked interview questions, which was published by Northwestern University, should be helpful (see Table 16). You can also practice interviewing by meeting with interviewers from companies where you're not considering employment. By interviewing with them, you can assess your strengths and weaknesses in an interview situation.

Before the interview, you should again review information about the company and remember key points. It will help to know the company's image and dress code. For example, if you are interviewing with a bank, would you wear blue jeans? Or if you are interviewing with an informal college department, would you wear a conservative three-piece suit?

Your interview may be a structured, rambling, group, or consecutive one. In the structured interview, the interviewer has prepared a set of questions which she will fire at you. In the rambling or in-depth interview, your personality, background, and a wide range of topics will be explored. In this type of interview, remember that you are being judged and you should put your best foot forward. In the group interview, several people from the company will collectively interview you. One person in the group, generally, will be hardest to impress, and you must locate and win her over. These group interviews are tricky and intimidating, but be relaxed and confident.

In consecutive interviews, you will have several interviews with company people and must impress each one. You should prepare for each one of these interviews seriously, because it is possible to impress two

* Parts of this section first appeared in the author's article "A Job Is Not Forever," *Essence,* September 1977.

TABLE 16

FREQUENTLY ASKED INTERVIEW QUESTIONS*

---

1. What are your long-range and short-range goals and objectives; when and why did you establish these goals; and how are you preparing yourself to achieve them?
2. What specific goals, other than those related to your occupation, have you established for yourself in the next ten years?
3. What do you see yourself doing five years from now?
4. What do you *really* want to do in life?
5. What are your long-range career objectives?
6. How do you plan to achieve your career goals?
7. What are the most important rewards you expect in your business career?
8. What do you expect to be earning in five years?
9. Why did you choose the career for which you are preparing?
10. Which is more important to you: the money or the type of job?
11. What do you consider to be your greatest strengths and weaknesses?
12. How would you describe yourself?
13. How do you think a friend or professor who knows you well would describe you?
14. What motivates you to put forth your greatest effort?
15. How has your college experience prepared you for your career?
16. Why would I hire you?
17. What qualifications do you have that make you think that you will be successful in your career?
18. How do you determine or evaluate success?
19. What do you think it takes to be successful in a company such as ours?
20. In what ways do you think you can make a contribution to our company?
21. What qualities should a successful manager possess?
22. Describe the relationship that exists between a supervisor and those reporting to him or her.

* Source: Northwestern Endicott Report. Published by Placement Center, Northwestern University, Evanston, Ill. 60201. Reprinted with permission.

23. What two or three accomplishments have given you the most satisfaction? Why?
24. Describe your most rewarding college experience.
25. If you were hiring a graduate for this position, what qualities would you look for?
26. Why did you select your college or university?
27. What led you to choose your field of major study?
28. What college subjects did you like best? Why?
29. What college subjects did you like least? Why?
30. If you could do so, how would you plan your academic study differently? Why?
31. What changes would you make in your college or university? Why?
32. Do you have plans for continued study? An advanced degree?
33. Do you think that your grades are a good indication of your academic achievement?
34. What have you learned from participation in extracurricular activities?
35. In what kind of work environment are you most comfortable?
36. How do you work under pressure?
37. In what part-time or summer jobs have you been most interested? Why?
38. How would you describe the ideal job for you following graduation? Why?
39. Why did you decide to seek a position with this company?
40. What do you know about our company?
41. What two or three things are most important to you in your job? Why?
42. Are you seeking employment in a company of a certain size? Why?
43. What criteria are you using to evaluate the company for which you hope to work?
44. Do you have a geographical preference? Why?
45. Will you relocate? Does relocation bother you?
46. Are you willing to travel?
47. Are you willing to spend at least six months as a trainee?
48. Why do you think you might like to live in the community in which our company is located?
49. What major problem have you encountered and how did you deal with it?
50. What have you learned from your mistakes?

out of the three and not get the position. To help pass these types of interviews, ask someone in the organization to brief you on each person.

During the interview, you should be enthusiastic, confident, and leave a good impression. You should always be positive. For example, if the interviewer asks about your weaknesses, turn it around and say, "I am a workaholic" or "I work later than everyone else." Even if there are problems in the interview, for example, if the interviewer does not like you, is shy, or talks too much, you should calmly get your point across. If questions about age, marriage, or children are brought up, politely redirect the question by establishing that you are a responsible career woman and consider your career a priority. You should never say, "Would you ask that of a man?" Handle these sticky situations diplomatically.

After each interview, recall your strengths and weaknesses. Were you too nervous? Did you talk too much? Did you get your points across? Did you establish rapport with the interviewer? There are many reasons why people get and don't get jobs. If you do not get your dream job, try to determine why. To help you analyze, the Northwestern Endicott Report tells some of the reasons people don't get jobs (see Table 17). After each interview, promptly send a polite thank you letter, which may win you points.

If you get the job, salary negotiations are important. When money is discussed, do not take the first offer. Employers often offer the bottom price in a salary range. Because you have done your homework on the field and position, you will know the salary range. You should always negotiate for a higher salary and not be afraid to discuss money.

Let's hope after such thorough preparation you will work in the career of your choice. It's not easy to accomplish this goal, but with good planning, it's likely that you will.

TABLE 17

REASONS PEOPLE DO NOT GET JOBS*

1. Poor personality and manner; lack of poise; poor presentation of self; lack of self-confidence; timid; hesitant approach; arrogance; conceit.
2. Lack of goals and ambition; does not show interest, uncertainty and indecisiveness about the job in question.
3. Lack of enthusiasm and interest; no evidence of initiative.
4. Poor personal appearance and careless dress.
5. Unrealistic salary demands; more interest in salary than opportunity; unrealistic about promotion to top jobs.
6. Poor scholastic records without reasonable explanation for low grades.
7. Inability to express oneself well; poor speech habits.
8. Lack of maturity; no leadership potential.
9. Lack of preparation for the interview—failure to get information about the company and therefore unable to ask intelligent questions.
10. Lack of interest in the company and the type of job they have to offer.
11. Lack of extracurricular activities without good reason.
12. Attitude of "what can you do for me, etc."
13. Objection to travel; unwilling to relocate to branch offices or plants.

* Source: Northwestern Endicott Report. Published by Placement Center, Northwestern University, Evanston, Ill. 60201. Reprinted with permission.

2

Career Changing in the Eighties

"Career changing" conjures up disapproving thoughts of job hopping. To some, it is going against the grain. To others, it is the freeing mechanism from unwanted jobs. The American career-changing phenomenon is exploding. In the coming years, millions of Americans will change careers. Boredom, frustration, career burnout, limited mobility, and poor salaries will be chief complaints. Black women in particular are likely career-changing candidates. Although many Black women have successfully moved into corporate jobs, many still want to work for private industry. This section is particularly for them. For the woman in the private sector who wants to or has been forced to leave her job, this chapter can also help.

Many Black women career changers may look to private industry for employment. Yet the search for corporate employment may be short-lived. Corporate employers rarely envision the "soft" skills of teaching, counseling, and social and community work as viable or transferable.

They seek "hard" skills: financial, accounting, data processing, marketing, and analytical. To counteract this low acceptance of "helping" skills, Black women must develop airtight strategies for moving into the corporate sector.

The first strategy step is to thoroughly examine your needs, values, and goals. Many community and social service workers have great social consciousness. The financial emphasis of the business world is often a contradiction. Questions should be asked. Are there areas you can go into and still have a social commitment? Are there some corporations which have a greater social commitment than others? You must also assess the benefit losses of moving into the corporate world. For example, a supervisor may lose seniority and a large staff to begin as a trainee in a new field. Teachers will have to give up summer and winter holidays. Some career changers may experience salary cuts in new careers.

After assessing your values and goals, plot the shortest route to successfully switching careers; this is your second strategy step. Are there careers you can move into without getting additional education? Are there careers that require going back to school for a short period of time? Which careers offer the greatest career mobility and salary advancement? What careers can be equally dead-end as your present job? What career will best utilize your skills?

The astute career changer sets goals: short-term, long-term, lifelong. Beginning with short-term goal setting (six months to a year), write down and commit to memory accomplishments hoped for in this period. Get detailed, but be realistic. For example, a career changer wanted to enter pharmaceutical sales. She wanted a "career," flexible hours, independence, a company car, and an expense account. Her short-term goals were to research and talk to people in the field, interview with several pharmaceutical firms, and attend "Careers for Women" seminars which aid prospective saleswomen. In her notebook, she detailed a goal-setting log, set a schedule for accomplishing these goals, and set aside family, personal, and social time.

After six months, she had accomplished most goals. There were several interviews at pharmaceutical firms but no job offers. Field research disclosed that she needed some science training in her background to get a job, and her choppy work history was also a disadvantage. In the next six months, she shifted gears. To work in the pharmaceutical industry meant getting additional educational training. Educational costs would cripple her family budget and keep her away from the children in the evenings. The financial and personal sacrifices were too much. She sought help. A career counselor helped her focus on her true occupational wants and needs: job freedom, company car, expense account, and "real career."

The career counselor helped this career changer reassess her goals. There were many sales areas; most did not require additional training. There was no real reason for clinging to pharmaceutical sales. The career changer took a sales representative job with a company which produced advertising items (calendars, matchbooks, pens) for companies. In several months, she had built up a good sales record and was able to move into the marketing arm of a bank. She now persuades store owners to purchase the bank's credit card machines for customer convenience. She has a brand new company car, expense account, job freedom (she works in the field), and flexible hours.

Goal setting helps you get from point A to point B. It records firmly in your mind where you're going and how. If you follow the activities in a goal-setting log (a loose-leaf notebook), you will avoid procrastination but still have plenty of time for other activities. If your initial goals are not realistic, scrap them and make new ones. After you have planned and completed short-term goals, set five-, ten-, twenty-five-year and lifelong ones.

The third strategy step is assessing the most transferable fields. Human resources, personnel, and employee assistance programs offer good career-changing opportunities. These departments offer the best opportunities for psychologists, social workers, and counselors. "Helping" skills are directly transferable because of employer interest in aiding "troubled" employees. Employees with drug, alcohol, depression, and career burnout problems affect the company's productivity. Helping professionals are needed to counsel and aid these employers. Corporations are also concerned with unhappy employees. Unhappy employees do poor jobs and slow down production. Many corporations have also determined that unsatisfied workers should have the option of moving to other fields or companies and have instituted exit counseling procedures. Helping professionals are needed in this area, too. Be aware, however, that some corporations may want you to have corporate experience.

Teachers may find employment opportunities in the training components of personnel or human resources departments. If you look at teaching broadly, it is training. Let's look at some of the skills the Dictionary of Occupational Titles lists for educational trainers: "Formulates teaching outline in conformance with selected instructional methods utilizing knowledge of specified training needs and effectiveness of such training methods as individual coaching, group instruction, lectures, demonstrations, conferences, meetings and workshops; selects or develops teaching aids such as training handbooks, demonstration models, multi-media aids and reference works." A personnel trainer performs many of the same duties. (For more information, see the section on careers in personnel in chapter 13.)

A good cross-over career is sales. The M.B.A. degree is generally not required but prior sales experience is a plus. If you look broadly at your employment, volunteer, and community service work, you may uncover sales experience. For example, the teacher who raised $50,000 in door-to-door sales for a community group has transferable selling skills. Or the boutique sales worker who increased the sales volume by 60 percent has proven sales ability. Or the direct sales representative who sells cosmetics, jewelry, or Tupperware can redirect that selling to other sales areas. You may have to start at a small company and work up to a bigger one. (For more information on sales, see "Soft-Sell Careers: Sales.")

Educational publishing sales should appeal to teachers. Educational publishing sales people sell elementary, secondary, and college textbooks and other relevant materials to schools, colleges, and universities. A bachelor's degree is usually required. Prior sales experience is a plus, but you can learn sales techniques in company sales training classes. (For more information, see "A Career That Gets the Word Across: Communications.")

Communications can offer interesting career challenges. Teachers may want to lend educational expertise to educational television stations. Other career changers may want broadcast technician jobs like engineering or camerawork; FCC licensing will best prepare you for these lucrative jobs. (For more information, see "A Career That Gets the Word Across: Communications.")

Insurance is a good career bet. The career changer may take licensing examinations to become an agent. But there are other opportunities in the field. For example, a former math teacher may move into insurance's actuary work. (For more information, see "Soft-Sell Careers: Insurance.")

Some career changers may be intrigued by entrepreneurship. A special talent or skill can become the seed for a small business. Business ownership is fascinating but difficult. Monetary and personal sacrifices must be made but the rewards can be fulfilling. (For more information, see "A Career of Your Own: Starting Your Own Business.")

New technological fields like computers can offer many career opportunities. For example, a math teacher who has taken computer courses can find corporate employment. Other technological fields may be windfalls for career changers who get training in these fields. They are new. You can start on the bottom and work your way up as the industry develops.

Some career changers will opt for law or medical careers. Qualifying for law school means having good undergraduate grades and taking the Law School Admission Test (LSAT). Once accepted, you must spend three years (full-time) and four years (part-time) pursuing the J.D. (For more information, see "An Advocatory Career: Law.") Those who want medicine can take one of two routes. If you meet the medical school requirements, you can take the Medical College Admission Test (MCAT) and apply for admission. Those without prerequisites can independently take them at local colleges and universities or enter structured post-B.A. programs. (For more information, see "Helping Hand Careers: Health Services.")

Step four in your career changing strategy is assessing skills, deciding the organization where you want to work, interviewing with people in the field, and successfully marketing yourself. Start by assessing your skills. Tables 18, 19, and 20 list secretarial, teaching, and social work skills. On the left side of each table, you'll find typical job duties. On the right are these duties' expanded meanings. For example in Table 18, item one on the left states that a secretary "relieves executive of various administrative duties." The expanded meaning takes it one step further. On the right, "these duties translate to" states: "Being of service to, being sensitive to boss, able to work under pressure, etc."

The tables can help you reveal many hidden skills. If you expand the left side of the table to include other job tasks, you may discover other job functions. You may be more of an administrative assistant than a secretary. Or a trainer rather than a teacher. Or an administrator rather than a social worker. Similar charts can be written for each job in your employment history. You may discover that you have five hundred or more hidden marketable skills.

TABLE 18

SKILLS ANALYSIS: SECRETARIES*

DUTIES

1. Relieves executive of various administrative duties.

2. Coordinates and maintains effective office procedures and efficient work flows.

3. Implements policies and procedures set by employer.

4. Establishes and maintains harmonious working relationships with superiors, coworkers, subordinates, customers or clients, and suppliers.

5. Schedules appointments and maintains calendar.

6. Receives and assists visitors and telephone callers and refers them to executive.

7. Arranges business itineraries and coordinates executive travel requirements.

8. Takes action authorized during executive's absence and uses initiative and judgment to see that mat-

SKILLS REQUIRED:

1. Being of service to, being sensitive to boss, able to work under pressure, etc.

2. Gets the job done, has ability to move others to get the job done, able to persuade, able to facilitate.

3. Orderly, keeps records, able to process information, can do many tasks.

4. Takes initiative, has people-management skills, relates well to public and fellow employees/boss, has ability to effectively deal with many people.

5. Coordinates, able to persuade when difficulty arises, able to evaluate.

6. Has diplomacy skills, sensitivity to others, is patient and fair, is comfortable with many different kinds of people, is liaison for boss and others.

7. Is helpful, good at organizing details and written material, makes arrangements for others, responsible.

8. Able to follow through, able to assist and lead in absence of boss, able to assume other duties, able to

ters requiring attention are referred to delegated authority or handled in a manner so as to minimize effect of employer's absence.

direct others, able to communicate effectively.

9. Takes manual shorthand and transcribes from it or transcribes from machine dictation.

9. Takes shorthand. Able to transcribe.

10. Types material from longhand or rough copy.

10. Types, analyzes, edits, corrects, and obtains information from boss or others to complete the job.

11. Sorts and reads incoming mail and documents and attaches appropriate file to facilitate necessary action; determines routing, signatures required, and maintains follow-up.

11. Able to sort, read, file, and observe. Gets the task done. Able to do follow-up and detail work.

12. Composes correspondence and reports for own or executive signature.

12. Writes well, able to compose letters.

13. Prepares communication outlined by executive in oral or written directions.

13. Able to follow directions.

OTHER DUTIES

14. Gathers information from various sources.

14. Able to do research. Able to get information from others.

15. Schedules conferences and meetings.

15. Schedule, communicate to others, and take others' plans into consideration.

16. Handles sticky situations with diplomacy.

16. Has diplomatic ability. Able to handle difficult situations.

DUTIES	SKILLS REQUIRED:
17. Analyzes information.	17. Able to analyze.
18. Has good writing and speaking skills.	18. Speaks and writes well.
19. Saves time for boss and self.	19. Is efficient. Can get the work done.

* Source: "Prototype Secretarial Job Descriptions." Copyright © Professional Secretaries International. Reprinted with permission.

FIELDS TO TRANSFER SKILLS TO

TRAVEL—Need good secretarial skills, flair for language, knowledge of particular country or area. Should have patience and experience in dealing with hard-to-please customers and the public in general. Also need organizing skills, writing and speaking skills, and an ability to follow through on projects.

COMMUNICATIONS—Best bets: radio engineer, accounting clerk, secretary and research assistant in small radio company or radio-affiliated company and try to move up. For TV, try broadcast technician/engineer. Or start off as production secretary in television.

PUBLISHING—Many go in as trainees/secretaries. In some companies, everyone starts off as a secretary. Competition will be rough and bachelor degrees are pluses. If you are interested in writing, you can do what one woman did, which is become a secretary/receptionist in an area in which you want to write, e.g., children's books.

MAGAZINES—Many editors started off as secretaries or editorial assistants, as they are called on some magazines. Then many move up the ladder from these entry-level jobs. You may, however, need a college degree. But remember that the road to editor, senior editor, and other top editorial jobs is slow. One Editor-in-Chief estimated that it takes from six to ten years to move up. Also, be prepared for low salaries in magazine and publishing jobs.

INSURANCE—With some small companies, you can work as an underwriter or underwriter/trainee. You can also work in the clerical area doing claims and work your way up. Or you can be an insurance agent (at first you may get a small salary, but soon you may have to live on your commissions).

LEGAL ASSISTANT—A legal assistant falls somewhere between a legal secretary and a lawyer and helps relieve the lawyer of some of the work. If you are working in a law firm, this may be a good way to boost your position and salary. You may have to take a course especially designed for legal assistants. Such courses are given at several colleges and universities and institutes in your area.

OWNING YOUR OWN BUSINESS—Take your knowledge of the firm you are working for and translate that into a business of your own. For example, if you are working for a boutique, in your off hours or during slow times you can ask questions and learn the total business. Then later, with a little knowledge, advice from professionals, and your own capital or money from investors, you can go into the boutique business for yourself.

REAL ESTATE—Since there are no specific academic requirements for real estate saleswomen, you should take a course to prepare for the real estate exam, find a broker to work for, pass the exam, and start selling. Your best bet, after you have accumulated some basic experience, is to break into traditionally male areas, e.g., commercial real estate. A poor economy, however, has severely affected this economy.

SALES—This field's requirements vary according to the type, size, and location of the company. Your experience with salesmen and buying supplies should give you some knowledge of what to expect. If you want to make the switch, start talking to the saleswomen and men who frequent your office now.

RETAILING—You need at least a two-year degree. You can take that while working at a retail store as a secretary or a salesperson. After your schooling is completed, apply to your company's or another executive training program.

OTHER FIELDS OF INTEREST—Nontraditional blue-collar jobs, such as in construction. (These jobs generally pay more and many secretaries are switching to fields of this type.) Many secretaries and clerical workers are finding good job opportunities on transportation carriers, such as the Long Island Rail Road, which pays a good starting salary. Also, look for civil service jobs which incorporate your background and interests, but will help you break out of the secretarial slot.

TABLE 19

SKILLS ANALYSIS: TEACHERS

DUTIES	SKILLS REQUIRED:
1. Trainer.	1. Ability to talk in front of group. Teaching. Able to persuade. Able to promote own idea. Can lead. Able to design programs. Can guide.
2. Proficient in curriculum guides and learning resources.	2. Ability to read and digest materials. Have the ability to summarize. Able to review and evaluate. Able to know what interests others.
3. Sets objectives.	3. Ability to work on own with little or no supervision. Plans. Researches. Makes priorities.
4. Plans classroom activities and makes assessment of the success of instruction.	4. Plans. Good at organizing. Able to carry out plans. Keeps record of progress. Able to review, evaluate, and judge.
5. Motivates and stimulates students.	5. Ability to influence others. Is sensitive to others. Creates an environment for learning and intellectual exchange. Has ability to encourage and stimulate. Good with groups.
6. Helps children become aware of their self-worth.	6. Ability to establish good rapport. Able to show others their self-worth. Able to dig deep to help people know themselves. Able to design activities to help others determine their self-worth.
7. Expands and develops students' abilities.	7. Ability to develop. Able to look at situations and people and decide those activities and materials which might help them advance. Able to appraise and move on. Able to size

DUTIES   SKILLS REQUIRED:

up people and create alternatives to speed up progress.

8. Analyzes students' grades to determine progress.

8. Can determine, analyze, diagnose.

9. Proficient in the basic skills of particular subject.

9. Ability to read, write, and do math. Proficient in particular subject area, such as language (Spanish, French), music, art, home economics, etc.

10. Creative and innovative in projects.

10. Imaginative, good at coming up with original projects. Good at drawing and putting things together. Good at getting the job done.

11. Is skillful in interpersonal relationships.

11. Ability to help others. Able to talk things through. Able to command respect. Can help people work better together. Can help people cope with school and others.

12. Develops own tests.

12. Is creative. Able to determine the needs of others and translate this understanding into methods which are most conducive to learning. Able to develop tests. Able to predict whether others can adapt their learning to particular tests. Able to conceptualize.

13. Interprets tests and reports to parents or students.

13. Ability to interpret tests and translate these results into meaningful analysis for students and parents. Good communication skills, both in writing and speaking. Ability to tactfully explain results. Ability to deal with potentially sticky situations.

14. Reads and prepares materials.

14. Ability to read, interpret, and analyze.

15. Makes referrals.

15. Able to size up situations and act in the best interests of others. Ability to get all of the facts and make an assessment. Ability to be fair. Has negotiating skills. Is persuasive.

16. Handles difficult students or those with problems.

16. Is diplomatic. Sensitive. Has ability to get others to do what is wanted. Good at problem solving.

17. Knows how to work with young children, adolescents, or young adults.

17. Good people management skills. Knows how to get younger people to work effectively with each other.

18. Knows how to organize time.

18. Has good time management skills. Good at organizing. Ability to get job done.

FIELDS TO TRANSFER SKILLS TO

BUSINESS—A good combination is a math teacher who has taken some courses in computer science. Since math is considered a technical field, stressing your math background can help you to transfer to business with computer training. You can start off as a programmer.

INSURANCE—If you are a math teacher, you can become an actuary. For those with bachelor's degrees in liberal arts fields, you can start off as a claims representative, underwriter, or insurance agent.

ADVERTISING—Journalism or English majors may be able to find jobs in advertising as copywriters. However, you must have a portfolio (samples of ad campaigns that you've developed) for most copywriting jobs. Once you are accepted for employment, many agencies have training programs. For art teachers, you can begin free-lancing for agencies as an artist, or try to get an assistant art director, artist trainee, or production position.

RETAILING—You can join the executive training program of a major store and move up to a buyer position. Be prepared to take a salary cut; retail salaries are traditionally low.

OWNING YOUR OWN BUSINESS—If you can come up with the idea and get the financing and good professionals (lawyer, accountant, and management personnel) to help you, then business ownership is possible. There's good help available for new business owners.

TRAVEL AGENT—Start off by being an outside sales agent for a travel agency. For example, if you know a lot about Jamaica, you can approach an agency and tell them you are interested in taking a group there. Then, approach the teachers in your school or the people in your church or your women's groups and set the trip up. You can eventually take a home study course and become a Certified Travel Counselor and seek employment on a full-time basis.

REAL ESTATE—Take a preparation course for the real estate exam at one of the colleges or universities in your area which offer it. Then approach a broker, take the test, and begin working. A word of caution:

You will have to save up some money. Most real estate agents must work on commission. A poor economy, however, has affected this industry.

WRITER—Start off on a free-lance basis. Write articles about experiences you have had while teaching or of interest to parents. For example, you could write about how to find a good neighborhood school. Although most writers cannot support themselves on writing alone, you might consider trying to get a job teaching in your subject area at a junior or community college or four-year college (depending on your qualifications) to augment your writing. After writing numerous articles, you may be able to write a book.

TABLE 20

SKILLS ANALYSIS: SOCIAL WORKERS

DUTIES	SKILLS REQUIRED:
1. Interviewing.	1. Develops rapport and trust; keeps confidences or confidential information; has good verbal/communications skills; able to encourage communications.
2. Assessing clients' needs.	2. Sensitive to others; remembers people and their preferences; understands human motivations; can size up situations; understands political realities.
3. Arranging for services, e.g., food stamps, medical care, educational opportunities.	3. Resource expert; can make and use contacts effectively; good at compiling; skilled at clarifying problems or situations; adept at gathering information, analyzing; good at processing information; organized and orderly; good at keeping track of information; collects data accurately.
4. Record keeping.	4. A good detail person; has keen and accurate memory for details; keeps track of information; has high tolerance for repetition or monotony; collects data accurately.
5. Is an advocate for clients.	5. Change agent; promotes another individual; leads others; brings people together in cooperative efforts; renders service to others; treats people fairly; has unusual ability to represent others.

6. Good listening skills.

6. Determining; figuring out; evaluating; diagnosing; hearing accurately; perceptive; treats others as equals.

7. Does placement.

7. Able to assess, appraise, and screen others' feelings; able to make successful "work marriages"; able to develop warmth over the telephone.

8. Programming.

8. Planning; developing; has systematic approach to goal setting; able to formulate policy; able to interpret; good at program development.

9. Evaluating.

9. Revising; analyzing; recommending; makes good use of feedback; able to judge.

10. Empowering people.

10. Helps people identify their own intelligence; encourages people; motivates others; able to raise people's self-esteem; able to help others express their views.

11. Has administrative and leadership skills.

11. Able to take charge; able to work alone; able to organize others and bring people together in cooperative efforts; schedules; assigns; coordinates operations and details; directs others; makes decisions about others; able to take initiative; excellent at organizing own time; shows courage; role model.

12. Informing.

12. Communicates well; makes assessments; filters out information; adept at two-way conversation.

13. Able to handle unexpected or unpleasant stress.

13. Able to ignore undesirable qualities in others; deals patiently, sympathetically with difficult people; handles super-difficult people without stress.

14. Understanding.

14. Relates well to people; is intuitive; establishes rapport/trust; warm and responsive to others' needs.

DUTIES	SKILLS REQUIRED:
15. Good writing and oral skills.	15. Good communications skills; organized; clear in thought; able to communicate for self and others.
16. Thinking critically.	16. Analytical; reviewing and evaluating; decision making; diagnosing; problem solving.
17. Acting objectively.	17. Able to act in unbiased manner; can evaluate information.
18. Counseling.	18. Sensitive to others' needs; mediates between two conflicting parties; advocate; caring, warm; able to act in best interest of others; able to help others act for themselves.

FIELDS TO TRANSFER SKILLS TO

PERSONNEL—Social workers can directly transfer their skills to Human Resources Departments (Personnel). Private industry is placing more emphasis on helping individuals with personal problems.

MANAGEMENT CONSULTING—You can work with management consultant firms or start your own.

OWNING YOUR OWN BUSINESS—Business ownership is a good option for social workers.

REAL ESTATE—In the area of property management, you can use social work skills in tenant-landlord relationships. You can also enter real estate sales.

The second part of the secretarial, teaching, and social work charts (see Tables 18, 19, and 20) indicate fields where transferable skills can be applied. For example, many secretarial tasks are performed by travel agents: arranging itineraries, scheduling arrivals and departures, and phone work. A sharp secretary with knowledge of a particular continent or country could move into travel work.

Skills assessment should be followed by skill selection. Of the skills that you have, which ones do you want to transfer to new fields? For example, a social worker may have writing skills but prefers not to transfer them to a journalism, public relations, or advertising career. She knows writing is important to any career but prefers to emphasize her organizational and people management skills in the job hunt.

After skill selection, determine the industry or industries to work in. Is it beauty, fashion, communications, publishing, or banking? Selecting one or two industries will help you focus. After selection, begin the company research that is discussed in chapter 1.

After industry and company research, talk to and make contacts with people in the field. This is particularly crucial for career changers. Informational interviewing will help you discover marketable transferable skills; extra educational or training needs; résumé and interview tips; salary ranges; and referrals to others in the field.

Another way to reach people in your prospective field is to contact professional and trade organizations (both general-membership and minority group); many of them have rosters of women and minorities in the field. Or, browse through college alumni directories. You may uncover many people in the field, and alumni are always glad to talk to other graduates.

You should set your sights on one or two organizations, learn as much as you can about each, and begin job hunting. The career changing process is not easy. It can take a great deal of planning and time, but the effort is worth it.

Let's look at how one career changer, Carolyn Hughes, managed the switch.

CAROLYN HUGHES

Carolyn Hughes is a former New York City public school teacher. Today she owns a business! Painstakingly, she has calculated each career move to reach her goal. Hughes left teaching to work in Tanzania for the All African Trade Fair and developed a desire to do agricultural work for underdeveloped countries. Realizing that more educational training was needed, she returned to the States to pursue a master's degree in agricultural economics at Cornell University.

With degree in hand, she landed a researcher position with a Wall Street commodities firm. From there, she went on to do research at another firm. Setting her goals higher, she sought employment at banks but was unsuccessful. A mentor suggested working in agribusiness, specifically with Continental Grain, one of the industry's largest companies. The career move meant relocating to Chicago.

Hughes was hired as a merchandiser-in-training. She learned the mechanics of buying and selling corn and soybeans. After two years of developing her agribusiness skills, she again approached banks and received offers from several. After a few months of reassessing her career goals, she decided banking was the best career. She approached Chicago's Continental Illinois National Bank and was hired. Hughes left banking and started a business, Our Place Tavern and Restaurant in Henderson, North Carolina. She is enjoying business ownership and is currently on the board of directors of the Chamber of Commerce in Henderson.

The M.B.A.

Some career changers may find that they need additional training or education. This may be particularly true for the Black woman career changer. For years, Black women have needed credentials three times as good as other job seekers'. This is true for private-sector jobs too. The most marketable private industry degree is the M.B.A. If an M.B.A. will help you get a job or help you advance in one, it should be included in educational and career plans.

Once it was labeled the "ticket to success," but many corporate Blacks now see the M.B.A. degree as a qualifying credential. But it does not guarantee immediate advancement up corporate ladders. The M.B.A., however, does offer high starting salaries. Yet many factors will influence M.B.A. graduates' starting prices. Those with scientific and technical undergraduate degrees enjoy higher salaries; men's starting salaries often outdistance women's; prior work experience also counts.

The M.B.A. advantages are not an equal asset to all. M.B.A.s from the more prestigious schools enjoy the employment edge. Schools like Harvard, Stanford, M.I.T., and the University of Pennsylvania generally carry more weight in the interviewing process. Graduates of less prestigious schools can find corporate entry as rough as some non-M.B.A.s. The exceptions are those who already work in the business world. Many are discouraged that this "miracle" degree has not proved so marketable.

Yet most industry observers feel that Blacks should definitely arm themselves with the M.B.A. The career changer may experience difficulties with this. Many of them will not be able to return to school because of the immediate need for paychecks and the escalating cost of graduate business education. One answer is to seek a fellowship from the Consortium for Graduate Study in Management, which is designed to help minority students finance M.B.A. educations.

The Consortium for Graduate Study in Management provides graduate M.B.A. students who are pursuing full-time study with financial aid opportunities for the cost of education. The Consortium schools are the University of Texas at Austin, New York University, University of Wisconsin at Madison, Indiana University, University of Southern California, University of North Carolina, Washington University, University of Rochester, and the University of Michigan. The Consortium's address is 1 Brookings Drive, Box 1132, St. Louis, Mo. 63130.

Other financial aid alternatives include getting a corporate job and using company tuition reimbursement plans or attending a graduate school which offers flexible schedules for full-time workers. For example, one school allows students to maintain the same schedule for the program's duration. A student then knows the times and days for the next two or three years that will be devoted to school and can plan schedules accordingly. Another school has a structured program where corporations release employees to attend classes.

Admission to M.B.A. programs is competitive. After acceptance, the program is rigorous. Some schools require that you take a core curriculum and then specialize.

Full-time students should include a summer internship in their educational plans. It will give them the edge in job hunting. It shows prospective employers that they are highly motivated and have prior working experience in the field.

Once you graduate, prepare for a competitive job market. Many are pursuing M.B.A.s and in the future years, the degree may lose some of its magic. It may eventually become a prerequisite for entering the business field.

The College Degree

For many career changers the M.B.A. will be a long-term goal. First, some must complete college degree programs. Today, many Black women are returning to school. Accessibility of urban colleges and universities has helped, and many companies, organizations, and unions are encouraging it. Those returning to school have several options including attending a two-year or four-year college. The two-year program leads to the Associate in Arts degree (A.A.), Associate in Science (A.S.), or the Associate of Applied Science (A.A.S.). Many associate degree programs lead directly to careers. For example, the woman who wants to become a fashion industry designer can take an associate's degree and gain employment in the field. Or the woman who wants to switch to nursing can complete a two-year nursing program and be qualified to take state licensing examinations.

Advantages of the associate degree programs vary. But one is that after two years, you have a degree. At a four-year college, two years of study does not qualify you for a degree. Another advantage of an associate's degree is that it offers you a feeling of accomplishment in a shorter period of time.

The four-year college program is taken at a college or university. At one time, a bachelor's degree offered many career possibilities. Today that degree in a liberal arts subject (history, sociology, anthropology, et cetera) is not as marketable.

The most marketable four-year degrees are in engineering, accounting, computer science, and business administration. But the bachelor's degree is the prerequisite for entry into many fields and graduate and professional schools. For the Black woman, it is advisable to pursue it. The degree will give you more career flexibility.

Today there are several nontraditional approaches to getting a college degree. Today's Black woman can choose from several options: credit by examination; correspondence school or independent study; credit for noncollegiate instruction; credit for experience; and part-time degree programs (on and off campus).

Taking proficiency examinations can lead to college credit without traditional classroom attendance. There are two major programs: College Level Examination Program (CLEP) and the American College Testing Proficiency Examination Program (ACT-PEP). The College Level Examination Program is administered by the College Entrance Examination Board. This program evaluates college level knowledge. Satisfactory scores can translate into college credit at more than 1,800 institutions. For CLEP information, write to CLEP, College Entrance Examination Board, Box 1822, Princeton, N.J. 08541.

The American College Testing Program's ACT-PEP examinations are available throughout the country and at worldwide military bases. In New York State, the ACT-PEP examinations are called the College Proficiency Examination Program (CPEP) and Regents External Degree Examinations (REDE), and they were specifically designed for the Regents External Degree Program. For information about CPEP or REDE, write to the New York State Department of Education, Room 1919, 99 Washington Avenue, Albany, New York 12230. For information about CPEP or REDE outside of New York State, write to ACT-PEP, P. O. Box 168, Iowa City, Iowa 52240.

Another nontraditional college method is the Regents External Degree Program, which is nationwide. The Program allows students to get college credit by combining prior college credits, proficiency examinations, military education programs, special assessment of knowledge or performance skills, courses offered by nonacademic organizations, and other methods. For Regents External Degree Program information, write to the New York State Department of Education, Room 1919, 99 Washington Avenue, Albany, New York 12230.

A student can get college credit from correspondence or independent study courses. A wide range of courses are available for home study. Completed assignments are evaluated by university classroom standards. Some seventy-three colleges and universities that are National University Extension Association (NUEA) members give college credit by this method. For more information, write for the *Directory of Accredited Home Study Schools* (free), National Home Study Council, 1601 Eighteenth Street NW, Washington, D.C. 20009.

Many employees take courses at businesses, government agencies, labor unions, and volunteer and professional organizations. Some courses are equivalent to college level work and warrant college credit. To facilitate this, the American Council on Education's Office on Educational Credit evaluates courses and determines which are approved for credit. For more information, write for the *National Guide to Educational Credit for Training Programs* ($37.50), Project on Non-Collegiate-Sponsored Education, American Council on Education. You can order it by calling Macmillan Publishing at this toll-free number: 800-257-5755.

Another alternative way to get college credit is Project CAEL (Cooperative Assessment of Experiential Learning), which was designed by Educational Testing Service (ETS) and two hundred educational institutions. Through six assessment stages, the student's prior learning experience is evaluated. The Council of National Organization for Adult Education has also devised methods to evaluate home and volunteer experience: fourteen "I Can" lists. By using these lists, a student can determine skills developed from her volunteer or homemaking work and get college credit. For CAEL information, write to CAEL, 10840 Little Patuxent Parkway, Suite 203, Columbia, Md. 21044. For the booklet *How to Get College Credit for What You Have Learned as a Homemaker and Volunteer ($5.00 paper)*, write to Project Have Skills, Education Testing Service, Princeton, N.J. 08541.

There are also many on and off campus degree programs for part-time students. Some require residency periods of one to two weeks. Others require no classroom attendance whatsoever. For example, Empire State College of the State University of New York has both associate and bachelor degree programs, but learning in most programs does not take place in the classroom. Students sign contracts with faculty advisors ("mentors") and complete work on their own. There are also nontraditional graduate programs. For more information about on and off campus programs, send for *Directory of External Degrees from Accredited Colleges and Universities* from ETC Associates, 507 Rider Road, Clayville, N.Y. 13322 ($12.95).

Careers to Build On: For Those Who Don't Want to Change Careers

Many of you may not be forced to or want to change careers. You may want to creatively career path in present ones.

JOYCE DUDLEY

A career to build on is counseling. Joyce Dudley, who was assistant director of the Education Department/Coordinator of Counseling at District Council 37 (American Federation of State and Municipal Employees) in New York, headed up the counseling division. A creative career-pather, she has carved a career in an alternative counseling setting, and feels counselors must soon consider alternatives. Budget cuts, shrinking elementary and secondary school populations, and college layoffs have affected counseling. Future employment forecasts don't predict many openings in the area; only employment and rehabilitation counseling are expected to have viable opportunities.

To help counselors carve new career niches, Dudley recommends that they don't look narrowly at their acquired counseling skills. She feels that analytical, listening, evaluative, technical (test administering), resource brokering, helping, and emphasizing skills learned by counselors can be transferred to a variety of settings. One setting is private industry. Today, more business organizations are becoming concerned about employees who have emotional problems or are alcohol or drug abuse victims. Dudley feels that counselors can be helpful particularly with these problems. However, she cautions that some companies may require prior corporate experience.

Dudley also feels that counselors can move into consultant work by marketing their skills. For example, a counselor can become a consultant to government, private industry, or nonprofit organizations. A counselor can also open up a private career counseling service or do résumé writing for résumé writing and career planning companies. And Dudley practices what she preaches. After a year as deputy city personnel director for the New York City Department of Personnel, she is pursuing a free-lance career consulting career.

ROSALIND JEFFRIES

There are other work settings for counselors. Take the example of Rosalind Jeffries, who is director of the Human Resources Development Department at Washington Hospital Center in Washington, D.C. She does career counseling and helps hospital workers upgrade their educations by advising them on suitable educational courses and training to take. She does exit counseling for those workers who no longer want to work in the health field and conducts seminars in supervisory and management development training and career planning. She is also the owner of RJ Associates, a guest-relations consultant firm.

ESTHER WYNN

Secretaries can also creatively expand their careers. Take the example of Esther Wynn of the Women's Center in New York. After working as a secretary and administrative assistant for many years, she moved into an organizer's position for the Center's popular Debtors Anonymous group. Wynn's career movement was prompted by her own financial problems. She suggested that the Center start a group for debtors, and she has subsequently helped turn "Debtors Anonymous" into a nationwide success. Wynn has shown that secretaries can sometimes move from their traditional roles, and even start businesses. She has recently opened a beauty salon in New Jersey, and is on leave from the Women's Center.

A secretary can also upgrade her skills by taking courses in word processing, a field of the future. It is predicted that many companies will switch over to the word processing system, and to keep pace secretaries will be required to master word-processing skills.

There are many ways to creatively build upon a career. Look broadly at your skills, and think of the many ways that they can be put to use in another area of your career.

Part Two

The Careers

3

An Advocatory Career

LAW

When Charlotte E. Ray stepped across the stage to pick up her diploma from Howard University's law school in 1872, she became the first American Black woman to graduate from a law school. Many others followed, building and expanding on her example; Jane Bolin went on to become the nation's first Black female judge; Constance Baker Motley, the first Black woman to enter the federal judiciary; and 107 years after Ray's entry into the legal profession, Amalya Kearse became the highest-ranking Black woman judge, taking her place on the Second Circuit Court of Appeals.

Although we've had our victories in the field of law, it has not always been easy for us. We have often had to overcome seemingly insurmountable obstacles to become professionally and economically viable. Many of us were never able to overcome the discriminatory practices and policies of licensing organizations like the state bar examiners, and we were, therefore, unable to practice our profession.

Many Black lawyers nearly starved to death as they struggled with dying private practices. Some have had to augment their practices and support themselves by taking on other jobs or businesses. Others just simply gave up and went into more "suitable" careers like teaching and social work. Indeed, the continuation of many of these discriminatory practices prompted the NAACP Legal Defense Fund to file legal suits against about twenty states which discriminated against Blacks in bar examinations.[1] But according to the NAACP Legal Defense Fund, this legal battle has been unsuccessful.

Even today, the struggle has not disappeared. We still represent a small percentage of all practicing lawyers in the country. We have not made significant progress in establishing ourselves in large law firms.

We have also been plagued by the cries of "reverse discrimination" because we have managed to get a few law school seats. We have been misled by the theory that there will soon be an oversupply of lawyers. Yet we know there will probably never be enough lawyers to adequately service our communities.

We should know that as social problems deepen, lawyers are needed to add legal perspectives to community problems: crime, housing, health and environmental concerns, poverty, labor conflicts, wife beating, child abuse, and the escalating divorce rate. We should understand that lawyers are needed outside the country to lend legal expertise to developing countries and help in international conflicts. And yes, we are also needed in corporations to gain valuable business experience, because our communities desperately need this expertise.

Look Before You Leap into Law

Before you can decide where you best fit in the field of law, you must understand the nature of it. Being a lawyer usually isn't as glamorous as television would have us believe. If your idea of law is predicated on watching Perry Mason's leisurely afternoons spent driving long distances, hopping planes to see clients, or lazing around with them all afternoon in luxurious restaurants—forget it! If you see yourself cleverly trapping witnesses into revealing that they are indeed the culprit, thus freeing your client in the name of humanity for huge fees—forget that too. Sure, there are superstars, but their numbers are few.

Most lawyers spend their time researching and passing hours in less than glamorous courtrooms, defending clients in less than sensational cases—and after ten years of experience, most lawyers have only comfortable salaries.[2] Their primary focus is advocacy. They are the confidants and technicians in daily legal battles.

Most lawyers work in private practices.[3] Their area specialties include poverty, criminal, labor, tax, corporate, entertainment, real estate, or international law. Others go on to become judges, teach, or work for or outside the field.

Once You Understand the Nature of the Field, Learning How to Best Market Yourself

Many of us are drawn to law for different reasons. Some attend law schools because of deep social concerns. Many want status and economic security. Others want to follow in the footsteps of mothers, fathers, aunts, or friends. Still others want to enter law because they would like to correct injustices they see in present legal administrations.

Building Impressive Academic Records

Competition for law school seats is still keen. To prepare ourselves for law school admission, we must begin to build impressive academic records early. Thinking of ourselves as future lawyers early in our college years will help us begin to lay a sound foundation that will enable us to get into law school.

First you should determine from your advisor what counseling services are available for prelaw students. What is the best approach for law school admission? What is the acceptance rate for your college's prelaw students to law schools? Of those accepted, what are their majors, grade point averages (GPAs), and Law School Admission Test (LSAT) scores? What specialized activities are available for prelaw students, i.e., clubs, seminars, recruiter's visits? How many times a year should you as a student confer with your advisor?

Selecting a Major

There are a lot of misconceptions about the best majors for law school admission, but a well-rounded liberal arts education is really the best preparation. Old beliefs that history and political science are the best majors are outdated. Students with math, English, engineering, physics, sociology, psychology, and a host of other majors have successfully made it into law schools.

What is most important for law school admission is that you choose a major you like and can do well in. The best preparation for law school study is taking courses which prepare you for the work which lawyers engage in. You will need to take courses which especially strengthen your verbal and written skills and those which help you think logically.

Many of us become so concerned with selecting the best majors that we sometimes mistakenly choose areas of study because they seem "right" for law school admission. We are so busy listening and accepting peer advice that we find ourselves stuck in the "right" major getting the worst marks. If you solicit curriculum advice, get it from the expert, the prelaw advisor. Don't take courses at random.

Let's be realistic. Law school admission is competitive, and whenever there is competition, a strong academic record—good grades—are the primary consideration. Trying and failing doesn't count in law school admission. Only the best-informed and academically substantial students survive; those with bad advice or poor grades end up on rejection lists. But getting good grades is only half the battle.

Polishing Up Academic Records with Extracurricular and Other Activities

Extracurricular activities are also important criteria for law school acceptance. Law schools are interested in students who are well rounded. Therefore, you should become active in prelaw clubs, particularly minority ones, if your campus has them. Minority prelaw clubs can invite minority legal professionals and law school officials to specifically talk about the problems you might have in getting into law school and about current trends for Black students, and they can often be helpful to you in the admission process.

If there are no minority prelaw clubs on your campus, you should get a group of other aspiring lawyers together and organize a club of your own. If you organize a club or have an officer's position in it, you will convey to prospective law schools your leadership abilities. If you are active in prelaw clubs, it will indicate that you are highly motivated to become a lawyer, and that you are interested enough in the field to spend extra hours learning about it.

Properly structured prelaw clubs can give you a wealth of information. You may find your prelaw club a good vehicle for setting up internship programs in law offices, poverty law agencies, or within the court or prison system. All of these extras will add "sparkle" to your academic records. Community or political involvement will also help. But remember, none of these extras will take the place of a strong academic record.

Picking a Law School

Although freshman and sophomore years are good times to lay foundations for law school admission, it is not until the junior year that you will actually begin the technical part of the process. Your junior year should be set aside for exploring law schools.

There are many different reasons for choosing a law school. You may want to go to a prestigious one for status as well as its educational benefits. You may want to attend the alma mater of parents, siblings, or friends. Or you may consider only those close to home. Whatever your reason for selecting the law school of your choice, your overriding consideration should be your chances for admission.

If you have a low grade point average, are the ivy league schools likely to embrace you? Can you match up to the competition if your LSAT scores are low? If a law school is geared toward poverty law, should you consider it, if tax law is on your mind? If a law school is prone to accept only state residents, will you have a chance as a nonresident?

You should apply to a wide variety of schools depending on your academic ability and LSAT scores. Your first consideration in selecting a law school, however, is to determine whether your chosen law school is accredited by the American Bar Association. If it is not, you may receive a law degree but not be able to practice law in the state of your choice.

You should also consider the state in which you want to practice. Bar examinations, those qualifying examinations taken after graduation from law school, include questions on both local and basic law. If you go to law school in a state other than the one you wish to practice in, you will have to take additional crash courses to pass the local part of the bar examination. If you go to a school which focuses on general law, you will also have to brush up on local law.

You may want to choose a law school that combines law with other specializations. Combined degree programs are offered in law and business (J.D.-M.B.A.), law and public administration (J.D.-M.P.A.), law and a master's degree (J.D.-M.A.), and other areas.

The Application Process

Application to law school generally begins one year prior to admission. Part of this application process is taking the Law School Admission Test, administered for the Law School Admission Council by the Law School Admission Service. The LSAT should be taken as early as possible. It is recommended that you take the admission test in the June before your senior year. The LSAT is generally given in October, December, February, and June. If you are already out of school, you should take the test one year before you plan to enter law school.

If you take the LSAT and do not do well, you may take the examination again. The possibility of having to retake the LSAT is also a good reason to take it as early as possible—to give you time to study for your second chance. The advantage of taking the exam early is that it allows you a head start in the admission process. By the time you are ready to apply to a law school in September or October, you will know your scores and can then make more realistic school selections.

Since the LSAT and your grade point average will be the two most important criteria used for admission, let's now talk about the exam. The Law School Admission Test is a rigorous, standardized examination consisting of two parts, the LSAT proper, which measures reading, verbal, quantitative, and symbolic reasoning; and a second section which measures writing ability.

The LSAT section is scored on a range from 10 to 48; the writing sample isn't scored. Because so much depends on scoring well, many prospective law students prefer to prepare for it. LSAT exam preparation books can be purchased in local bookstores. The LSAT preparation courses are also popular, offering classes in LSAT test-taking procedures.

Law school admission is usually based on the rolling admissions concept, which means the best candidates are accepted first and the least qualified rejected immediately. The average candidate is then placed in another group along with a new batch of applicants, and again the best and least qualified are accepted or rejected. The process continues to rotate until the law school has chosen all its first-year students. Therefore, it is to your advantage to apply early.

You should fill out your application carefully and completely. Once you know to which schools you are applying, the Law School Data Assembly Services (LSDAS), another service of the Law School Admission Service, will compute your grade point average, report your LSAT score, and send personal data about you to the law schools you choose.

Another Law School Admission Service program, the Law School Candidate Referral Service (LSCRS), will give you opportunities to provide law schools that you haven't applied to with sex, age, ethnic group, and socioeconomic background information. These schools will review LSCRS applicants and might become interested in those with good credentials. As a result of using LSCRS, which also provides grades and LSAT scores, some of you may receive invitations to apply to certain schools.

The law school interview can be another part of the application process. Generally, law schools do not give interviews, but in some cases, law school officials may want to talk to minority students. If you are invited for an interview, you should first contact the law school's Black American Law Student Association (BALSA) to find out what kind of students the school is looking for. You should also find out from BALSA how large the minority student body and faculty are, and what the retention rate is for minorities. Many law schools have BALSA chapters on campus and they can usually be contacted by writing to:

President, Black American Law Student Association (BALSA), with
the name and address of the law school.*

Financing Law School Education

Unless your prospective law schools offer attractive financial aid pack-
ages, you may have to turn to federal aid, loans, or to the few financial
opportunities that exist.

The Council on Legal Education Opportunity (CLEO) Program is
probably one of the most popular financial aid sources. Although
CLEO offers financial aid to its students, it is also a program to give
students a head start on law school. Through its summer institute program that is given at seven sites, students are taught courses similar to
those in law school curriculums and given intensive writing help. For
those students who have not received law school acceptance by the end
of the six weeks, CLEO tries to find places in its consortium law
schools. Then while you are in law school, CLEO provides stipends.
CLEO can be contacted at:

> 818 M St. NW, Suite 290, North Lobby,
> Washington, D.C. 20036.

For other financial aid sources, contact your prospective law school.

What to Expect Once You Get into Law School

Acceptance into a law school is only the beginning. Law school itself
can be the most debilitating step of your career path. It requires endurance, top-notch study skills, and serious minds to conquer the massive
volumes of school work. "Many Black students," says Marianne Sprag-
gins, a former adjunct associate professor of law at New York Law
School, "do not recognize the degree of discipline and concentration
that it is going to take. We become overwhelmed, get into a cycle of
losing ground, and never get out of it."

The first year of law school is the most difficult. It is a year that tests

---

* Some campus BALSAs may have other names. In that case, please check with individual law schools.

endurance. Some students may have to repeat this year or leave. Others will master it, go on to less stressful second and third years, and then graduate.

The hurdle after graduation will be passing the bar examination which will permit you to practice law. It is to be hoped that the new Multi-State Examination that is used in some states and legal pressures will effectively eliminate any residual discriminatory practices and boost the number of Blacks passing the bar examination.

What Will You Earn as a Lawyer?

Recent law school graduates have commanded salaries from $10,000 in some public interest programs to more than $40,000 in some larger law firms. Starting salaries for lawyers in private industry averaged $29,000. In the same year, experienced lawyers in private practice averaged $88,000.[4]

CAREER PROFILES

Golden Johnson-Burns and Mary Welcome represent today's growing breed of Black women lawyers. Both have made significant contributions to their profession and serve as inspiring role models.

Golden E. Johnson-Burns
Judge, Municipal Court, Montclair, New Jersey
and Attorney, East Orange, New Jersey

Golden Johnson's childhood fantasies focused on growing up to become a doctor. But, like many Black children, she was told by high school counselors to take nonacademic courses and redirect career dreams to a beautician's career. Johnson's parents insisted that their daughter take academics and go to college.

A good student, Johnson was accepted to Douglass College in New Jersey and studied bacteriology. After graduation, she began work as a microbiologist at East Orange, New Jersey's Veteran Administration Hospital. At the height of her career, she reassessed her goals. Already at the highest level that she could go, to advance she would have to get a doctorate and research experience with a prestigious research lab. She decided against it and toyed with her initial dreams of becoming a physician.

A friend introduced her to law. "My friend was a lawyer and encouraged me to consider law. I applied and was accepted by Rutgers, the State University School of Law," Johnson recalls.

Early in law school, she began plotting the future. To augment her legal education, she participated in several internships. "One summer, I was an intern with the Newark Legal Services. I gained a great deal of experience working with clients in landlord/tenant disputes, small claims court cases, welfare situations, domestic relations, and consumer protection cases. It taught me a lot procedurally," Johnson remembers. A second summer internship would further impact on her career plans. "The next summer, I was an intern in the United States Attorney's office, District of New Jersey," she says. As a result of the political climate in Newark and some landmark cases, she started formulating plans to work in the political arena. "Working in the Attorney's office helped me focus on some of those plans," she recalls.

After graduation, the ambitious lawyer became a Deputy Attorney General in the financial section for the state of New Jersey. "My duties included handling legal work for the Division of Taxation, the Lottery Commission, and the Department of Agriculture. I was also responsible for court appearances and administrative coverage," she remembers.

Afterward, she went to the community as project director for the Community Legal Action Workshop (CLAW), a privately funded division of the American Civil Liberties Union (ACLU). "It was a single-attorney law office in the Newark Black community. We handled discrimination matters which were directed against the poor and minorities. We handled illegal methods of process serving and wrongful obtaining of default judgments," she says. "We also handled racial and sexual discrimination in employment, landlord/tenant, and welfare rights cases. I also served voluntarily as assigned counsel for indigent people in Newark's Municipal Court once a month." Her two years with CLAW would lay the foundation for her ultimate judgeship appointment.

In April of 1974, she became an attorney for Hoffmann-La Roche, Inc., one of the largest pharmaceutical companies in the world. "Rumor had it that they were looking for a Black woman attorney with a science background. I'm sure there were not too many of us who could fit the bill. I applied, was very impressed with the person who interviewed me, thought I could learn from him, and took the job," she recalls. "I worked in the corporate acquisitions area. Our department aided in the legal aspects of acquiring other companies. We became involved from the moment an idea left our corporate planning department, during the acquisitions process of a company until after the closing took place or a determination of legal infeasibility was made." Johnson also assisted as in-house counsel for newly acquired companies in such areas as food and drug laws.

When Newark's former mayor, Kenneth A. Gibson, wanted a Black woman judge for Newark's Municipal Court, Johnson became an easy choice. There were only a handful of Black women lawyers in the area and she had grown up and worked in Newark. She took a leave of absence from Hoffmann-La Roche and started the judgeship.

Johnson's life would change dramatically because of the appointment. She was no longer citizen Johnson but Judge Johnson. "Being a judge isn't as glamorous as it sounds. It's very difficult to decide people's lives and know your decisions will affect them the rest of their lives," she recalls. "It's also lonely because you're always on display. If you go out, people say 'What's a judge doing here?' or if you have a run in your stocking, they question it. It was difficult going places without being scrutinized. And although I'm no longer a sitting judge, I still have to be extremely careful of what I do," she stresses. Her family's and friends' support prevented the judgeship from being a lonely experience.

But Johnson learned a great deal during the judgeship. In Newark's court system, the municipal court is the largest, busiest municipal court in New Jersey. As one of its six judges, Johnson divided the court's duties with the others on a rotating basis. "We handled criminal judicial cases, traffic matters, and municipal ordinances like housing, shoplifting, neighborhood disturbances, prostitution, and arraignments," she says.

After three years as a judge, she wanted to enhance her legal skills and abilities in terms of growth as a lawyer. She resigned and exercised an option in a leave of absence agreement, and returned to Hoffmann-La Roche as a general attorney. When she returned to the company, she was encouraged by many people both on and off the job to enter politics. After active participation in Senator Bill Bradley's campaign, she decided to enter the political arena. Last year, she ran unsuccessfully against Congressman Peter Rodino (Tenth Congressional District). But she'll probably try again.

Johnson, a career planner, has always known exactly where she wanted to be in one, three, or five years. She left nothing to chance and recommends developing a career strategy to advance. "Many lawyers who become tired of trial work look longingly towards a judgeship. But you must have your politics together. Plus you must become visible by being politically active in professional groups and community development groups. Join organizations, churches, or the local girl scouts," she advises. "It is also important to join the local bar association. My memberships in the Golden State Bar Association, Essex County Bar Association, National Bar Association, New Jersey State Bar Association, and other professional organizations were extremely valuable. Establish a network. Getting appointed is a result of who talks to who and suggests whom."

Judge Johnson now sits on the bench at the Municipal Court in Montclair, New Jersey, and is in private practice in East Orange, New Jersey.

Mary Welcome
Attorney
Baltimore, Maryland

The brutal Atlanta children murders shocked the country. When Atlanta police arrested Wayne B. Williams, pint-sized dynamo Mary Welcome was one of his first lawyers.

It is not the first news blitz she has witnessed. Welcome's triumphant march against prostitution and pornography made local headlines during her tenure as Atlanta's first city solicitor. Her "corrective surgery" on Atlanta's municipal and criminal court systems made the city take notice.

Welcome's climb to national celebrity status began in her native Baltimore, Maryland. Born to a politician mother and physician father, she nurtured a love of politics. "At thirteen, I decided to become a lawyer. When my mother campaigned, she took me along. She believed in 'pressing the flesh' by going out and ringing doorbells," she remembers. "It was amazing so many people did not know their constitutional or credit rights. Those experiences helped formulate my decision to study law, preferably constitutional law."

Following that dream, Welcome went to Morgan State University to major in political science. She graduated, but wanted to delay law school. The job search produced a low-salaried position and the disappointed Welcome hurriedly applied to Howard University's law school.

Setting her career sights on constitutional law, she eased into difficult law school studies but soon became bored. "After my first year, I considered dropping out. It was boring. I wanted to become involved in the actual learning process, not read outdated cases," she recalls. "One of my law professors saved me by offering a research job—helping him with writing, managing estates, and real estate. Suddenly, law came alive. I enjoyed it because I was getting practical experience."

The work kept Welcome in school. Upon graduation, she delayed taking the bar examination to take an assistant housing coordinator position with a federally funded program. She organized for tenant rights.

A vacation in the Virgin Islands changed Welcome's life. She did not return to the activist position, but married a Virgin Islander lawyer and moved to his home. She settled into marriage, a clerkship with a local judge, took and passed the bar, and gave birth to a son. Soon, she was tapped for Assistant Attorney General for the Virgin Islands and her career began moving.

When the marriage collapsed, Welcome and son relocated to Atlanta. She took a law firm position while preparing for the Georgia Bar. Former mayor Maynard Jackson sensed a competent professional and appointed her the City Solicitor. "I oversaw the prosecution of the 67,000 municipal and criminal division court cases annually. I immediately developed a system where every prisoner was listed. If they were jailed too long, I had them brought before the court. If the police didn't have a case, I dismissed it. Prosecutors have the discretion to prosecute or not," she stresses. "There were times when a person was charged with eight or nine offenses, each one carrying a bond. You could, for example, have someone incarcerated for hitting someone and have a total bond of $10,000 because he said bad words or didn't move quickly enough. If he didn't have a previous record, I requested taking the best two offenses, dropping the rest, and reducing the bond."

Welcome felt bond reduction would not result in skipping bonds. "Historically, people show up for court appearances because they don't like being looked for," she insists. "If they're going to escape, they will, even with a $50,000 bond."

She was also instrumental in creating a pretrial release program based on a point system, but her cause célèbre was fighting against prostitution and pornography. "Police complained prostitutes were immediately set free after arrests and back working on the streets. The business community also complained about the prostitution houses in the Peachtree area," Welcome remembers. "We checked the property titles and then published the names of landlords of these houses. We wanted the public to know these landlords didn't care about Peachtree Street or they would evict these tenants. Our first case was dismissed, but the second was won. Members of the hotel associations, insurance companies, city council members, and police officers rallied behind me."

Welcome's fervor against prostitution and pornography was controversial and brought her to public attention.

As her clout grew, she set about another arduous task: professionalizing the municipal court. The case load had grown to 76,000 cases but Welcome managed the feat. "Previously, everything was carried around in people's heads. The court system didn't even have court reporters. I set about professionalizing the system by establishing court rules: spectators' conduct; filing system for court papers; court hours. Also I arranged for a computer system to record data on each prisoner," she says.

With her mission nearly complete, Welcome left the City Solicitor's office to enter private practice at Garland, Nudkolls, Kadish and Cook. She had given the system her best; it was time to move on. "Criminal work grew tiring. I wanted to do something different," she says. "I was asked to become Inspector General with the Environmental Protection Agency in Washington, D.C., but declined. The position would have made me the youngest Inspector General, but I wanted to pursue private practice, try corporate law." Ironically, criminal law has not evaded her. The Williams case has put her back in that arena. But Welcome did other cases: divorces, business incorporations, equal employment opportunity, and malpractice cases. In 1978, she opened a law firm, Welcome & Associates. She has since left Atlanta, and is now in Baltimore, Maryland.

Looking back on an impressive career, Welcome's thoughts turn to the former City Solicitor's position. Her career advice centers on those prosecuting days. "I would like to stress to law students and lawyers that being a prosecutor isn't necessarily a 'bad guy' role. Most students want to be defense attorneys because they believe that they're the 'good guys.' But a prosecutor determines which cases get tried," she says. "She can go into those jails, find people who are unjustly charged, and make sure justice prevails."

Career Aids

Books and Pamphlets

1. *Pre-Law Handbook* ($5.00) is available from:
   The Law School Admission Service
   Box 2000
   Newtown, Pa. 18940
2. For information on schools, financial aid, etc., write and ask cost of publications from:
   Information Services
   American Bar Association
   750 North Lake Shore Drive
   Chicago, Ill. 60611
3. For information on legal education, contact:
   Association of American Law Schools
   1 Dupont Circle, NW
   Suite 370
   Washington, D.C. 20036

Professional Organizations

1. The National Conference of Black Lawyers
   126 West 119th St.
   New York, N.Y. 10026
2. The National Bar Association
   1275 11th St., NW
   Washington, D.C. 20001-4217
3. The National Association of Black Women Attorneys
   508 Fifth St.
   Washington, D.C. 20001

All addresses and prices are subject to change.

4

Helping Hand Careers

SOCIAL WORK

Social welfare programs are being severely cut back at a time when our cities are suffering economic and unemployment problems. The poor and disadvantaged are, of course, the victims. They are lost in the shuffle between those who would neglect them until steaming ghettos erupt, others who would extend aid but are rendered impotent by the cutbacks in allocations for social service programs, and still others who advocate Band-Aid solutions for ailing populations.

Caught in the midst of this social catastrophe, the social worker must deal with bureaucracies and suffering populations. She must deliver social services to the poor, elderly, sick, disadvantaged, incarcerated, mentally ill, drug and alcohol abusers, as well as orphaned, abandoned, or abused children. She must direct her clients through a system which is often racially and sexually biased and indifferent to those in need.

And she must fight through bureaucratic red tape knowing the battle can't always be won.

As our cities become more plagued with rising crime rates, unemployment, cutbacks in essential services, housing deterioration, hospital closings, and the decline of school systems, the social worker must somehow cope and assist. She must intervene to relieve the crises and advocate policies sensitive to the needs of her clients. And through it all, she must struggle to empower the powerless—guiding them toward personal independence.

In recent years, the social worker has seen a change in her role and sphere of activity. Social workers are involved in the areas of drug and alcohol abuse, rape prevention and counseling, child abuse, wife beating and family violence, suicide prevention, and rehabilitation. They work in hospitals, mental health facilities, schools, colleges and universities, prisons, family and child care agencies, day care centers, private practices, orphanages, juvenile correction centers, and consultant firms. Social workers have drifted into private industry to help employees cope with job-related stress, and they are becoming more vocal in their advocacy for better delivery of services to their clients.

As social work has expanded, so must our view of it. Although our sensitivities are needed in working with individuals, families, and groups, we are particularly needed in administrative and top decision-making roles to formulate, plan, and direct social service programs which will benefit the community at large.

Career Pathing in Social Work

Social workers have three traditional approaches: casework, group work, and community organization. Caseworkers assist individuals and families. Using interviewing techniques, they help them to better understand and cope with problems. As a caseworker, you may place an abused child in a foster home, provide a terminally ill patient with home nursing care, counsel a prisoner returning to society, or guide a family to proper medical services.

Social workers who specialize in group assistance focus on guiding group members through exercises that help them cope with their problems, with other group members, and their society. They might work with teenagers at a community center, the elderly in a senior citizens' center, or prisoners in a correctional center.

A social worker connected with community organizations endeavors to combat neighborhood social problems by proposing solutions and programs to religious, political, and civic groups.

Social workers are also employed in administrative and research positions; they work for educational institutions, consulting firms, and in private therapy practices.

To prepare for social work, you may pursue several degree paths: B.S.W., M.S.W., or the ultimate degree of professional competence, the Certification of ACSW.

If you are interested in entry-level social work positions, the Bachelor of Social Work degree (B.S.W.) is now increasingly accepted. However, some graduates with majors in psychology, sociology, or other related fields have managed to get entry-level jobs. To gain more career leverage, the Master of Social Work degree (M.S.W.) is recommended.

The M.S.W. usually requires two years of study plus supervised field work beyond the bachelor's level. With this degree you can become a researcher, administrator, or do supervisory work. There are many agency-level jobs which require this advanced degree.

If you want to teach, an M.S.W. backed with experience and appropriate expertise may serve you well. However, a degree as a Doctor of Social Work (D.S.W.), will provide more leverage.

For further professional recognition, you may want to obtain the ACSW (Academy of Certified Social Workers) credential, bestowed on those members of the National Association of Social Workers who pass ACSW examinations, have master's degrees, and have at least two years of work experience at the post-master's level.

Thirty-three states require that you be licensed to become a social worker. Licensing requirements include specified educational training, work experience, and/or the passing of an examination. Contact the state where you plan to work to determine requirements.

What Will You Earn as a Social Worker?

As in most socially oriented jobs, your salary as a social worker will not make you rich but will allow you to live comfortably. Your earnings will depend on your degree, position, the agency you work with, and where you live.

In a recent survey by the International Personnel Management Association, B.S.W.-holding caseworkers made $15,700; casework supervisors who held M.S.W.s averaged salaries of $20,100; average salaries for social workers in the federal government were $30,800, according to the Occupational Outlook Handbook.

CAREER PROFILES

Joan Adams and Patricia Matthews-Juarez are two seasoned social workers. Early in their careers, both followed traditional social worker career paths. Today, each is following different pursuits. Adams has strengthened her social work background with psychotherapeutic and psychoanalytical training and has a private practice. Matthews-Juarez is program administrator for the Department of Family Medicine, Charles R. Drew Postgraduate Medical School.

Joan Adams, M.S.W., CSW
Social Worker/Psychotherapist/Psychoanalyst
New York, New York

Joan Adams does not represent the typical social worker. She has discovered ways to improve her career by strengthening clinical skills. The desire seemed practical; her work experience leaned toward clinical work. After getting a graduate degree from William Smith College in Geneva, New York, and an M.S.W. from Fordham University, she went into clinically oriented areas: a social worker position in Harlem Hospital's In-Patient Psychiatric Services; a counselor's position at Queens College.

To move toward her ultimate career goal, she took family therapy courses at William Alanson White, a psychoanalytical training institute.

That experience narrowed her goal. She wanted to improve her skills as a psychotherapist and begin a private practice. There were several routes to becoming one: completing a clinical psychology doctoral program; seeking further employment at an agency or clinic with a good in-service training program, or attending a psychoanalytic training institute. She was impressed with the Postgraduate Center for Mental Health. It was the first psychoanalytic training institute to accept and train nonmedical analysts: social workers and psychologists, et cetera. She took a leave of absence from Queens to concentrate on her studies.

Getting psychoanalytic training is not easy. The curriculum is based on learning psychoanalytic and psychotherapeutic principles. "At the Institute, we learned to understand human behavior and emotional development through psychoanalytic principles and theories. We learned that our developmental experiences—those experiences and interactions between parents, siblings, and peers—shape the way we are today," she says. "We also learned to understand the kinds of emotional problems, both conscious and unconscious, that bring people to therapy. Classes and supervision focused closely on psychoanalytic and psychotherapeutic techniques for helping people understand their feelings and behavior, and make changes in themselves."

The training took Adams four years. "The first three years of study operate on a trimester basis. Each trimester, I took three courses for a total of nine a year," Adams says. "In addition, each week psychoanalytic candidates are required to do ten or more hours of clinical work with adults in the Institute's clinic. During the first two years, there are required twice-weekly sessions with supervisors, and third- and fourth-year candidates meet in both one-to-one and group supervisory sessions. Because an important trademark of psychoanalytic training is that students be in analysis, we were required to attend three-times-a-week sessions. The program was very stimulating and demanding but it resulted in a great deal of personal growth."

In the third year, the Postgraduate Center requires a community mental health project. "Since I was interested in clinical training which relates to the Black community, I felt my community project should be done in that community," she says. "My project was working at a New York Public Health Department clinic to help administrative and other staff focus on job-related problems. The project gave me the type of experience and training that you don't get in a more traditional psychoanalytic training institution."

Upon graduation, Adams became a certified psychoanalyst and psychotherapist. She feels both designations are important, but that she will get more career mileage from being a psychotherapist. "Psychotherapy gives me a broader base to use in a private practice. Training in just psychoanalysis is too limiting and restricting. People seem not to be interested in looking as deeply within themselves as they must in psychoanalysis. It's also a time consuming process—three-to-five-times-a-week sessions and a number of years to complete. And it's expensive," she stresses. "On the other hand, psychoanalytic psychotherapy, while emotionally demanding, is more flexible for the client. People are seen once or twice a week, usually for a period of one to three years."

Adams has begun a two-year advanced program in doing analytic group therapy. She feels that combined individual and group therapy is extremely helpful to many clients. She is building a psychotherapy practice which includes a multi-ethnic group of patients and is particularly interested in reaching more Black patients. She knows, however, that dispelling myths about psychology is required. "People must have a fair degree of mental health to seek therapy or analysis. They may have problems which interfere with a desired way of functioning, but it doesn't mean they're crazy," she says. "That's one myth I'd like to dispel in the Black community."

Adams has realized a career dream. She is now assistant director of the Adult Therapy clinic at the Postgraduate Center for Mental Health. Her responsibilities include coordinating, supervising, and teaching a unit of graduate social work students. She also teaches community health consultation to third-year candidates at the center. Other social workers who want to build upon clinical skills can follow Adams's lead or take alternative approaches to becoming a certified psychotherapist. The road is not easy, but it is rewarding.

Patricia Matthews-Juarez, M.S.W., Ph.D. in Social Policy
Program Administrator/Assistant Professor
Department of Family Medicine
Charles R. Drew Postgraduate Medical School
Los Angeles, California

Patricia Matthews-Juarez has seen many sides of social work. She was a planner and community organizer, psychiatric social worker, supervisor, consultant, and professor. Recently, she completed a doctoral program at the Florence Heller Graduate School for the Advanced Studies in Social Welfare at Brandeis University. "Getting the doctorate is important. In social work, there's a hierarchy. Having a Ph.D. facilitates career mobility and allows me to be in decision- and policy-making positions," she says. "Decision- and policy-making positions are two areas where Blacks are needed. We must prepare ourselves for policy-making positions in areas which impact upon our communities."

Matthews-Juarez entered social work via college and graduate school. With a B.A. in psychology from Fisk University and an M.S.W. from New York University, and studies at the London School of Economics, she established herself as executive director of a Brooklyn-based day care center before entering social work. Her first professional social work experience was as community organization specialist at the Community Church of New York's outreach program, RENA-COA. Afterward, she continued community work as a psychiatric social worker and supervisor of community outreach programs at the Washington Heights Inwood-West Harlem Council's Mental Health Center in New York.

The confident and competent Matthew-Juarez soon moved to the consultant level. She became a consultant for the Inter-Organization Vietnam Agency, an organization which placed Black Vietnamese children in this country. After that she became the administrative supervisor to the National Parent Unit for Harlem Dowling Children Services. She also worked as a senior social work consultant at Youth Consultation Services.

To round off an impressive career, she took on the challenge of acting director of the Social Welfare Sequence/Department of Sociology at Hampton Institute. Her task was to bring the department in line for accreditation from the Council on Social Work Education. Having accomplished this, Matthews-Juarez was invited to join the faculty at Norfolk State College's School of Social Work in Norfolk, Virginia, as an assistant professor in social administration and clinical group methods.

Teaching was rewarding, but Matthews-Juarez sensed the American agenda with regard to economic and social problems and decided to enroll in a graduate program.

A social work career is one desired by many Black women. It has been a field that has accommodated us. But Matthews-Juarez suggests that you put a great deal of thought and planning into pursuing the field. "If you want to go into social work, be sure you're committed to helping people. The commitment must be rooted in a genuine caring and concern for people," she advises. "Social work is not a field of glamour or one where you can make a lot of money. Social work is hard 'humanity' work. It is both exhausting and rewarding."

Another consideration is getting credentials and selecting appropriate training grounds. "You must get the necessary degrees, but don't just go to any school. Select and evaluate the school you plan to attend. The school's philosophy will determine your philosophy as a social worker," she says. "For example, I went to NYU, which had a generic approach which prepared us for casework, group work, and community organizing. But some schools are psychoanalytical in nature, with few courses, if any, in administration and community organization. So your schooling as well as the agency you work for will determine your perspective in the field."

Matthews-Juarez also recommends that every social worker work in the inner city: "Many social workers have never worked in the inner city, and unfortunately, some of them are making policies which directly affect inner city populations."

Matthews-Juarez is now program administrator and assistant professor for the Department of Family Medicine at the Charles R. Drew Postgraduate Medical School in Los Angeles, California. As second in command in the department, she helps administer a department with a three-million-dollar budget and eighty employees, and trains twenty-two physicians a year in the specialty of family medicine. She also assists in residency selection, faculty appointments, coordination of research and grants, and supervises the operation of two clinics (one county and one private) and the hospital-based EmergiCenter. She considers this position "her perfect job."

She is married to Paul Juarez and is the mother of two children, Erin Patricia and Kristin Danielle.

Career Aids

1. Career information is available from:
The National Association of Social Workers
7981 Eastern Ave.
Silver Spring, Md. 20910

2. For information on accredited B.S.W. and M.S.W. programs,
   contact
   The Council on Social Work
   1744 R St., NW
   Washington, D.C. 20009 for *Directory of Accredited BSW Programs* and *Directory of Accredited MSW Programs* ($5.75 each).

Professional Organizations

1. The National Association of Black Social Workers
   271 West 125th St.
   Room 317
   New York, N.Y. 10027

All addresses and prices are subject to change.

HEALTH SERVICES

MEDICINE

Medicine has long held a fascination for us. From the days in 1864
when Rebecca Lee was the first Black woman to receive medical training in the United States to the early 1870s when Susan Smith McKinney Steward became the first Black woman to receive an M.D. degree,
we have made our mark in the field.

We think of medicine as a field where we can make lucrative salaries,
gain professional status, and be of great benefit to our communities. The
field offers all of that and in addition is an area where we are desperately
needed. We need more Black physicians if our communities are to be
adequately serviced.

There are problems, however, associated with our becoming doctors.
Discrimination is practiced against Black students enrolled in premedical courses. There has been a history of discriminatory practices in
medical school admissions. It is felt that the Bakke case set us back
somewhat as nervous medical school officials became reluctant to en-
force special quotas established for minorities during the sixties. In fact,
in the post-sixties years, our numbers in medical schools have declined.

Yet we must pursue careers in medicine with determination and dedication. The lives of our communities are literally at stake.

Career Pathing in Medicine

Admission Requirements

Medical school preparation starts as early as high school. You should select a high school curriculum which is academically oriented and includes courses in biology, chemistry, physics, algebra, geometry, and trigonometry.

After high school, you must take college courses that will make you eligible for medical school admissions: one year of biology (with lab); one year of inorganic chemistry (with lab); one year of organic chemistry (with lab); one year of physics (with lab); one year of math, preferably calculus, is highly recommended; and one year of English.

Most premeds major in biology, chemistry, or physics, but some are English or psychology majors and also take courses to meet medical school requirements. A small percentage obtain bachelors' degrees in liberal arts areas and then take medical school prerequisites on a nonmatriculated basis or in special post-B.A. programs which allow students to just take required medical school courses in a structured program.

Good study habits, a good memory, discipline, and time management all will prepare you for the rigors of medical school. You should also try to get the best grades and to participate in extracurricular activities (e.g., becoming president of the campus premedical club) that will show your leadership abilities. You should also pursue activities that will give you clinical experience, such as working in a hospital, clinic, or doctor's office.

There are a number of special tutorial programs throughout the country developed to help minorities strengthen the academic skills needed for success in medical school. These programs, usually summer ones, are competitive. To learn about these programs, contact your premedical advisor.

The Admission Process

The actual admission process usually begins in your junior year when you will, in some cases, take the Medical College Admission Test (MCAT), which is required or recommended by many schools. There is fierce competiton for medical school seats and your examination results will count heavily in medical school admissions along with your grade point average, in schools which use these criteria. This exam will test your cumulative knowledge in the areas of biology, reading skills analysis, chemistry, physics, science problems, and quantitative skills. It should be taken about eighteen months before you plan to enter medical school.

You should prepare diligently for the exam since so much is at stake. Some students may take preparatory courses from independent test preparatory centers, which are located in several major cities. Other students may prepare for the exam by purchasing MCAT preparatory books. You should use some method to study for the exam.

The premedical committee is a vital part of the admission process and is usually composed of a body of campus science and math professors including the premedical advisor. The committee prescreens and rates premedical students. If your campus has one, you cannot bypass it. This committee interviews students and collects and forwards composite recommendations of premed students to medical schools, along with ratings for each student.

Since recommendations play an important part in the admission process and since many of your science or math professors may be on the committee, you should cultivate relationships with your professors so that they know both you and your work. You should also develop a good relationship with your premedical advisor, who will not only give you sound advice on the admission procedure but can also provide a reference.

The Application Process

You should begin applying to medical schools one year before you plan to attend, or as early as June or July before your senior year. The American Medical College Application Service (AMCAS), which is used by some schools, will help. AMCAS, a central processing service, receives your application and transcript and summarizes the information, which is then disseminated to the schools of your choice. Many medical schools use the service, but if your school does not, then you must apply directly.

AMCAS also provides the Medical Minority Applicant Register (Med-Mar), which will give you an opportunity to have vital biographical information about you sent to all medical and other health professional schools. If these schools are interested in you, you may be invited to apply.

To avoid missing deadlines, get your applications in early. Remember that medical schools start selecting their new classes early and you don't want to wait until these classes are nearly filled. Also make sure your applications are neat in appearance, grammatically correct, and complete. Depending on your qualifications, you may hear from the schools early or as late as the summer before you plan to attend.

What Will You Earn as a Physician?

It is generally felt that physicians earn very high salaries. However, your location, the economic ability of your patients, and your skill and reputation will influence how much money you will make. The American Medical Association reports that physicians in pediatrics and family or general medicine have an average income of $71,000; the average income of a surgeon is $152,000.[1]

OSTEOPATHIC MEDICINE

This fast-growing profession can offer you many opportunities. Doctors of Osteopathy (DOs) diagnose and treat diseases, but are given training in an extra dimension—the musculoskeletal system.[2] They use structural diagnosis and manipulation of the bones and muscles by hand to aid in the treatment of disease. They should not, however, be confused with chiropractors, who also use manual manipulation. The profession has a holistic approach to health care. They also treat diseases by traditional medical methods like surgery and drugs.

The majority of osteopathic physicians practice family medicine. The largest number of these physicians are found in Florida, Michigan, Pennsylvania, Missouri, New Jersey, Ohio, and Texas.[3]

Career Pathing in Osteopathic Medicine

Requirements for admission to one of the fifteen schools of osteopathic medicine is generally three years of college, but most applicants have four years. Courses in English (6–8 semester hours), general chemistry (8 semester hours), organic chemistry (6–8 semester hours), biology (8–12 semester hours), and physics (8 semester hours) are mandatory. You are generally required to take the Medical College Admission Test. Osteopathic medical schools also like to see backgrounds of participation in civic activities dealing with the health of a community, sensitivity to individual, family, and community health needs, and clinical experience, particularly in osteopathic hospitals or clinics.

Admission to osteopathic colleges is competitive. You must have good grades, recommendations, and MCAT scores. You must also understand the nature of osteopathic medicine and have a commitment to it. Those students who pass preadmission screenings will be invited for interviews.

After a successful interview, you may be accepted. Osteopathic medical education generally takes three or four years to complete. To successfully complete training and become a Doctor of Osteopathy, you should have perseverance, good study skills, and discipline.

All states and the District of Columbia require that osteopathic physicians be licensed. Licensing requirements include graduation from an approved osteopathic medical school and passing a state board examination.[4] Most states require a post-osteopathic medical training period (residency). During this period, you will be exposed to many areas, including medicine, surgery, obstetrics, anesthesiology, radiology, and clinical pathology. You can then go to a residency for specialization or fellowship.

What Will You Earn as an Osteopathic Physician?

Most osteopathic physicians are in family practices and enjoy salaries comparable to other professionals'. Specialists tend to make more. Salaries vary according to ability, years of experience, and location. Recent studies indicate that the average income for physicians is approximately $108,000.[5]

DENTISTRY

There is a shortage of Black dentists to properly service the Black community. Therefore, you should consider a career as a dentist. As a dentist, you can help children and adults maintain good dental health by diagnosing and treating diseases and abnormalities of the teeth and supporting structures.

Dentists examine teeth and surrounding tissues of the mouth, take X-rays, clean teeth, treat gums, remove teeth, and perform corrective surgery. If you have visited a dentist lately, you know that dentistry has become more advanced in recent years.

As a woman, you should note that dentistry will allow you to combine a family and career because a dentist's hours are flexible, which will allow you to work and raise children. It can also be a lucrative field which will allow you to be financially independent.

Career Pathing in Dentistry

Admission to dental school requires two to four years of predental work, but most of those admitted have four years. You need biology, chemistry, physics, math, and English and social science subjects, and you must take the Dental Admission Test (DAT), which is required of all applicants. For schools which use it, the American Association of Dental Schools Application Service (AADSAS), a centralized application service, must be used.

Dental schools, like medical schools, are competitive, and your grade point average and DAT scores are weighed heavily. Other factors considered for admission are leadership ability and community and health activity involvement. Good recommendations from science faculty members and the premedical committee are also important factors.

Dental school education is usually four years, though some schools have three-year programs. Your first two years will be spent in classroom and laboratory activities learning the basic sciences; the last two years are spent primarily in a dental clinic working with patients. After successful completion of dental school coursework and clinical work, you will be awarded the Doctor of Dental Surgery (D.D.S.) or the equivalent of Doctor of Dental Medicine (D.D.M.).

After graduation, you may open your own office or go for additional postgraduate training in a specialty. There are eight specialties recognized by the American Dental Association:

1. Dental Public Health
2. Endodontics
3. Oral Pathology
4. Oral Surgery
5. Orthodontics
6. Pedodontics
7. Periodontics
8. Prosthodontics

To practice dentistry, you must be licensed. Licensing requires that you be a graduate of an American Dental Association–approved dental school and pass a written and practical examination. Forty-nine states and the District of Columbia allow candidates to partially fulfill state licensing requirements by successfully passing a written examination by the National Board of Dental Examiners. If you want to specialize, sixteen states and the District of Columbia require two or three years of graduate work and in several instances you must pass a special state examination.[6] In the other states, you must have graduate training and your practice will be regulated by the dental profession.

What Will You Earn as a Dentist?

Dentists can make lucrative salaries depending on their locations, type of patients, and if they are in specialties. The average salary of a dentist is approximately $60,000 a year; those who specialize earn approximately $95,000.[7]

PODIATRY

There is a severe shortage of Black podiatrists. Many of us do not consider podiatry because of the lack of role models in the field. Many do not know of the vital work which podiatrists perform: treating and caring for conditions of the human foot; fitting corrective devices; prescribing drugs, physical therapy, or proper shoes; treating corns, bunions, ingrown toenails, skin and nail disorders; treating deformed toes and arch disabilities; and performing corrective surgery. Persons suffering from bowlegs, club feet, corns, bunions, flat feet, and other foot and lower body extremity disorders are thankful to these primary care physicians.

Podiatry is a good field for women. The hours are flexible, allowing time for family and career.

Surprisingly, Black women have been in the field of podiatry for decades. Dr. Mildred Dixon, a podiatrist who is interested in preserving the history of Black women in the field, has chronicled our involvement in a paper called "The Long Walk."

Career Pathing in Podiatry

The minimum requirement for admission to colleges of podiatric medicine is three years of college, but over 90 percent of first-year students have bachelors' degrees. Admission standards are competitive. To gain admission to one of five colleges of podiatric medicine, you should have course work in chemistry, biology or zoology, physics, mathematics, and English. You are also required to take the Medical College Admission Test.

According to some experts, there is a need for more Black and minority podiatrists. Robert T. McDonald, health educational consultant and former assistant dean for Student Affairs at the New York College of Podiatric Medicine, says, "Today, there's a tremendous health man/woman power shortage in the profession of podiatric medicine. There are about 8,500 podiatrists in the United States. There is a need for more podiatrists in general and for more minority podiatrists in particular. There is only one podiatrist for every 23,000 Americans. However, there are fewer than 400 minority podiatrists, with Blacks accounting for only 275 or three percent of all practicing podiatrists."

It takes four years of training in a podiatric medicine college to become a podiatrist. The first two are spent in classroom and laboratory activities, the last two are spent in clinic work and the classroom.

After successfully completing training, you will be eligible to obtain the Doctor of Podiatric Medicine degree (D.P.M.). To practice, you must become licensed. Licensing requirements include graduation from an accredited school and passing written and oral state board proficiency examinations.[8] New Jersey, Michigan, Virginia, California, Arizona, Rhode Island, Oklahoma, and Georgia also require a one-year residency in a hospital or clinic.

What Will You Earn as a Podiatrist?

The average salary for practicing podiatrists is approximately $50,000, according to the Occupational Outlook Handbook.

OPTOMETRY

Optometrists specialize in examining people's eyes and diagnosing vision problems, diseases, and abnormalities. They prescribe lenses and give care to those who wear corrective lenses. About 4 percent of today's practicing optometrists are Black.

Career Pathing in Optometry

To become an optometrist, you must have a minimum of two years of college, though some schools require three years and a considerable number of candidates have bachelors' degrees, master's degrees, or more advanced degrees. With the competition for seats, it is wise to prepare yourself maximally. To be competitive with other candidates for admission, you will need courses including English, mathematics, physics, chemistry, and biology or zoology. You must also take the Optometry College Admission Test (OCAT).

The four-year optometry school or college curriculum is rigorous, and successful completion of it will require discipline and good study habits. After graduation, you will receive the Doctor of Optometry, but you will have to be licensed by the state in which you wish to practice. Licensing requires graduation from an accredited optometric school or college and passing a state board examination. In some states you may take the exam of the National Board of Examiners in lieu of passing part of a state exam.[9]

What Will You Earn as an Optometrist?

New practicing optometrists make average salaries of approximately $27,000 a year, but experienced ones average approximately $55,000 a year.[10] Many optometrists make much more, depending on their type of practice, the location, and the type of clientele. Some optometrists work in group practices, for the government, teach, or do research, and their salaries reflect where they work and what they do.

VETERINARIANS

There are very few Black veterinarians in the United States. It is not a field that many of us think of, but it is one where we can add substantially to the well-being of those in our community. In their work, along with diagnosing, examining, treating, performing surgery, and controlling diseases and injuries in animals, veterinarians also inspect meat and other animal products which we eat. Their work is used in medical research, the space program, and environmental pollution.

Career Pathing in Veterinary Medicine

There are twenty-seven accredited colleges of veterinary medicine. To be eligible for admission, you must have at least two years of preveterinary study in the physical and biological sciences, but most candidates have at least three to four years of preveterinary study. You must also take the Veterinary Aptitude Test (VAT) for admission. Competition for admission to these schools is keen. Most colleges prefer their state's residents, but some arrangements have been made particularly for those students in the South and West to participate in regional educational plans which allow them to attend designated regional schools.

Once admitted to veterinary medical college, you will find the course work tough. But once you complete the four-year professional program, you will be conferred with a Doctor of Veterinary Medicine degree (D.V.M. or V.M.D.).

After graduation, you must be licensed. After licensing, you can go into private practice or work at a hospital, farm, ranch, zoo, or teach in veterinary college, or do research for the federal government, animal food companies, or pharmaceutical companies.

What Will You Earn as a Veterinarian?

Starting salaries for new graduates in private practice range from $19,000 to $21,000. Experienced veterinarians average $46,000. The average salary for those in the federal government is $40,000.[11]

NURSING

There have been many Black role models who are nurses, therefore, it is a field to which many Black women have aspired. Our role models have been fine examples of career women: Mary Mahoney, the first Black nurse; Martha Franklin, founder of the National Association of Colored Graduate Nurses; Adah Thoms, a high-ranking administrator of the Lincoln School for Nurses and campaigner for professional equality for Black nurses.[12] It is an honorable area which is and has been a source of steady income.

Nursing becomes an automatic career choice in the health field because many of you are people oriented and care about others. Today, there is a nursing shortage, and the field offers exciting career opportunities and job possibilities.

Career Pathing in Nursing

To become a Registered Nurse (RN) you must be a high school graduate, and you must qualify for one of the types of nursing programs. Two programs, the associate degree and bachelor's degree programs, are of particular interest.

In the associate degree program, you will enroll in a two-year college program at a junior or community college and receive an associate degree upon completion. With the bachelor's degree program, you will enroll in a program which will generally take four years to complete, but some take five. In the future, nurses with bachelor's degrees will have the best employment opportunities. The bachelor's degree will also qualify you for managerial or administrative positions. A master's will enhance your marketability in teaching, consultation, and specialization.

All states and the District of Columbia require that you obtain a license to practice. Licensing requirements include graduation from an approved school of nursing and passing a written state board competency examination.

Once licensed, you may work in a hospital, nursing home, school, government agency, visiting nurses' association, clinic, private industry, a doctor's office, or on private duty.

What Will You Earn as a Nurse?

The median salary for registered nurses is $21,000 a year. The top 10 percent of nurses—most of them supervisors—make more than $31,000, according to the Occupational Outlook Handbook.

OTHER HEALTH OCCUPATIONS

There are more than two hundred different health and health-related occupations: dental assistants; dental hygienists; dental laboratory technicians; electrocardiograph technicians; electroencephalographic technologists and technicians; emergency medical technicians; medical laboratory workers; medical record technicians and clerks; operating room technicians; optometric assistants; radiologic (X-ray) technologists; respiratory therapy workers; physical therapists; physical therapists' assistants and aides; occupational therapists; occupational therapy assistants; speech pathologists; radiologists; dieticians; dispensing opticians; health service administrators; medical record administrators; and pharmacists. For a description of some of these health workers, see Table 21.

TABLE 21

OTHER HEALTH WORKERS*

PHARMACISTS—dispense drugs and medicines prescribed by physicians and dentists.

To become a pharmacist, you must be licensed. Licensing requirements include graduation from an accredited pharmacy degree program, which requires study five years beyond high school, passing a state board examination, and completing an internship or getting practical experience.

Prepharmacy courses should include biology, chemistry, physics, mathematics, humanities, and social science. After graduation, you can work in community pharmacies, hospitals, for industry, or teach or do research. According to a recent survey by *Drug Topics* magazine, the average starting salary for pharmacists in chain drugstores is $32,200 a year; median earnings are about $29,000.

MEDICAL TECHNOLOGISTS—work under pathologists, do tests including analyzing blood, tissues, and human body fluids.

Medical technologists usually complete four years of college including specialized medical technology training.

After the completion of training and state examination, you can be certified as a Medical Technologist (MT ASCP) by the Board of Registry of the American Society of Clinical Pathologists, or as a Medical Technologist (MT) by the American Medical Technologists, or as a Registered Medical Technologist (RMT) by the International Society of Clinical Laboratory Technology. Medical technologists in Florida, California, Hawaii, Nevada, and Tennessee must be licensed.

An Executive Compensation Service, Inc., study states that the average starting salary for chief medical technologists is between $25,300 and $31,000.[13]

PHYSICAL THERAPISTS—help those with disabilities caused by nerve, muscle, joint, and bone diseases or injuries overcome their problems. They work with patients to help them regain the use of muscles after an

---

* Parts of this chapter appeared in the author's article "Allied Health Needs You," *Essence,* August 1977.

amputation, stroke, or an attack of crippling arthritis. In treating patients, water, massage, light, and heat are used.

To become a physical therapist requires completion of an approved four-year bachelor's degree program. If you have a bachelor's degree in another field, you can apply to an approved clinical program to receive a certificate, or pursue another bachelor's degree in this field, or take a master's degree in the field.

You must be licensed to practice. Licensing requirements include having a degree or certificate from an accredited program and passing a state examination. After licensing, you can work in a hospital, nursing home, rehabilitation center, school for the handicapped, physicians' office, public health agency, research organization, or you can teach. Some physical therapists are in private practice.

The average starting salary for physical therapists is $19,000 a year, and supervisory therapists earn more than $35,000, according to a University of Texas medical branch survey.[14]

OCCUPATIONAL THERAPISTS—work with people with emotional or physical problems by giving them educational, recreational, and vocational activities to help them adjust and cope with their disabilities. You will work in a hospital, clinic, psychiatric facility, or special school.

To become an occupational therapist, you must have a bachelor's degree and certification. Some schools have a two-year program for those who have already completed two years of college. Others have shorter programs for students with bachelor's degrees in other fields. In these programs you can get certificates or master's degrees. A graduate of an accredited program can take an examination to become a registered occupational therapist (OTR).

A survey by the University of Texas medical branch states that occupational therapists begin with an average salary of $18,900; some experienced ones make up to $25,700; some administrators make up to $33,000.[15]

EMERGENCY MEDICAL TECHNICIANS (or ambulance attendants)—save lives during medical emergencies like heart attacks, automobile accidents, or poisonings.

To become an emergency medical technician (EMT), you should include a 110-hour training program designed by the Department of

Transportation, and offered by police, fire, and health departments, in hospitals, and at some medical schools, colleges and universities.

Graduation from an approved EMT program, having specified experience requirements, and passing a written and practical examination for the National Registry of Emergency Medical Technicians can earn you the designation of Registered EMT-Ambulance. The National Registry also registers EMT-Paramedics. This designation requires EMT-Ambulance registration or state certification, completion of an EMT-Paramedic training program, six months of EMT-Paramedic field experience, and passing a written and practical examination. All states have some certification procedures.

A survey by the *Journal of Emergency Medical Services* indicates that annual earnings for EMT-Ambulance are $14,520; for EMT-Intermediates $14,716, and for EMT-Paramedics $18,540.[16]

HEALTH SERVICE ADMINISTRATORS—are managers of medical and health care facilities including hospitals, nursing homes, and clinics.

Usually the first step to becoming a health services administrator is to become associate or assistant administrator. A master's degree in health or hospital administration will prepare you for this position. A master's degree in public health may prepare you for work as a program analyst or program representative in public health departments, as well.

Hospital administrators' salaries vary greatly.

CAREER PROFILES

Muriel Petioni and Donna Mendes are women with impressive medical careers. Dr. Petioni has a history of serving the Black community. For more than three decades, she has worked in New York's Harlem community and been an active member of civic and community groups. Dr. Mendes is a new breed of Black woman physician. She has chosen surgery and is in vascular surgery.

Dr. Melba Adams Wilson is a dentist specializing in periodontics. She is a role model for those wanting to pursue dentistry.

Dr. Mildred Dixon has career pathed in podiatric medicine. Currently, she is semi-retired.

Dr. Adriane E. Murray is one of the few Black women optometrists, and is in private practice in Little Falls, New Jersey.

Muriel Petioni, M.D.
Physician
New York, New York

Muriel Petioni is one of the Black women medical crusaders. After graduating from Howard University College of Medicine in 1937, she began a long and impressive career. Petioni was inspired to study and practice medicine by her physician father, a former Trinidadian radical newspaper reporter. "In 1918, my father was invited to leave Trinidad and came to this country to study medicine. He encouraged us to study a profession so we could be independent," Petioni recalls.

To tackle premedical studies, she enrolled in New York University, but later transferred to Howard University. After graduation, she went to Howard University College of Medicine. After medical studies, she returned to New York to do an internship at Harlem Hospital. "I chose Harlem Hospital primarily because it had a good reputation, but also there really was little choice. At the time, there were not many hospitals taking Blacks. Even at Harlem, the physicians were mostly white," Petioni remembers. "I took a two-year internship: the first year, department rotations occurred, the last six months of the second year were devoted to a speciality. I chose Obstetrics-Gynecology. If I had stayed a third year, I would have taken what is now called a residency. But I did do something similar to a residency in Ob-Gyn at Homer G. Phillips Hospital in St. Louis, Missouri." She received twenty dollars a month for her services.

After post-medical training Petioni delayed starting a practice to become college physician at Wilberforce University. "I was not ready to go into private practice. I was rushed through school and graduated from medical school at age twenty-three. At the time, you could go to medical school after three years of college and at the end of the first year, receive a bachelor's degree," she says. "My father pushed me because he was anxious to help me and my brother and sister while he could. He was not a wealthy physician and needed help financing my brother's and sister's education."

A staff cut at Wilberforce made Petioni reassess her career goals. She could go into private practice or locate to another college position. She chose the latter and moved into a college physician position at Alabama State Teachers' College (now Alabama State University). The new position led to job happiness, personal satisfaction, and marriage. She remained at Alabama State for two years before transferring to Bennett College in Greensboro, North Carolina. Afterwards, she took another college physician slot at Hampton Institute in Virginia.

When World War II broke out, Petioni's husband joined the Armed Forces and she faced life alone. After the war's end, he returned and they moved to Chicago. There she became pregnant with their son, Mal Woolfolk, and retired from medicine. Her newly created housewife status disturbed her aging father. He wanted her to become an active physician. "My father was worried that I was wasting my medical degree. As a result, I decided to come back to New York. I took the boards and began practicing in my cousin's 123rd Street office in Harlem. When my father died in 1951, I took over his practice and have been here ever since," she recalls.

Private practice was difficult; a Black physician's life was not easy. "When I first started practicing, I received five dollars for an office visit. If the patient was on welfare and housebound, I was paid three dollars. Even if the whole family was sick, I was still paid three dollars for the house call," she remembers, "but we were glad to get the three dollars. Back then, I could earn about four hundred a month by making three-dollar house calls, which kept me going and paid my rent. It's a lot easier now."

Medicine has become a more viable career opportunity for Black women; the opportunities have increased. "When I came out, you could only go into general practice. Now if a woman wants, she can go into a medical speciality, and is paid from nineteen thousand to twenty-five thousand dollars a year while studying. She can even go into a speciality where she works nine-to-five or part-time and still have time for a family," says Petioni. "A woman doesn't have to feel that medicine will interfere with her personal life."

Yet a woman physician can experience difficulty managing family and career. Petioni and her colleagues discovered a unique way to help one another. "Years ago, the number of Black women physicians in New York was so small that we all knew each other. We needed each other because we had special problems. We had problems with practicing medicine and having husbands and children," she says. "As our numbers grew, we had no way of coming into contact. I thought it was a shame we didn't know and couldn't help each other. One day in 1974 we called a meeting and the Susan Smith McKinney Steward Medical Society was formed. We have held seminars and a luncheon that honored women who had been in medicine over fifty years. We coordinated a national job announcement system." She is also active with the Coalition of 100 Black Women's Health Committee.

Petioni feels women can now better manage medicine. "Of all the professions I know, medicine has the most flexibility and variety. But it's demanding. You must like people and be willing to involve yourself totally in your work. If you can, it's a rewarding profession," she advises.

Donna Mendes, M.D.
Vascular and General Surgeon
Clinical Instructor
Columbia University, College of Physicians and Surgeons
New York, New York

It's a long and difficult road to becoming a physician. Becoming a surgeon is twice as hard, but Dr. Donna Mendes has chosen surgery as a specialty. It's been eighteen years since she began training. There will be many more years before she reaches her career height, but she continues her struggle.

As an undergraduate at Hofstra University in Hempstead, New York, Mendes dropped speech therapy to pursue premedical studies. Between study time and classes, she helped other Black premedical students by helping to organize a premedical club. As president of Hofstra's minority premedical group, she helped motivate others and served as a role model.

In 1973, she graduated and enrolled in Columbia University's College of Physicians and Surgeons. That first year was difficult. "At Columbia, there were many first-year students who had graduated at the tops of their classes, and this created a very competitive atmosphere. Fortunately, there were eleven Black students in our class, and we helped each other by studying together," she remembers. "After the first year, things eased up. The next three years were subsequently easier; the last year was easiest."

In 1977, the group of eleven Black Columbia medical students graduated, received the M.D. degree, and went on to do their postgraduate first years (internships). Mendes began an internship at St. Luke's/ Roosevelt Hospital on New York's Upper West Side. St. Luke's/Roosevelt is a teaching hospital, one affiliated with Columbia University, and she felt that it would give her a great deal of clinical experience. Like many Black physicians, she wanted a chance to help Blacks and other minorities. The hospital is based in a community that houses a mixture of ethnic groups.

The first-year internship was rough. Her life revolved around the hospital. There was little time for sleep or socializing. "As an intern, you are known as the 'scut person,' someone who does everything that the chief resident requests. It was my responsibility to admit patients, start i.v.'s, insert catheters, and take care of wound victims," she says. "I was exposed to the clinic and emergency rooms and performed minor surgical procedures." She spent spare time constantly reading to keep abreast of the medical field. It was a difficult year, but she managed.

It was this internship year, however, that confirmed her idea of pursuing surgery. Surgery is a difficult medical subspecialty to pursue. In the past, few women have career pathed in this male-dominated area. Traditionally, it has taken an exceptional woman to tackle one of the profession's most prestigious and lucrative specialties. Today, more women are entering the field.

With surgery confirmed as an ultimate career goal, Mendes entered postgraduate year two. "In that year, I received more responsibility. Second-year postgraduate students are the first called to the emergency room for major trauma and diagnostic surgical problems. I assisted with open heart surgery cases and took care of clinic patients. If I had any questions, I called the fourth-year postgraduate students," she recalls. "In my third postgraduate year, I instructed interns on minor surgical procedures like breast biopsies. I took care of acutely ill patients in the surgical intensive care unit and was responsible for taking care of the entire ward. After the chief resident went home, I was the most senior person on the ward in the evening. And the chief resident was responsible for advising me on certain cases."

The fourth year brought more responsibility as Mendes climbed the medical hierarchy. "I was responsible for patient care on the ward and advising second-year students on emergency room and bedside procedures, instructing interns on admitting procedures and everything that was done in the evening, and making sure that the ward ran smoothly," she says. "A fourth-year postgraduate student is also the most senior in terms of heart surgery. My other responsibilities included balancing things between the chief resident and the attending physicians. I also did surgical consultations for nonsurgical subspecialty departments that needed advice on surgical problems."

In July of 1981, Mendes became chief resident in general surgery. In order to become board certified, she had to have a tenure as chief resident. "As chief resident, I had the power to decide which surgical procedures I wanted to perform, and when. I had to make on-the-spot clinical decisions and judgments about what should be done with evening trauma patients who have gunshot or knife wounds," she says. "I was the overseer and coordinator, who made sure that things run smoothly."

Throughout her surgical career, she has performed numerous operations including kidney transplants, pediatric surgery, mastectomies, lung and stomach resections, and neurological procedures. She is a highly skilled surgeon.

In July of 1982 Mendes began a fellowship in vascular surgery at Englewood Hospital in Englewood, New Jersey. Since completing the fellowship, she has worked as a clinical instructor at Columbia's College of Physicians and Surgeons, is also a junior assistant attending at St. Luke's/Roosevelt Hospital and is in private practice.

For those who want to follow a surgical career path, Dr. Mendes says: "The field is very demanding, but can be very rewarding. Don't let anyone talk you out of pursuing surgery because it's hard. It can be very difficult, but you should give it a try. If you want surgery, investigate the field by taking a surgical internship."

Mendes represents the growing number of women surgeons. She is intelligent and hard-working. "To survive in surgery, you must have a strong ego. You have to be assertive by saying what you feel, but also be open to suggestions," she says.

Mendes's assertiveness, professionalism, and integrity have pushed her up the medical hierarchy to success. She has struggled, survived, and become one of our finest surgeons. She is soon to become a fellow of The American College of Surgeons.

Dr. Mendes lives in New York with her husband, Ronald LaMotte.

Melba Adams Wilson, D.D.S.
Houston, Texas

While at Fisk University, Melba Adams Wilson began as a premedical student but switched to predental studies. "I had observed the demands that medicine placed on my physician father's time. In contrast, I had observed my uncles, who are dentists, and found that their hours were less demanding. I thought that dentistry and its nine-to-five hours would allow me to combine career and family," she recalls.

After graduation, Wilson completed dental training at Meharry Medical College School of Dentistry and went to Wilmington Medical Center in Delaware to do a summer's internship. From there, she did three years of postgraduate training at the Goldman School of Graduate Dentistry of Boston University.

Now a periodontist practicing in Houston, Texas, Wilson specializes in preventing, diagnosing, and treating diseases of the supporting structures of the teeth, such as gums, bone, cementum (coverings of the root), and periodontal ligaments. The only Black woman periodontist in the state of Texas, Wilson is a former assistant professor and periodontal consultant for the Department of Community Dentistry at the University of Texas Health Science Center in Houston, and currently a visiting professor and consultant at Meharry.

"Dentistry is a good profession for women. With it, you can maintain an independent financial status or augment your family's income. It affords you professional status and all the benefits which go along with being a health professional. Dentistry also provides a needed and vital service to the community and it is not devastating toward your personal life. I usually work an eight-to-ten-hour day. I don't regret going into dentistry instead of medicine. The pay is good, the life-style satisfying, and dentistry also fulfills my commitment to quality patient health care."

Mildred Dixon, D.P.M.
Podiatrist
Tuskegee Institute, Alabama

A Black female podiatrist persuaded Mildred Dixon to choose podiatry. It was, she said, a stable, secure profession. Curious and ambitious, Dixon investigated the field and applied to the Ohio College of Chiropody in Cleveland. She managed the curriculum well and graduated in 1944. She met and married a college professor and moved with him to Tuskegee Institute, Alabama. They had two children. Dixon then settled into practicing from a home office. She took on another practice in the nearby town of Opelika.

"In the early years, I drove to one of the neighboring towns to see patients. The referring physician arranged for me to use his office on an off day. When my second child was born, I gave up the second office and concentrated on a home practice," Dixon remembers. "For a woman, a home office has certain advantages. It keeps you in closer contact with family and allows a flexible schedule and more time for the PTA and community programs."

In the early days, health professionals like Dixon did not always have lucrative practices. "Pay wasn't always in dollars and cents. I can think of a sack of peas, home canned fruit, a live chicken, and sometimes just a plain 'thank you' from some of the rural patients," recalls Dixon. "For me, it was the satisfaction of having helped them that paid off."

In the late forties and fifties, Southern-style discrimination also took a toll on Black health professionals. For the podiatrist, discrimination came in many forms. Dixon explains one: "When I first came South, I was not permitted to join the state society which meant that I could not join the national society. This was true of all southern Black podiatrists. I contacted some other podiatrists and in 1949 we organized a group of Black podiatrists from Alabama, Florida, Georgia, and Louisiana. The organization was called the American Chiropody Association."

By the late fifties, Dixon was able to move into a full-time position with the Veterans Administration Hospital making her the first full-time female podiatrist in the V.A. system. "They assigned me to a room on the orthopedic ward and gave me an old barber chair until a podiatry chair could be ordered."

During her tenure in Tuskegee's V.A. system, Dixon witnessed the making of impressive inroads in the health care area in the state of Alabama. "We have come a long way. For example, in 1975, the V.A. approved an externship program at our facility with the Ohio College of Podiatric Medicine. Those assigned to the program spent six weeks working with me in the clinic. The first student to complete this program is now practicing in Montgomery, Alabama," she says. "And the V.A. has the only podiatry residency program in the state. In June of 1980, the first resident completed his work. The following year, we added a second resident. In 1982, the approved program had two residents plus externs, who spend four weeks with us."

Dixon, who has been active in persuading Blacks to become podiatrists, points to Black women's impressive role in the field which is chronicled in her research paper, "The Long Walk." "In 1913, Dr. Sarah Childs was the first Black to graduate from the New York Institute of Podiatry. In 1920, Dr. Emily Charlton was the first Black honor student to graduate from the same institution. Drs. Julia Johnson, Bertha Williams, Alma Haskins, and Vera Campbell were also graduates from that institution," she says. "In Cleveland, Ohio, Drs. Beatrice Gaines, Jewel Merchant, and Mabel West were early podiatrists. In Illinois, Dr. Flossie H. Valentine, her daughter, Dr. Joan Valentine, and Dr. Hettie Martin Stevens were graduates of the Illinois College of Chiropody." Drs. Haskins, Johnson, and Campbell, says Dixon, organized the Pi Delta Mu Sorority for Black women podiatrists, who were not welcomed into white sororities. Today, the sorority still offers a yearly scholarship to a prospective Black woman podiatry student.

Dixon hopes Black women will continue to enter the field. "As we older Black women retire or die, we are concerned about the future. Will there be enough young Black females to fill the void?" she asks. "It would be tragic if Black females do not continue in the field of podiatry."

Adriane E. Murray, O.D.
Optometrist
Little Falls, New Jersey

During undergraduate days at Virginia Union University, Adriane Murray was introduced to optometry. "I became interested in optometry after meeting a Black optometrist at a premed club seminar. Although I was always interested in a health career, I became interested in optometry after speaking with him and other optometrists," she recalls.

After graduating, Murray pursued the field at Indiana University's School of Optometry. "Optometry school was very difficult. The first year was particularly difficult but once I mastered the routine, it became a little easier," she remembers. "Going to school in a conservative state like Indiana contributed to the difficulty. A friend and I were the first Black females to ever attend and we experienced problems of finding others to talk and relate to or understand some of our needs."

But Murray's persistence paid off; she graduated from the School of Optometry in 1976 with a Doctor of Optometry degree. "After I graduated, I returned to the East and worked as an optometrist with a Brooklyn ophthalmologist."

Murray decided to get a license and open a practice in New Jersey. "The licensing requirements vary from state to state. Some states will recognize the National Board of Examiners' optometry examinations in lieu of their own written examinations. Some states, however, do not give a written examination and you must take and pass the National Board to practice," she says. "But all states have a practical or clinical examination. You have to pass the national or state written examination, then the practical or clinical. For example, New York does not have a written state examination so you have to pass the National Board in order to take the practical. But in my opinion, the National Board is harder to pass."

Murray has a thriving practice. "As an optometrist, I examine eyes and related structures, take care of vision problems, diagnose eye diseases, give vision therapy, prescribe lenses and contact lenses. My work is different from that of the ophthalmologist, an M.D. who does a residency in diseases and surgery of the eye. Or the optician, who fills prescriptions given by the optometrist and ophthalmologist and works with lenses making sure glasses are correctly fitted."

As a Black woman optometrist, she would like to see more of us in the field. "There is a great need for Black women in optometry. From conversations with other Black women optometrists, we estimate that there are less than fifty of us in the country," she said. "A Black woman interested in optometry should investigate the field completely. Go to an optometrist's office and ask to sit and observe. If possible, arrange to visit an optometry school and talk with some of the faculty and students."

Murray discourages premeds, who want medicine, from going into optometry. "Some people go into optometry as a second choice to medicine. I think if you really want medicine, optometry can be frustrating. In most states, you are not able to treat any of the diseases you are trained to diagnose," she explains. "You know the medicines used in treatment because you've taken pharmacology courses. Yet state laws say you have to refer the patient to the ophthalmologist."

For those who have investigated and want optometry careers, Murray advises contacting the National Optometric Association, a national organization of minority optometrists, which is interested in the recruitment and retention of minority students. (For more information, see "Career Aids.")

Career Aids

Books and Pamphlets
MEDICINE

1. For career information, contact the American Medical Association, 535 North Dearborn St., Chicago, Ill. 60610.
2. *Medical School Admission: U.S.A. & Canada* ($7.50) *and Minority Student Opportunities in United States Medical Colleges* ($7.50), available from Membership and Subscriptions, Association of American Medical Colleges, 1 Dupont Circle, NW, Washington, D.C. 20036.

Professional Organizations

1. Student National Medical Association, 1012 10th St., NW, Suite 1000, Washington, D.C. 20001.

2. Minority Student Information Clearinghouse, Association of American Medical Colleges, 1 Dupont Circle, NW, Suite 200, Washington, D.C. 20036.
3. National Medical Association, 1012 10th Street, NW, Washington, D.C. 20001.
4. The Susan Smith McKinney Steward Medical Society, c/o Dr. Muriel Petioni, 114 West 131st St., New York, N.Y. 10030.

Professional Examination Information

1. For MCAT registration information: MCAT Registration, The American College Testing Program, P. O. Box 414, Iowa City, Iowa 5224–3.
2. For the MCAT Student Manual ($7.00, Plus $1.00 per book for fourth-class postage): Membership and Subscriptions, Association of American Medical Colleges, 1 Dupont Circle, NW, Suite 200, Washington, D.C. 20036.
3. For AMCAS Information: Association of American Medical Colleges, 1 Dupont Circle, NW, Suite 200, Washington, D.C. 20036 Att: AMCAS

Books and Pamphlets
OSTEOPATHIC MEDICINE

1. For career information, contact American Association of Colleges of Osteopathic Medicine, 4720 Montgomery Lane, Suite 609, Washington, D.C. 20014.

Professional Organizations

1. The American Osteopathic Association, Department of Public Relations, 212 East Ohio St., Chicago, Ill. 60611.

Books and Pamphlets
DENTISTRY

1. For career information, contact Council on Dental Education, American Dental Association, 211 East Chicago Ave., Chicago, Ill. 60611.
2. *Admissions Requirements of U.S. and Canadian Dental Schools* and *AADSAS Brochure* (for applications of the American Associa-

tion of Dental Schools Application Service) available from the American Association of Dental Schools, 1625 Massachusetts Ave., NW, Washington, D.C. 20036.

Professional Organizations

1. National Dental Association, 5506 Connecticut Ave. Suite 24–25 NW, Washington, D.C. 20015.

Professional Organizations
PODIATRY

1. The American Association of Colleges of Podiatric Medicine and the American Podiatry Association, 6110 Executive Blvd., Suite 204, Rockville, Md. 20852.
2. The Podiatric Medical Students' Ethnic Minority Organization (PMSEMD), located at each college of podiatric medicine.

Books and Pamphlets
OPTOMETRY

1. *Information for Applicants to Schools and Colleges of Optometry* (limited quantities available free) from the American Optometric Association, 243 North Lindbergh Blvd., St. Louis, Mo. 63141.

Professional Organizations

1. Association of Schools and Colleges of Optometry, Suite 410, 600 Maryland Ave., SW, Washington, D.C. 20024
2. National Optometric Association, 2830 South Indiana Ave., Chicago, Ill. 60616.

Professional Organizations
VETERINARY MEDICINE

1. The American Veterinary Medical Association, 930 North Meacham Rd., Schaumburg, Ill. 60196.

Professional Organizations
NURSING

1. Communications Department, National League for Nursing, 10 Columbus Circle, New York, N.Y. 10009. For networking with other Black nurses, contact:
2. National Black Nurses Association, Inc., 818 Harrison Ave., House Officers Bldg., Room 413, Boston, Mass. 02118.
3. American Nurses Association 2420 Pershing Rd., Kansas City, Mo. 64108

Professional Organizations
PHARMACISTS

1. The American Association of Colleges of Pharmacy, Office of Student Affairs, 4720 Montgomery Ave., Suite 602, Bethesda, Md. 20814.
2. The American Pharmaceutical Association, 2215 Constitution Ave., NW, Washington, D.C. 20037.
3. National Pharmaceutical Association, P. O. Box 934 Howard University, Washington, D.C. 20059.

Professional Organizations
MEDICAL TECHNOLOGISTS

1. The American Society of Clinical Pathologists, Board of Registry, P. O. Box 12270, Chicago, Ill. 60612.
2. American Society of Medical Technology, 330 Meadowfern Drive, Houston, Tex. 77067.
3. American Medical Technologists, 710 Higgins Rd., Park Ridge, Ill. 60068.

Professional Organizations
PHYSICAL THERAPISTS

1. American Physical Therapy Association, 1111 North Fairfax St., Alexandria, Va. 22314.

Professional Organizations
OCCUPATIONAL THERAPISTS

1. American Occupational Therapy Association, 1383 Piccard Drive, Rockville, Md. 20852.

Professional Organizations
EMERGENCY MEDICAL TECHNICIANS

1. National Association of Emergency Medical Technicians, P. O. Box 334, Newton Highlands, Mass. 02161–0334.
2. National Registry of Emergency Medical Technicians, P. O. Box 24233, Columbus, Ohio 43229.

Professional Organizations
HEALTH SERVICE ADMINISTRATORS

1. American College of Hospital Administrators, 840 North Lake Shore Drive, Chicago, Ill. 60611.

All addresses and prices are subject to change.

PSYCHOLOGY

Many people in the Black community are skeptical of psychology and psychologists. Some feel mental illness is not our biggest problem. Others feel that the field is not oriented to the unique mental problems of Blacks in this society.

However, as the economic situation worsens, poor people and poor Black people particularly will suffer most from the ravages of unemployment, the high cost of living, poor housing conditions, rising crime rates, drug and alcohol abuse, and cutbacks in essential services—all of which will result in increasing stress, tension, and emotional trauma.

Black psychologists will be needed to help us cope with these conditions. If more of us become psychologists, our presence, sensitivities, and concerns will help persuade the profession to focus more on the psychological needs of Black men, women, and children. We will be able to join forces with those few Blacks who are teachers and students in graduate schools of psychology as well as those who are professionals in mental health facilities and researchers in social and behavioral science facilities.

Career Pathing in Psychology

There are several career paths in psychology: clinical, experimental, social, psychometric (quantitative), industrial/organizational, personnel, engineering, educational, developmental, community, counseling, child clinical, and school (see Table 22).

Typically, a doctorate in psychology will give you the most career leverage, and the Doctor of Philosophy (Ph.D.), Doctor of Psychology (Psy.D.), and Doctor of Education (Ed.D.) are three types of doctoral degrees available in the field.

The Ph.D. is geared toward research and usually takes four or more years to complete.[1] You must write a dissertation or original research paper which will contribute to the field and, in most cases, you must take a one-year internship before completing requirements. Because of discussions about the relevance of the Ph.D.'s research orientation for those who want to become therapists, the Psy.D. was developed to give more practical experience.[2] The Ed.D.'s orientation is primarily toward education rather than research or practical therapy training.

After graduate training at the doctoral level, psychologists who want to go into private practice must become certified and licensed in all states and the District of Columbia. Licensing requirements vary but usually include the doctorate, two years of professional experience, and successfully passing a written examination.

To obtain more credentials, you can secure diplomas from the American Board of Professional Psychology in clinical, counseling, individual or organizational, and school psychology. Qualifications for these diplomas include a doctorate, five years of specified experience, recommendations, and completion of an examination.[3]

Although the field is geared toward completion of the doctorate, a master's degree in psychology may qualify you to work as an assistant under a psychologist, or as a counselor, researcher in some fields, or community college teacher. To enter some master programs, your undergraduate degree should be in psychology, while others require degrees in related fields.

TABLE 22

PSYCHOLOGY SPECIALTIES†

CLINICAL

In the largest psychology specialty, you may work in mental health facilities like hospitals or clinics or in private practice helping those with mental or emotional problems cope with their lives. You will be involved in test administration and interpretation, provision of therapy to clients, or, in some instances, you will do research. In most instances, clinical psychologists have doctorates.

EXPERIMENTAL

In this area, through research with human beings and animals like monkeys or rats, you will study behavior. Your area of expertise may be learning and retention, motivation, sensory and perceptual processes, or genetic and neurological factors in behavior, and you will typically be known as a psychologist of your area of expertise, e.g., learning psychologist. The Ph.D. is required for these research-oriented positions.

SOCIAL

Social psychologists study how we, as individuals within groups, behave with others in our social settings. As this professional, you may work in the areas of group behavior, dependency relationships, or leadership. You may be involved in research or teaching.

PSYCHOMETRIC

As a psychometric (quantitative) psychologist, you will work in the area of analyzing and developing tests to measure behavior. Typically a Ph.D. and a good background in math, statistics, and computers are needed for this area.

INDUSTRIAL/ORGANIZATIONAL

As an industrial and organizational psychologist, you will work in the area of personnel assessment, research, policy, planning, training and development, organizational development, and other activities which study the relationship between workers and employment. You may work in private industry, government, or higher educational institutions, and you must have a doctorate.

PERSONNEL

As a personnel psychologist, you will focus on the personnel functions of organizations: interviewing, testing, and selecting and promoting employees, and you will be involved in such activities as assessing and updating selection criteria. A background in psychometrics is a plus and a doctorate is usually required, though some with lesser degrees can get entry-level positions.

ENGINEERING

As an engineering psychologist, you will be concerned with our living and working environments and will design methods to enhance both. For example, you may design an office space for graphic artists, taking into consideration that they must have large drawing boards, proper lighting, and comfortable environments to increase creativity. Typically a Ph.D. is required.

EDUCATIONAL

As an educational psychologist, you may develop instructional or training materials, analyze and come up with effective conditions for learning, and evaluate educational programs. A doctorate is a plus for obtaining positions in educational systems.

DEVELOPMENTAL

Developmental psychologists are concerned with people's various development stages from childhood to old age. Your chances for employment will increase if you have a doctorate.

COMMUNITY

Community psychologists analyze the relationship between individuals and their communities. A doctorate is also a plus in this area.

COUNSELING

As a counseling psychologist, you will use interviewing and testing to assess people with everyday problems: academic, vocational, social, and personal. You may counsel, teach, do research, or become an administrator or consultant. The doctorate is generally required.

CHILD CLINICAL

As a child clinical psychologist you will work primarily with preteens, helping them cope with emotional or mental problems. A doctorate is required in this area.

SCHOOL

As a school psychologist, you will work with school-age children helping them work through emotional difficulties, adjust to school, and cope with learning and social problems.

OTHER PSYCHOLOGISTS
   Environmental
   Personality
   Evaluation
   Population
   Physiological
   Consumer

† Source: Adapted from the American Psychological Association, *Careers in Psychology.* Copyright © 1986.

There are some bachelor degree programs that will qualify you to work in some psychological settings or teach in secondary schools. There are also associate-degree training programs which offer you a chance to work in testing and interviewing in the mental health area under psychologists or other professionals.[4] However, since little is known about this training, you may find difficulty in obtaining positions.

What Will You Earn as a Psychologist?

As a psychologist, your salary will vary according to the level of your position and the type and location of your employer.

A recent survey by the National Research Council states that the median salary for psychologists with doctorates is approximately $35,800. In educational institutions, the median is $33,600; in government (state and local), approximately $32,300; in nonprofit organizations, $29,800; in private industry, $48,000. In the federal government, the average salary is about $39,800, according to the Occupational Outlook Handbook.

CAREER PROFILE

Dr. Nancy Boyd-Franklin is a highly skilled clinical practitioner. She is a clinical psychologist, teacher, wife, and mother, successfully balancing her four roles.

Dr. Nancy Boyd-Franklin, Ph.D.
Clinical Psychologist
Private practice in Brooklyn, New York
Clinical Assistant Professor, The College of Medicine and Dentistry
of New Jersey and
Supervising Psychologist at the Community Mental Health Center,
Child and Adolescent Unit
Newark, New Jersey

Becoming a clinical psychologist is an accomplishment, particularly for a Black woman. Nancy Boyd-Franklin has become one, and hopes others will follow in her career path.

As a psychology undergraduate at Swarthmore College, Boyd-Franklin spent many spare hours counseling fellow students. She enjoyed it and decided to combine an interest in helping adults and children. "While in school, I became interested in children's development and learning problems. I had education training and began to think of ways to work with children, families, and adults. But after being dorm counselor I realized that I wanted to do something broader than teaching. I wanted to do something that would combine work with children and young adults," she remembers. "I wanted a flexible field that included teaching, counseling, and therapy and an opportunity to work with different age groups. One day, a counselor suggested a degree which would allow me to do many different things and have a great deal of flexibility: the degree was a Ph.D. in clinical psychology."

Boyd-Franklin applied to several graduate psychology programs; her major selection criteria was locating a program housed in a school of education. Harvard and Columbia's Teachers College became first choices. She chose Teachers College.

Teachers College's four-year clinical psychology program was challenging. "In the first two years, we did basic studies including diagnostic testing, development, interviewing techniques, different types of psychotherapy, and clinical therapy. I was exposed to child and adult (family, individual, and group) therapy," Boyd-Franklin remembers. "The program is 'technically' four years. But during this period, you should complete course work, take a practicum where you do therapy under supervision, a full year's internship, and the dissertation."

Boyd-Franklin was able to get her doctorate by setting a four-year goal, completing course work on time, and promptly completing an internship in Family Therapy. She applied and was accepted to a year's internship at Philadelphia Child Guidance Clinic. Many Black graduate psychology students are stumped by the internship. Those who work full-time must quit and cut back on expenses to accommodate the often low internship salary.

Boyd-Franklin also graduated on time because there were many Black professionals that helped. "I worked at community agencies all the way through school. During the first two years, I worked at Harlem Interfaith Counseling Services. The staff was very supportive and helped teach me about psychotherapy with Black people," she emphasizes. "Another important support network was the Association of Black Psychologists. Prospective students should get in touch with them immediately. They offer dissertation seminars to help you. Thanks to the Association, I finished my program in four years. Now those of us who went through graduate programs are helping the next group."

Boyd-Franklin feels that Black students must utilize Black professionals to help answer questions concerning therapy for Blacks. "Programs can't give you all the answers. The field is just in its beginning stages of treating Blacks. Many internship programs, for example, have never treated or had Blacks on the staff. Therefore, it's difficult for them to answer your questions about the treatment of Blacks," she advises. "That's why building a network of Black mental health professionals is essential to your survival. They can help you build on the basics of school training. You must then go out and find your own answers and ways of working with our people."

After graduation, Boyd-Franklin set definite career goals to find answers. First, she wanted to delve deeper into serious mental illness and went to work at Bronx Psychiatric Center in Bronx, New York. To diversify her training and include work with children, she moved to Montefiore Hospital and worked as a child psychologist and pediatric liaison in the Child Psychiatry Department.

She found working with children exciting, but limiting. She also wanted to balance the work with treating adults. To accommodate these needs, she opened a practice in Brooklyn, New York. "My private clients are mostly Black women, but I see their families in conjunction with their treatment," she says. "Many Black women struggle with being the child bearer, child rearer, and breadwinner—these conditions can cause tremendous emotional stress." She now also runs therapeutic support groups for Black women in which these issues can be addressed and collective support given. In her practice, she also works with couples and families.

In the last ten years, Boyd-Franklin has developed her professional reputation in the area of family therapy, which she teaches at the University of Medicine and Dentistry of New Jersey. She is clinical assistant professor and a supervisory psychologist at the Community Mental Health Center, Child and Adolescent Unit. She is also the author of numerous articles on therapy with Black families, and is working on a book on the subject.

Boyd-Franklin would like to see other Black women avoid some of the pitfalls in getting the clinical psychology doctorate. "Graduate clinical psychology programs are very competitive, but I feel that minorities have a good chance for admission. Many of the doctorate programs are based in urban areas and many clinics need minority psychologists to work with increasing minority populations and their problems. As a result, we are needed in the field. Psychology is therefore a field Black people should consider," she recommends.

Ideally, it should take four years to complete the program. "Many people have taken six, seven, or ten years to finish," she explains. Many Black students may experience financial difficulties that cause study disruption. Some leave their studies to find full-time employment. Others have problems at internship time. Many internships are low-paying, below many students' life-style requirements. But they are required for graduation and some part-time students cannot easily afford to interrupt full-time jobs to pursue internships.

"After receiving the doctorate, there is a certification process for psychologists. Early in your graduate years, check the licensing procedures for your state. It's important to build that into your career objective—it will allow you to choose a program leading to state certification. They are really tightening up and there are now many state and federal laws pertaining to the practice of psychotherapy. In the past, many have hung out shingles without having proper credentials. Now, in states like New York, you can't administer psychological testing or call yourself a psychologist without licensing," Boyd-Franklin says. "But the problem is each state has its own licensing procedures, and that's one of the things they're working on—trying to standardize licensing procedures."

With proper planning and willingness to seek employment, getting through a clinical program can be eased. Like Boyd-Franklin, you must develop a support network and develop ways to complete your studies on time. If you're successful, you can enjoy a satisfying career.

"Clinical psychology is a wonderful career for a woman who wants to combine a satisfying and rewarding career with marriage and family. Since I have had a child, I have been able to develop flexible hours in order to spend more time with him. This flexibility has allowed me to be active in my professional life and at the same time to enjoy being in a relationship with my husband and child. It is difficult managing all of the roles, but it can be very rewarding," says Boyd-Franklin.

Boyd-Franklin lives with her husband, Dr. A. J. Franklin, who is also a psychologist. She is mother to Jay and stepmother to Deidre, Tunde, and Remi.

Career Aids

For career information, contact:
1. The American Psychological Association
   1200 17th St., NW
   Washington, D.C. 20036
2. The Association of Black Psychologists
   P.O. Box 5599
   Washington, D.C. 20040

For scholarship information, write to:
The American Psychological Association
See address above.

All addresses are subject to change.

5

Careers for the Advancement of Mankind

ENGINEERING

As little Black girls, we were propagandized by the myths that plague the field of engineering. Only recently has there been a massive effort to correct the many misconceptions and misunderstandings about the field.

Let's clear up some of these misconceptions and misunderstandings. First, engineering seems to us to be overwhelmingly difficult, highly technical, and mathematically intricate because as children, the majority of us were not geared toward the sciences and math. In many urban junior high and high schools, we were either told to go into or opted for easier programs that avoided algebra, geometry, trigonometry, physics, chemistry, and biology. Many of us felt we would land in the social sciences in college anyway, so why bother with the "heavy" stuff. Even if we took these courses, it was usually to get academic diplomas rather than a serious attempt to master them.

Many women view engineering as male-oriented. We envision engineers as men who stomp around in hard hats, tinker with machines, and build bridges. We can't imagine ourselves in these roles because we are told it is unfeminine to wear hard hats, unladylike to dirty our hands with machines, and too macho to build bridges.

But the field of engineering is widely diversified. Many engineers are inside designing and problem solving. Many do not work directly with machines or engines. And engineers design bridges rather than build them.

Because we do not view engineering as socially oriented, many of us cross it off our lists as unacceptable. However, the field of engineering is geared toward making things better for people. Where would we be without the engineers who create and are constantly improving many of our modern conveniences? Without the engineer we wouldn't have the design and manufacture of automobiles. We wouldn't be able to launder our clothing in washing machines, or enjoy the luxury of dishwashers, or cook with microwave ovens. Without the engineer's designs, we couldn't communicate with others through telephones or hear music on our stereos or watch television or listen to radios.

Traveling from city to city is made easier because of engineering concepts—airports, airplanes, highways, transportation arteries, and vehicle designs—all are the work of engineers.

Without their work in environmental health, pollution would be more hazardous to our collective health. They have also facilitated the commercial use of computers, heat for our homes, and processing of rubber products and medical devices like pacemakers and patient-monitoring machines.

Engineering has given us many diversified products which have bettered our lives in their own unique and specific ways. And there are other advantages to this field as well.

Engineering as a career offers us diversity in the number of specialties we can select; there are as many as twenty-five areas we can choose from. And within these areas we can often combine two interests. For example, if we are interested in the health field, we can become biomedical engineers working to improve the quality of life for hospital patients.

Engineering graduates make the highest starting salaries of all college graduates![1] Those who go on to graduate M.B.A. programs command more money after graduation than those with liberal arts backgrounds.

Engineering offers many career opportunities because there is a strong move to increase Black representation in the field. As a result, a great deal of scholarship money is pumped into the many programs established to guide us into engineering careers.

Career Pathing in Engineering

Within the more than twenty-five engineering specialties, there are more than eighty-five subdivisions, but let's explore aerospace, agricultural, biomedical, ceramic, chemical, civil, electrical, industrial, mechanical, and metallurgical.

Aerospace Engineer: As an aerospace engineer, you would be involved in the design, development, testing, and production of all types of commercial and military aircraft. You might work with passenger planes, helicopters, satellites, or rockets. You might specialize in structural design, navigational guidance and control, instrumentation, or communication methods. Your work will help us feel safer when we step aboard any aircraft, secure in the knowledge that our commercial aviation defense systems are performing protectively and with maximum efficiency. You might work in one of the federal government agencies, such as the National Aeronautics and Space Administration, the Department of Defense, in private industry, at home, or abroad.

Agricultural Engineer: Your focus as an agricultural engineer would be to design machinery and equipment to facilitate the production, processing, and distribution of our agricultural and food supply.[2] You would be concerned with energy conservation, continuous maintenance of water and soil, and other environmental factors. In this engineering specialty, you will probably work for farm equipment manufacturers, electric and utility companies, farm equipment and supplies distributors, or the Department of Agriculture. You will be constantly at work, seeking ways to improve the production, processing, and distribution of agricultural products.

Biomedical Engineer: Although their numbers are small in comparison to other engineering specialists, their work is felt throughout the medical community. The work of biomedical engineers in the area of developing and designing medical instruments and devices has saved many lives. Many heart patients have survived because of the development of pacemakers. Many lives have been saved thanks to patient-monitoring machines. Many hospital mistakes have been avoided because of the systems that have been developed by biomedical engineers to help medical facilities operate smoothly, and minimize life-threatening mistakes.

Ceramic Engineer: When you serve meals on fine china dinnerware, you are benefiting from the work of the ceramic engineer. Ceramic engineers work to develop new ceramic materials and ways to use them —but they also do more. Ceramic engineers also work with heat-resistant materials for furnaces, electronic components, and nuclear heaters.

Chemical Engineer: Did you know that chemical engineers play a large part in using the findings of chemists to design useful chemically made products like aspirin, ball-point pen ink, and paint? Did you know that they are responsible for designing and developing chemical plants? These engineers facilitate the making of thousands of everyday products by producing "basic chemicals" that are used in them.[3]

Civil Engineer: When you travel across a magnificent bridge, do you ever think about who was responsible for its design? Have you ever thought about who designs the tunnels which allow us to drive many miles beneath large bodies of water, or who designs the sewerage systems? When you are aboard a plane speeding along a runway toward its lift-off point, have you ever wondered who designed the airport? Are you ever concerned about the buildings you work, visit, or live in, do you wonder about the soundness of their construction, their frames, and who made them so? If your answer is yes, then you have considered the work of the civil engineer. The civil engineer also plays a role in restructuring decaying cities by planning better communities and is vital in protecting our environment, water supplies, and perfecting our sewerage systems. If you plan to work as a civil engineer, you will be working in one of the oldest engineering specialties.

Electrical Engineer: Electrical engineers have designed many of the electrical products used today: televisions, toasters, lamps, shavers, air-conditioners, stereos, radios, and street lights.[4] Indeed, we would be in the dark ages without their work in telephone, telegraph, electric light and power companies, government agencies, construction firms, and engineering consulting firms.

Industrial Engineer: With today's inflation rates, employers want the maximum in productivity from workers, machines, and materials, and the industrial engineer if a master planner who designs systems to help achieve this goal. A people-oriented specialist, the industrial engineer must make sure work environments are conducive to the comfort and safety of workers, thereby increasing their productivity. This engineer designs plant layouts, makes sure that equipment parts are made in the correct order, and is concerned with overall productivity.

Mechanical Engineer: When you ride in an elevator or automobile, have you ever thought of who designed these conveyances? What about your use of printed stationery, brochures, or business cards, do you ever wonder who is responsible for the development of the printing press? All of these conveniences come to us through the labor of the mechanical engineer. They are also responsible for the development of jet and rocket engines. This professional works in the designing and developing of power-producing and power-using machines like internal combustion engines, and steam and gas turbines.

Metallurgical Engineer: There are three branches in metallurgical engineering: extractive; physical; and mechanical.

An extractive metallurgical engineer extracts the metal from ore, refines it, and processes it into useful metal.

The physical metallurgical engineer analyzes the physical nature, structure, and physical properties of metals and processes them into final products.[5] The mechanical metallurgical engineer works with the casting, forging, rolling, and drawing of metals. This engineer works to design new types of metal products which are so vital to our everyday existence.[6]

Getting an Engineering Degree

There are three kinds of college-level programs which you can pursue to enter the field of engineering: college-level program leading to an engineering degree; four-year program leading to a degree in engineering technology; and two-year program leading to an associate's degree leading to qualification as an engineering technician.

To best prepare you for these programs, your high school work should include algebra, plane geometry, trigonometry, physics, chemistry, and biology.

On the college level, there are several ways to become an engineer. You must take an approved engineering program in one of the accredited engineering schools. You may enter a four-year degree program which will allow you to land entry-level engineering jobs, or a five-year program which combines undergraduate and graduate training which will give you a bachelor's degree and a master's upon completion.

Many students who want to combine a liberal arts and engineering education can take dual programs studying for three years at a liberal arts college or university, and two years at the engineering school, and receive bachelors' degrees from each institution. Then there are five- and six-year cooperative programs which allow students to combine work experience and classroom study in alternate semesters. Some engineering graduates go on to pursue master's degrees and others who want to teach or go into research get Ph.D.s.

In all states and the District of Columbia, engineers whose work may affect life, health, or property and those who offer their services to the public must be registered—this requires a degree from an accredited engineering school, four years of work experience, and the passing of a state examination.[7]

Engineering and Related Occupations

Some people enter the field after getting degrees in related areas, work in companies doing related tasks, and ultimately have job titles indicating that they are engineers.

To become an engineering technologist, you must enroll in a four-year approved engineering technologist program, which will usually lead to a Bachelor of Engineering Technology degree. These programs are usually less demanding in math and science than engineering programs. After graduation, you may be able to land jobs similar to those of four-year engineering graduates or work closely with engineers in the sharing of duties, but the engineer is your superior.

If you want to pursue a two-year associate's degree, you can become

TABLE 23

ENGINEERING AND RELATED OCCUPATIONS
AVERAGE STARTING SALARY OFFER

BRANCH	AVERAGE STARTING SALARY
Chemical	$29,256
Civil	24,132
Electrical	28,368
Mechanical	27,864
Metallurgical	27,864

Primary source: College Placement Council. CPC's *Salary Survey* is a study of beginning offers and reports offers, not acceptances, made to graduating students during the recruiting period September through June. The data are submitted by a representative group of placement officers throughout the United States. Copyright © July 1986.

---

an engineer technician. After school, you will work under engineers, assisting them in various engineering tasks.

CAREER PROFILE

Dr. Lilia Abron-Robinson
Engineer, Owner of PEER Consultants
Rockville, Maryland

Dr. Lilia Abron-Robinson's Southern family expected academic excellence. She enrolled at Le Moyne-Owen College in Memphis, Tennessee, to pursue premedical studies. The doctor dream almost became a reality, but her sophomore year brought frog and other animal dissection. Dissection wasn't easy and like many premeds who encounter it, she changed majors. Looking for another suitable profession, she settled for chemical engineering and met resistance. "I was told that it was difficult for Black men to get engineering jobs and Black women could forget it," she remembers. Disappointed, but not dismayed, she reached for a sympathetic ear, a college professor who insisted she get engineering graduate school prerequisites.

Abron-Robinson spent a great deal of time reading career material. One day, she stumbled upon environmental and sanitary engineering information. "I found that it blended my interests of health and engineering," she remembers. "You see, environmental and sanitary engineers work with many medical aspects. For example, if there is a waterborne disease or problem which could affect human health, we are called in. Most of the time, we notify the proper authorities about our findings with fish and plants. Since humans feed on fish and plants, their diseases affect us. Environmental and sanitary engineers also work with other environmental problems such as pollution. We develop ways to isolate toxic and hazardous chemicals, detoxify them, and thus protect the environment."

Abron-Robinson liked the blend environmental and sanitary engineering offered; she applied to Washington University in St. Louis, Missouri. After obtaining a master's in environmental and sanitary engineering, she did what few Black women do: graduate with a doctorate in chemical engineering. A Ph.D. from the University of Iowa positioned her for college teaching; first at Tennessee State University, then at Vanderbilt University, and later at Howard University.

Teaching offered Abron-Robinson a unique opportunity to share knowledge with young, eager minds. Her practical experience as business owner gave students a well-balanced teaching professional. PEER, her pride-and-joy engineering consulting firm, allowed her to impart to students practical information from the real world.

"PEER's name," she says "has a double meaning. We are a minority firm meaning that we are peers or equals and it stands for our specializations of pollution, energy, environment, and resources. Our primary client is the federal government. As a result of our affiliation, our first four years we did fine." The company has afforded Abron-Robinson tremendous growth. She has moved from engineer to entrepreneur and from worker to administrator. She's developed management and planning skills which make her a more marketable and higher salaried engineer.

Her work at PEER is gratifying. "As a sanitary and environmental engineer, immediately I can see the fruits of my labor. Unlike working in a lab, where results take ten or fifteen years or longer, most of my work's results are immediate," she says. She encourages others to enter this area of engineering.

"Engineering is becoming more attractive to women. You don't have to stick to it after getting the degree. It teaches you intuitive and deductive thinking. You can take the degree and do many things like engineering research, teaching, going into business, working with computers or entering other professions like law. You have many options," she says. "Fortunately, the number of women engineering students is increasing. But I'd suggest that you have a good grounding in science and math, the ability to stick with it, and discipline."

Career Aids

Books and Pamphlets

1. For career information, contact:
   The American Ceramic Society
   65 Ceramic Drive
   Columbus, Ohio 43214
2. For career information, contact:
   The Metallurgical Society of the American Institute of Mining,
   　　Metallurgical & Petroleum Engineers
   345 East 47th St.
   New York, N.Y. 10017
3. *Is Civil Engineering for You?* (free) is available from:
   The American Society of Civil Engineers
   345 East 47th St.
   New York, N.Y. 10017
4. *A Profile of the Woman Engineer* is ($10.00) available from:
   The Society of Women Engineers
   345 East 47th St.
   New York, N.Y. 10017

Professional Organizations

1. National Society of Black Engineers
   1101 Connecticut Ave., N.W.
   Suite 700
   Washington, D.C. 20036
2. The American Institute of Chemical Engineers
   345 East 47th St.
   New York, N.Y. 10017

3. The American Society of Mechanical Engineers
   345 East 47th St.
   New York, N.Y. 10017
4. The Society of Women Engineers
   345 East 47th St.
   New York, N.Y. 10017
5. National Society of Professional Engineers
   1420 King St.
   Alexandria, Va. 22314

All addresses and prices are subject to change.

SCIENCE

We have often shied away from science because of myths that say it is too difficult, too hard to master. Our schools have often left us unprepared to pursue scientific careers. But in the eighties, as this country attempts to become less dependent on imported oil, we will be needed as geophysicists, to unearth petroleum and other minerals; geologists, for exploration and discovery of new resources; and life scientists, to preserve the natural environment and participate in medical research.

Women have made considerable impact in the sciences: Leona M. Libby worked on the first nuclear reactors; Jocelyn R. Gill was chief of NASA's in-flight space program; Libbie H. Hyman worked with invertebrate zoology; Agnes Fay Morgan worked with hormones and vitamins; Elizabeth T. Bunce has made contributions to oceanography; Joanne Simpson works in meteorology; and Lise Meitner worked with splitting the atom.[1] Black women have made their impact too, including Shirley Jackson, who was the first of us to graduate from the Massachusetts Institute of Technology in theoretical physics[2] and Jewell Plummer Cobb, a cancer researcher who is now a college president.[3] There are others: Annie Easley, energy researcher; Katherine Johnson, aerospace technologist.[4]

Scientific careers can be beneficial to humankind as well as to ourselves. It will take discipline, hard work, and advanced training to excel.

Our presence in the field is needed and we should begin early to prepare for these careers.

Career Pathing in Science

Most scientific jobs are classified into three major categories: environmental scientists, life scientists, and physical scientists. The bachelor's degree is the minimum requirement for work in the sciences but advanced degrees are required for certain types of employment, advancement, or work in administration or management positions.

ENVIRONMENTAL SCIENTISTS

Geologists: These scientists study factors relating to the earth's crust, structure, composition, history. With their hammers, chisels, compasses, and other tools, they examine surface rock and drill rock cores to understand more about rock types beneath the earth's surface and their distribution.[5] Their research helps us understand more about the earth's structure and history, which can have future impact on earthquake prediction. They also work in uncovering oil and other minerals. Some work in laboratories analyzing specimens, fossils, and the flow of water and oil through rocks. Others are advisers to construction companies and the government in determining the best sites for dam or highway construction. Still others teach or administer research and exploration programs.

There are several geologist specialists: petroleum geologists, engineering geologists, mineralogists, geochemists, volcanologists, geomorphologists, paleontologists, geochronologists, stratigraphers, astrogeologists, and geological oceanographers.

A bachelor's degree in geology or a related field is required for entry-level positions, but for career advancement, teaching, and some research positions an additional degree is recommended.

Geophysicists: These professionals are concerned with the makeup (composition and physical aspects) of the earth and its electric, magnetic, and gravitational fields.[6] Most specialize in either the solid earth, fluid earth, or upper atmosphere. Some, called solid earth geophysicists and exploration geophysicists, are concerned with locating oil and mineral deposits; solid earth geophysicists also study earthquakes. Seismologists probe the earth's interior, are helpful in determining the causes of earthquakes, can discover underground nuclear explosions, and give information for bridge, dam, and building construction. Geodesists are concerned with the exact mapping of the earth's surface. Hydrologists study underground and surface water and rainfall; some study water supplies, irrigation, flood control, and soil erosion. Geomagneticians are concerned with the earth's magnetic fields; paleomagnetists study rocks or lava flows to understand past magnetic fields; planetologists study the makeup and atmosphere of bodies within the solar system.

A bachelor's degree in geophysics or in one of its specialties or in a related scientific field or engineering will help get entry-level positions, but graduate training is advisable for research or supervisory positions. A Ph.D. is needed for teaching or basic research.

Good salaries and very good employment opportunities make geophysics an attractive career possibility.

Meteorologists: These scientists study the atmosphere. They are most familiar for understanding and forecasting the weather, but they also contribute to research on air pollution and trends in the earth's climate.[7] Meteorologists specialize in several areas. Synoptic meteorologists study weather information; physical meterologists study chemical and electrical properties of the atmosphere, rescarch the effects of the atmosphere on transmission of light, sound, and radio waves, or study cloud formation, rain, and snow; climatologists study climate trends, which affect the planning of heating and cooling systems and building design.[8]

Meteorologists work in weather stations, the National Oceanic and Atmospheric Administration (NOAA), the Department of Defense, private industry, for commercial airlines, private weather consulting firms, design and manufacturers of meteorological instruments, and in aerospace, insurance, engineering, radio, and television firms.

The bachelor's degree in meteorology is generally the minimum requirement for employment, but the degree in a related science or engineering field coupled with meteorology courses can prepare you for many jobs. For research and teaching jobs, an advanced degree in the field is generally required. However, a graduate degree in a related field and advanced courses in meteorology, physics, mathematics, and chemistry may qualify you for research and teaching in the area.

Oceanographers: These scientists study oceans by using mathematical natural science and engineering techniques [9] Their research is helpful in beginning fisheries, developing methods for weather forecasting, uncovering ocean resources, and upgrading national defense. Many do their work at sea, but others work in laboratories studying sea specimens or testing theories about the ocean.

There are several oceanographer specialists: biological oceanographers study oceanic plant and animals; physical oceanographers (physicists and geophysicists) study waves, tides, and currents, which can lead to accurate weather predictions; geological oceanographers (marine geologists) help in understanding the ocean's underwater mountain ranges, rocks, and sediments; chemical oceanographers study the ocean's chemical makeup; and oceanographic engineers design and construct instruments for oceanographic exploration. [10]

A bachelor's degree in oceanography, biology, earth or physical science, mathematics, or engineering will lead to employment in entry-level jobs. For many research, teaching, and top positions, graduate training, preferably the Ph.D. in oceanography or a basic science, is required.

LIFE SCIENTISTS

Biochemists: These workers examine the chemical makeup and behavior of living things; their work is often in their areas of reproduction, growth, and heredity. [11] They also work in the areas of examining the causes and cures for diseases and the effects of food, drugs, and hormones on different organisms. About 50 percent of all biochemists worked for colleges and universities in 1978; one fourth worked in private industry for cosmetic and drug manufacturers and insecticide companies; others worked for federal, state, and local government agencies or nonprofit research institutes and foundations. [12]

The advanced degree is needed for entry-level research or teaching jobs. The Ph.D. is needed for those pursuing serious research careers or administrative and management positions. A bachelor's degree in biochemistry or chemistry, or in biology with a minor in chemistry, may prepare you for entry-level positions as research assistants or technicians.

Life Scientists: Study living organisms by understanding the relationship of animals and plants to their environments.[13] Most life scientists are referred to by what they study:

Botanists: Study plants; some examine all phases of plant life; some identify, classify, or determine the causes and cures of plant diseases.[14]

Agronomists: Are interested in the mass development of plants, coming up with new ways of upgrading crop growth and controlling diseases, pests, and weeds for crop improvement, and retardation of soil erosion.[15]

Horticulturists: By working with orchard and garden plants, they attempt to upgrade plant culture techniques for community, park, and home beautification.[16]

Zoologists: Study animal life. Some do experiments with live animals; others dissect dead specimens to understand their structures. Zoologists can be classified by the animals they study: entomologists (insects), mammalogists (animals), ornithologists (birds.)[17]

Animal Scientists: Research the breeding, feeding, and diseases of domestic farm animals.[18]

Microbiologists: Examine the development and features of microscopic organisms like bacteria, viruses, and mold.[19] Medical microbiologists study the relationship between bacteria and disease and the result of antibiotics on bacteria.

Pharmacologists and Toxicologists: Do experiments on rats, guinea pigs, and monkeys to understand how drugs, gases, poisons, and other substances affect tissue and organ functioning.[20]

Pathologists: Study how disease, parasites, and insects affect human cells, tissues, and organs; some examine drug use and genetic variations.

Although a bachelor's degree can lead to many entry-level life scientists' positions, a graduate degree is needed for advancement. The doctorate is needed for teaching, independent research, and administrative positions.

PHYSICAL SCIENTISTS

Astronomers: Study the universe by exploring its origin, history, and evolution by using physics and mathematical principles.[21] Using instruments like large telescopes and radiotelescopes, they observe the universe. Although some of the astronomer's work is done in observatories, many spend time in offices and classrooms where they are involved in research or teaching. To become an astronomer, the Ph.D. is generally required for advanced positions, but some entry-level positions may be available without it.

CHEMISTS

These scientists investigate and apply new knowledge about substances.[22] Their work has lead to the development of synthetic materials, energy-saving processes, and pollution reduction. About 50 percent of all chemists do research and development, but some work in production and inspection, in colleges and universities, in private industry and government agencies, as consultants, and in marketing and sales, as representatives.

Chemists generally specialize in one of chemistry's subfields: analytical chemistry, organic chemistry, inorganic chemistry, and physical chemistry.

A bachelor's degree in chemistry or a related area will get you entry-level positions in government or private industry, but for teaching and many research positions an advanced degree is required.

PHYSICISTS

They mathematically explain the universe's structure and the interaction of matter and energy and devise theories about the fundamental forces and laws of nature.[23] Most work in research and development; some who are engineering-oriented help develop new products; others teach and do research in educational institutions, consult, or work in production-related positions.

You must pursue graduate training to obtain beginning positions and to advance. The Ph.D. is needed for teaching and administration. A bachelor's degree may allow you to get some applied research and development positions in private industry or with the federal government, or you may work in other scientific fields.

TABLE 24

SALARIES FOR GEOLOGISTS, GEOPHYSICISTS, METEOROLOGISTS, CHEMISTS, AND PHYSICISTS

GEOLOGISTS AND GEOPHYSICISTS—Those with bachelor's degrees in physical and earth science average starting salaries of $22,800; those with master's degrees make starting salaries of $29,300.

METEOROLOGISTS—Those with bachelor's degrees and no previous experience who work for the federal government make starting salaries of $14,390 and $17,824 a year, depending on academic records; those with master's degrees can begin at $17,824 or $21,804; those with Ph.D.s can begin at $26,381 or $31,619. The average salary for meteorologists working for the federal government is $39,400.

CHEMISTS—According to the College Placement Council, chemists with a bachelor's degree make starting salaries that average $21,000 a year; those with master's degrees start with $26,700; those with a Ph.D. start with $35,000.

An American Chemical Society survey indicates that their members with a bachelor's degree can earn an average of $34,000, if they are experienced nonacademic chemists in private industry; those with a master's degree earn $39,000; those with a Ph.D. average $49,000.

PHYSICISTS—In an American Institute of Physics survey, beginning physicists' salaries in private industry average approximately $30,000 for those with a master's degree or Ph.D.

Physicists with bachelor's degrees who work for the federal government can begin at $14,390 or $17,824, depending on academic records; those with a master's degree can begin at $47,824 or $21,804; those with a Ph.D. can start at $26,381 or $31,619. The average salary for physicists working in the federal government is $43,400.

Source: Department of Labor, Bureau of Labor Statistics, Occupational Outlook Handbook.

What Will You Earn as a Scientist?

Scientists make relatively high salaries. Table 24 shows salaries for each scientific category.

CAREER PROFILE

Daisy Hodge Ellis is a clinical project coordinator at Hoffmann-La Roche in Nutley, New Jersey. She pretests drugs for that company and is one of the few Black women scientists.

Daisy Hodge Ellis
Clinical Project Coordinator
Hoffmann-La Roche, Inc.
Nutley, New Jersey

Daisy Ellis, a native of the Virgin Islands, attended North Carolina Agricultural and Technical State University in Greensboro, North Carolina. Although she wanted to be a mathematics major, she switched to chemistry. "When I signed up for mathematics, I had no idea of the opportunities which mathematics majors could pursue in the future. Therefore, I switched to chemistry in hopes of preparing for a more marketable career."

After graduating as a chemistry major, Ellis came to New York to look for a job. "It was very difficult finding a job as a chemist. Most employers wanted someone with experience. But I couldn't get experience without finding a job," she says. "After pounding the pavement and looking continuously, I found a job as a junior chemist at Francis Delafield Hospital, which was then a part of Columbia University but is now closed. In this position, I worked with a chief cardiologist who did studies with emphysema patients. Although I was glad to have employment, I was underpaid because I wasn't aware of the salary range for scientsts."

Like many workers who feel underpaid, Ellis attempted to change positions. Even with experience, getting employment was not easy. She turned to the New York State Employment Service for help and was referred to Hoffman-La Roche Inc., a large pharmaceutical company in New Jersey. "At this time, Hoffmann-La Roche, like many companies, was approached by organizations like the NAACP to hire Blacks. As a result, the company interviewed me, found that I was qualified and offered me a position."

Ellis decided to work for Hoffman-La Roche Inc. and started as an assistant scientist I in the Animal Health Research Department. "We did drug clearance tests on animals which are eventually fed to consumers, like poultry. Before these animals can be sold to consumers, drugs must be out of their systems," she says. "We tested animal tissue to determine how long it took drugs to clear out of their systems."

Ellis was then promoted to assistant scientist II but left Hoffman-La Roche on maternity leave. In the winter of 1971, she returned to the same department but six months later switched to the Department of Biochemistry and Drug Metabolism. She remained there for about five years and in January of 1977, she was promoted to Clinical Research Associate and began working in the Department of Medical Research. In that position, she left lab work for desk work. "We do drug study monitoring. I work closely with physicians, who are in-house and in the field. Before a drug can be marketed, it must be tested for effectiveness and safety. The drug is pretested on human volunteers as well as patients with the disease for which the drug is to be tested. A summary of the results including the statistics from the testing must be sent to the Federal Drug Administration (FDA) for approval or nonapproval," she says. "I do the testing and preparation of the reports sent to the FDA."

In 1980, she was promoted to Senior Clinical Research Associate and recently to Clinical Project Coordinator in the same department but says her climb to the position was not easy. "It has not been easy. I'm a woman and a Black person. There are many problems for the Black woman scientist because Blacks are not thought to have the ability to be scientists," she says.

In light of these problems, Ellis feels Black women should plan their careers carefully. "You must think ahead because it's important to have a good idea of what you want to do with your career. If you work for a large company, you can become very comfortable with the money you are making without considering advancement possibilities," she says. "In a large company like Hoffman-La Roche, each professional category has a salary range that you fit into. For example, assistant scientist I's have a certain salary range. When you reach the top, you must show

that you have taken additional course work or can handle more com
plex work to proceed to the next professional category. It happened to
me. I knew I would reach the top of my salary range and if I didn't start
doing something my movement would be slow. I started taking master
level courses in chemistry at New York University. This enhanced my
movement.

"To teach, you must have the doctorate. If you choose to work for a
large company, you can get employment with a bachelor's degree and
simultaneously work on an advanced degree. But you should get the
doctorate regardless of which employment area you enter," she advises.
"If you want to become known in the field, you should have the doctorate, get published, become known to people who work in your area of
expertise, and develop an assertive personality that will make you visible," Ellis continues.

"When I was in college, I had this fantasy that as a chemist, I would
be working in a laboratory finding cures to all types of diseases," she
says. "The reality is that this doesn't occur. If someone is cured of a
disease as a result of some of my work, that information is never filtered
back to me. Scientists like me grind out the work and pass it along to
those who will ultimately get the credit. To get the credit, you have to
have the doctorate, spend many years in research, publish widely, and
become known in the field. A beginning scientist must be aware of this
reality."

Career Aids

Books and Pamphlets

1. For a book on careers in astronomy, contact:
   American Astronomical Society
   Astronomy Department
   University of Virginia
   Box 3818 University Station
   Charlottesville, Va. 22903

Professional Organizations

1. American Geological Institute
   4220 King St.
   Alexandria, Va. 22302
2. American Geophysical Union
   2000 Florida Ave., NW
   Washington, D.C. 20009
3. American Meteorological Society
   45 Beacon St.
   Boston, Mass. 02108
4. For work opportunities with the NOAA National Weather Service, write:
   National Weather Service/Personnel
   1-RAS/DC 23,
   Rockville, Md. 20782
5. American Society of Biological Chemists
   9650 Rockville Pike
   Bethesda, Md. 20014
6. American Institute of Biological Sciences
   1401 Wilson Blvd.
   Arlington, Va. 22209
7. American Astronomical Society
   Astronomy Department
   University of Virginia
   Box 3818 University Station
   Charlottesville, Va. 22903
8. American Chemical Society, Career Services
   1155 16th St., NW
   Washington, D.C. 20036
9. American Institute of Physics
   335 East 45th St.
   New York, N.Y. 10017

All addresses and prices are subject to change.

6

A Little Black Box Career

COMPUTERS*

As modern technology advances, the presence of the computer dominates our everyday existence more and more. Computers calculate our payroll checks, distribute our credit histories to potential creditors, compute our checking and savings balances, and store information concerning our hotel and motel accommodations. They are important to researchers, urban planners, doctoral candidates, stockbrokers, accountants, bankers, marketers, publishers, engineering architects, librarians, health workers, business owners, and to all workers who must deal with massive amounts of information. They are used to help protect us from foreign attack, count us for government projects like the Census Bureau's data collection, and improve our air transportation systems.

* Parts of this chapter first appeared in the author's article "Computer Technology: Careers with a Future," *Essence*, February 1982.

The computer field offers good starting salaries. It offers good career opportunities, because there is a steady demand for computer professionals. And if nonprofit or teaching professionals are willing to take computer training, the field offers a good career cross-over. Take the example of Yvonne Leonard, a former math teacher who took computer science courses where she taught. Like the graduating seniors, she began meeting with college recruiters and was able to land a management trainee position with Citibank. She is now a systems analyst. Her math background and computer science training were very marketable.

Although the computer field promises interesting and well-paying careers, many still shy away from it because of its highly technical aspects and training. Many feel that the course work will be too difficult and time consuming. Computer science or data processing may not be one of the easiest majors, but its training will give you a good technical base. And since most organizations or companies have computer systems or will soon convert to them, computer training can be marketed in a variety of ways.

Career Pathing in Computer and Computer-Related Careers

The computer field offers many career possibilities. Let's explore a few.

Analysis and Programming: The systems analyst is the industry's master designer and problem solver. In today's rapidly changing society, businesses and government agencies need professionals who can analyze problems, develop solutions, and persuade management to accept their recommendations. The systems analyst is the skilled computer expert with these capabilities.

The systems analyst begins this challenging work by meeting with management to discuss problems. For example, a company may want to update an antiquated accounting system. Perhaps their present system is done by hand, making it too time consuming and thus too costly. The company wants to change and update the old system; they want to computerize it. To accomplish this, they summon the systems analyst. The systems analyst must solve this problem by gathering facts. She must talk to those workers who are involved with the present system and assess their needs. She must design and develop a new procedure based on all the facts.

Next, she must record her perceptions in a written proposal that is presented to management. Like a saleswoman, she must present her analysis and gently persuade them to accept it. Her communicative skills, both written and oral, must be top-notch.

Once management has accepted the proposal and is convinced the budget can accommodate the new procedure, the systems analyst has to activate a system to achieve the desired results. She often turns to the computer to help solve the problem. Since the computer is capable of rapidly processing large amounts of data, she knows that it is the most efficient way to produce a new accounting system.

Her next step is to prepare instructions or technical specifications for programmers, who will write the step-by-step instructions for the computer to follow. The systems analyst will write specifications for the equipment that is to be used, the method by which the information will flow, and other vital information. Ultimately, she will help the programmer test the instructions (called programs).

The systems analyst is one of the industry's most creative people. She is free to be imaginative in designing systems. This creative input makes her invaluable to companies and a vital link between management and the computer division.

Educational requirements vary for systems analysts, but the Association for Systems Management recommends four years of study in information systems, computer science, or a business education degree with a computer science major. The Association suggests that additional study or a graduate degree in business administration is valuable.

A systems analyst should have other qualities. In addition to having good oral and written skills, she should have the ability to think and reason logically, analyze and solve problems, and persuade and sell.

Programmer: Many computer tasks are interrelated. The programmer's work is associated to that of the systems analyst. The systems analyst submits her problem specifications to the programmer, who must write the detailed step-by-step instructions for the computer. She must code these programs into highly sophisticated computer language.

The computer is a machine that can't think. Someone must tell it exactly how to achieve the desired results. A programmer performs this task. Let's oversimplify the programmer's work. Think of the computer as a "mini-brain" because it works in a similar way. If the programmer needs a simple math problem solved, she writes instructions to program the computer in a computer language, like COBOL or Fortran IV.

The programmer must make sure that her instructions work. Can the computer complete the task and give the desired results? She must test and retest the program. If there are errors, she must alter the program until it produces the correct results. This process is called "debugging."

There are several types of programming: business applications programming; scientific programming; systems programming.[1] A business applications programmer does business oriented programs, and most programming jobs are in this area. A scientific programmer solves scientific and engineering problems. The systems programmer develops programs that will facilitate the programming of computers.[2] She maintains the general instructions (software).

Requirements for programmers vary, but increasingly most businesses are requiring a four-year college degree for entry-level positions. Scientific applications programmers are generally required to have college degrees with computer, science, mathematics, engineering, or physical science backgrounds. Some scientific jobs require a graduate degree.

Senior level computer programmers may want to become certified. The Institute for Certification of Computer Professionals confers the Certificate in Computer Programming (CCP) to those who pass a five-part examination. The Institute also awards the Certificate in Data Processing (CDP) to business oriented data processing people at the supervisory and management levels. They are presently developing a Registered Business Programmer (RBP) and entry-level examination for data processing positions.

Other qualifications for programmers include the ability to think logically, be patient, and do detailed work.

A programmer's job is prestigious and challenging. She supplies the brainpower for the computer and is therefore in demand. The Department of Labor expects a continued demand for these professionals throughout the eighties. Being in demand means commanding top salaries, and programmers are among the highest paid professionals. Programming positions include trainee, junior programmer, programmer, senior programmer, and programming manager.

Computer or Console Operators: The computer or console operator must make sure that the computer is in tip-top running condition. She sets up the required equipment, examines the programmer's instructions, and starts the machine. She makes sure that it is properly loaded with the correct cards, magnetic tapes, or disks. She is concerned with the data to be processed, the instructions, and the results ("output").

While the computer is in operation, she looks for error lights that may indicate a problem. She must also act quickly if the machine stops. She must find the problem and correct it or scrap the program.

Computer or console operators are usually high school graduates. Many employers will provide on-the-job training. Some operators get training at vocational or business schools or community or junior colleges. Career movement in this area is usually limited to promotions to supervisory positions.

The Department of Labor reports a growth in the area that will "rise about as fast as the average for all occupations," but indicates that there will be a fairly strong need for computer or console operators.

Keypunch or Data Entry Operators: The need for keypunch or data entry operators is expected to decline. As technology advances and new ways of entering data are developed, the need for these professionals will decrease. The field, however, is worth mentioning because Black women work or aspire to work in it.

A keypunch or data entry operator deals with the "input." She transcribes data to punched cards, tapes, or disks that can be "read" by the computer. She operates a machine that is similar to a typewriter.

Keypunch or data entry operators generally receive on-the-job training and are usually high school graduates. The ability to type is also required.

Many people feel that keypunch or data entry operators can move into other computer related areas. Advancement, however, is limited. Some may move into supervisory positions in their area; very few move into console or computer operator positions. And it would be unlikely for them to become programmers without further educational training.

OTHER COMPUTER-RELATED CAREERS

Computer Design and Manufacturing: Computers must be designed and produced, and research must be done in the area. Scientists, mathematicians, and engineers perform these duties. A college degree, and often advanced training, is required for these jobs. Manufacturers also need a college degree and highly advanced skills.

Sales and Marketing: Sales and marketing representatives can work in business systems or scientific applications. Those in business systems must understand company organization and may be required to have previous sales experience or business educational training.[3] Scientific oriented representatives need technical skills. A college degree is usually required, and a scientific or engineering background is often needed.

The Field Engineer: Field engineers install and maintain computers.[4] A field engineer must know how to fix a malfunctioning computer and size up equipment performance. She should have at least two years of training in mechanical, electrical, electronic, or electromechanical subjects.

The Systems Engineer: This professional is not really an engineer, but a manufacturing company customer liaison. She must help the company's clients adjust to their computer machinery and help them with any problems. Most companies provide intensive on-the-job training. A college degree is generally required but a business-oriented degree is preferred.

New Emerging Fields: As computer technology grows, new career opportunities do too. For example, there is the field of computer graphics, which combines graphic arts with computer work.

There are also careers in computer journalism. Many computer-related magazines are entering the market, and computer personnel are often employed to man these publications' staffs.

What Will You Earn in the Computer and Computer-related Industry?

Most computer workers command high beginning salaries. Robert Half of New York, Inc., a placement agency, publishes an annual report on starting salaries for data-processing specialists (See Table 25).

CAREER PROFILES

Janet Flowers, Norrene Johnson Duffy, and Cecelia Jeffries are three women who are career-pathing in computer and computer-related careers. Flowers works for IBM; Johnson Duffy works for the City of Atlanta; and Jeffries works for Spelman College.

Janet Flowers
Advisory Forecasting Analyst
IBM Corp.
White Plains, New York

Janet Flowers's computer career demonstrates how social science training can qualify you for the field. While a senior psychology major at Fisk University, Flowers was approached by the placement officer to investigate a career opportunity at IBM. "I was all set to take a programmer's job with Honeywell's in Boston, but I wasn't really set on the idea of becoming a programmer. The placement director told me IBM was looking for a college recruiter," she remembers. "That offer was more attractive because it meant traveling around to college campuses throughout the country, interviewing students and inviting them to interview with IBM."

Flowers took the job and has since moved into many different IBM positions. "From college recruiting, I became a salary analyst and evaluated job levels and salary increases for employees. From there, I went into a marketing support position in the IBM division that manufactures office automation equipment," she says. "Afterwards, I returned to personnel as a staff program manager. My responsibilities included equal opportunity, affirmative action, and employee development. As a result of company reorganization, I went into an intensive year-long training program to become a systems engineer and worked in that capacity for five years in IBM's small computer division."

A promotion to regional marketing support programs administrator brought Flowers back to the division which manufactures office products. This time, new technology had made its impact. "The standard typewriters and copiers had evolved into sophisticated word processing machines and high speed printers that could communicate with a computer," she says. "In this position, I was able to combine my data processing background and experience as a systems engineer with my marketing expertise."

The position put Flowers in project management and honed her administrative skills. As a regional marketing support programs administrator, she had a variety of responsibilities. "I provided technical support to a staff of marketing support representatives who worked from the sales branch offices in the New York and Puerto Rican regions. The

TABLE 25

DATA PROCESSING STARTING SALARIES 1986

DATA PROCESSING—LARGE INSTALLATIONS	1986 SALARIES
Vice President, MIS	$65,000–$94,000
MIS Director	55,000– 75,000
Systems and Programming	
Manager	$38,000–$46,000
Project Manager	35,500– 45,000
Project Leader	33,500– 42,500
Systems Analyst	33,000– 41,000
Programmer Analysts	26,000– 35,000
Programmer	22,000– 28,000
Technical Services	
Manager	$39,000–$49,000
Systems Programmer	30,000– 40,000
Data Base Support	
Data Base Administrator/Manager	$35,000–$45,000
Data Base Analyst	31,000– 42,000
Telecommunications	
Manager	$36,000–$42,000
Telecommunications Specialist	33,000– 38,000
Operations	
Manager	$30,000–$40,000
Shift Supervisor	24,000– 31,000
Operator	17,500– 22,500
Input/Output Clerk	16,500– 21,000
Data Entry	14,000– 16,000

Source: Robert Half of New York, Inc. Copyright © 1986 R H International, Inc.

MSRs worked on a team with sales representatives," she says. "When a customer wanted IBM equipment, the marketing support representative would do a systems analysis of the customer's applications and work with their personnel in installing the new IBM equipment." Flowers also developed technical product training programs.

Like many corporate professionals, Flowers realized the impact that getting an M.B.A. would have upon her career. She took advantage of IBM's tuition refund program and pursued an M.B.A. in marketing and finance at Fordham University. "It took me three years to complete the two-year program because my liberal arts background did not include business courses like accounting and economics. The first year, therefore, was spent taking qualifying prerequisites," she says. "It was a sacrifice, but well worth it."

Flowers's education and experience has paid off: she was promoted to administrative systems advisor for Information Processing. "Instead of working with IBM customers, I advised an IBM division about what sophisticated word processing and computer equipment they should install to increase professional and secretarial productivity," she says. "My responsibilities included strategic planning and overall implementation planning. IBM is a leader in the office technology field. My job was to help the company put into internal use some of its own highly developed products." She is now Advisory Forecasting Analyst.

Norrene Johnson Duffy
Director, Office of Management Systems
City of Atlanta
Atlanta, Georgia

Originally trained as an engineer, Norrene Johnson Duffy uses her technical background to head up the Office of Management Systems, the centralized data-processing office for the City of Atlanta, Georgia. She reports to the city's chief administrator, Shirley Franklin, and is responsible for seventy-eight people. Her office has overall responsibility for the computer-aided dispatch for the police, fire, and water bureau. She also handles data-processing needs for other City departments. "We handle anything that's affiliated with the City that has to do with computers," Duffy says, "It's quite challenging work."

Duffy decided early on a technical career. Her educational training took place at Spelman College in Atlanta, Georgia. There she majored in physics and participated in a six-year dual-degree program between Spelman and Georgia Institute of Technology, and now she has two bachelors' degrees in physics and electrical engineering. To augment her undergraduate training, she enrolled in a master's level electrical engineering program at Stanford University.

Her first job was as an electronics engineer in the simulation science division of NASA (Mountainview, California). She designed controls to guide simulators that simulate airplane flights through the use of computers. That work involved a great deal of computer programming.

Then she combined computer knowledge with engineering in the position of software engineer for Lanier Business Products. "I designed software for many computer systems. I specialized in applications of signal processing," Duffy says. "I worked in the area of computer research and development. We looked into the future uses of computers and develop them." Duffy also worked as a software engineer for Digital Communications.

Duffy says people have many misconceptions about technical careers. "People think technical areas offer little diversity, but engineering has for me." She has gone from employment with the federal government to private industry to local government.

Duffy says women shy away from technical fields because of math. "People are afraid to pursue technical fields because they require a great deal of math. Fortunately, I had a strong math background. Others didn't, but they persevered, were able to conquer math, and are now in technical areas," she says.

She feels Black women are practically guaranteed a job in this technically oriented job market. "I recommend strongly that Blacks consider technical careers. To date, I have not gone job hunting. All my job opportunities have come to me," she states. "Technical careers are also lucrative; technical field graduates make top dollars."

Duffy is married to Eugene Duffy, assistant to the mayor in Atlanta.

Cecelia Jeffries
Assistant Director, Computer Center
Spelman College
Atlanta, Georgia

After graduating as a mathematics major from Fisk University in 1965, Cecelia Jeffries began her computer career as a scientific programmer at IBM. "I went into scientific programming at a time when jobs were plentiful, and there was a push to hire minorities," she recalls.

After two years at IBM, Jeffries became a scientific programmer at Lockheed. There she was promoted to scientific programmer senior. "As a scientific programmer, I wrote computer programs of a scientific nature for engineers who did not have the necessary programming knowledge to do their own programs. We were a service organization to engineers. For example, if an engineer wanted to use the computer to solve large mathematical equations, I would write programs, which are the instructions that the computer follows to achieve a desired result. A computer cannot think and must be programmed to function in a logical manner."

As a scientific programmer senior, Jeffries worked as a troubleshooter. "Many engineers do their own programs. When an engineer ran into a problem, he or she called on me. I determined what was causing the problem. Or if the desired results were not achieved I was called in," she says. "Or if there were internal or departmental programming needs, like determining how many people used the computer, I was called in to break that information down."

Jeffries feels that there are opportunities for Black women in programming, but says a college degree is necessary. "To do scientific programming, you should have a good foundation in mathematics. This is particularly true if you want to grow in the field," she advises. "I recommend strongly that you develop some area of expertise other than the computer, which will allow you to grow. You should know more than programming. For example, if you understand both finance and programming, and are programming for a bank doing an audit, you are in a much better position to understand the total picture. To me, there are two types of people who do programming. There are those who just code what someone else tells them, which is limiting. And there are those who deal with the whole picture."

Jeffries feels that women who want programming careers should be able to think logically and be able to pay attention to details. "Many people are interested in computer programming, but you must be a patient person, a stickler for details, and be able to think logically. You must be able to say, 'If this, then what?' Many people find they cannot do this, which is no reflection on a person's intelligence. But you must think logically to do programming."

Jeffries now works as assistant director at the Computer Center on Spelman College's Campus in Atlanta.

Career Aids

For career information, contact:

Association for Systems Management
24587 Bagley Rd.
Cleveland, Ohio 44138

Professional Organization

Data Processing Management Association
505 Busse Highway
Park Ridge, Ill. 60068

7

A Career That Gets the Word Across

COMMUNICATIONS

The fast-growing and exciting communications field is a popular choice for many college graduates. It appeals to those seeking glamour status and high salaries. Its many career possibilities lure us to consider jobs in newspapers, magazines, television, radio, publishing, and public relations; but too often we seek the highly visible positions such as television or radio announcers, writers, editors, or reporters. This section will also explore many less visible positions.

Career Pathing in Communication

JOURNALISM

One major area of journalism is writing and editing for the mass media such as newspapers, magazines, or electronic media. Now, a college degree is rapidly becoming the highly desirable tool to get positions in the competitive job market of journalism. Good writing skills are a must and graduate work can strengthen journalistic skills. Prior work experience can give you an edge in the marketplace and this experience can be obtained by participating in an internship program at a magazine, radio or television station, or newspaper.

Newspaper Journalism: A news-editorial major is the best preparation for newspaper work. Prior newspaper experience like work as a stringer (part-time reporter who is paid on a free-lance basis), internship with a newspaper, or high school or college yearbook or newspaper editorial work is helpful.

After you are employed, you will probably begin as a general assignment reporter or a copy editor. You may want to work for the large city papers, but most hire experienced reporters. Your best employment chances will be at weekly or small daily newspapers. As a general assignment reporter, your beat will most likely be covering community events, writing obituaries, and observing police court proceedings. As you advance, assignments may become more specialized.

Within the newspaper hierarchy, the publisher is the top honcho. In the newsroom, the editor-in-chief is responsible for editorial policy; the managing editor handles the day-to-day operations for the paper; the city editor oversees local news coverage; the wire editor selects foreign and national news items coming off wire services; and copy editors make sure the text is grammatically correct and story details are right. Reporters research and write the news.

Nonjournalism jobs with newspapers include jobs in the business area, advertising, promotion, circulation, research, and so forth.

Magazine Journalism: A college degree and good writing skills are needed to gain employment with magazines. If hired, you will probably begin as an assistant or associate editor depending on the magazine. This is not the field to expect high beginning salaries.

Beginning salaries are low because some feel magazines have traditionally attracted upper-middle-class white women who worked in these prestigious jobs before marriage. Since these women worked for prestige rather than money, the field has traditionally had low-paying starting salaries. It is only after you have advanced to senior positions that salaries may become lucrative.

Advancement within magazine publishing organizations is slow. Before moving upward, you must wait until someone is promoted or leaves. The magazine hierarchy is very structured and you must move step by step up the ladder. As with newspapers, the top positions are publisher, editor-in-chief, and managing editor. Copy editors perform similar duties to those of their counterparts on newspapers. Associate and assistant editors edit manuscripts sent in by free-lance writers and may be responsible for the editorial work for a particular column or department such as fashion. Most magazines rely on free-lancers to supply them with articles.

Nonjournalism jobs are similar to those in newspapers. One of the most lucrative nonjournalism positions in the magazine area is selling advertising space.

Technical Writing: Another journalism area is technical writing, which involves writing about scientific and technical information. For example, you may write about the work performed by scientists or engineers at research laboratories, universities, or chemical manufacturing companies for business or government.

To prepare yourself for this field, your college program should include writing and science. You should have knowledge of the technical areas for future employment. After college, the Society for Technical Communications can provide useful job hunting tips.

Free-lance Writing: Free-lance writing is another area of journalism, but supporting yourself as a free-lancer can be rough. Writing for commercial, trade, and professional magazines and journals or newspapers will probably be your best source of revenue and steady work.

To begin your free-lancing career, you should read thoroughly for content, style, and format the magazines, journals, or newspapers in which you hope to publish. Many beginning writers receive rejection slips because they fail to investigate thoroughly prospective publications and send in articles which are contrary to the publication's content, style, and format.

Next, you should send a query letter or a synopsis of your idea to the editor. If editors are interested, they will notify you of a tentative publication date.

As a free-lancer, you may also want to write a book. Many free-lancers peddle their manuscripts or ideas for books on their own; others secure an agent's help. First-time writers, however, may find difficulty in getting agents. Many agents do not handle novice writers. But regardless of the method used for approaching publishers, you will probably be required to present a detailed proposal or outline of the book to the publisher.

Free-lancers must constantly generate work for themselves and meticulous records and research notes must be kept. Although they are creative, successful free-lancers also find themselves performing independent business people's tasks, like bookkeeping.

BROADCASTING

Careers in broadcasting are primarily in television or radio. You may find employment at television or radio stations, with station representative firms, broadcasting-related trade and professional associations, or in educational institutions. With television and radio work, you can decide on careers in the highly visible positions such as announcers or as behind-the-scenes workers.

Getting a job is highly competitive, but the field offers opportunities for those with a variety of educational backgrounds. Some secretaries have moved up to producers' and announcers' slots. Those with high school degrees have moved into well-paying positions, particularly in the technical area.

Most experts feel that a beginner's best employment prospects are in small radio or television stations rather than in larger markets like New York, Chicago, or Los Angeles. In smaller stations, the competition is not as keen and once hired, you may be able to do tasks which would be restricted in larger stations by union regulations. For a description of nontechnical broadcasting jobs, see Table 26.

For information on technical jobs, you should contact the Federal Communications Commission, the watchdog agency that licenses and

TABLE 26

JOBS IN BROADCASTING

PROGRAMMING

A radio and television's programs are vital to its operations. Whether news, public affairs, interviews, religious, or children's shows are featured, radio and television stations' programming departments work to provide distinctive programs. With television, programs can originate from one of the three national networks, or from local stations, independent program producers, or syndication companies, which supply features or shorter films. With radio, programs come from the station, national radio networks, or independent producers.

PROGRAM DIRECTOR—Is in charge of the programming department and is responsible for what is broadcasted. This administrator develops and oversees the programming, schedules department personnel, plans and implements budgets, and works closely with the station's general and sales managers.

PRODUCTION MANAGER—Works under the program director. At television stations, she does tasks related to program production. She coordinates personnel, determines and arranges for space and equipment, and gets props for productions.

PRODUCER-DIRECTOR—Is responsible for the performers, sets, lighting, and props for one or more shows. She oversees production from beginning to the actual show.

MUSIC LIBRARIAN—Works for radio stations and is responsible for cataloging and storing records and tapes.

STAFF ANNOUNCER—Reads for commercials, makes many program introductions and station identifications.

SPECIAL PROGRAM PERFORMERS—Are specialists who either give the news, sports, public affairs, or, in radio stations, are disc jockeys.

FILM DIRECTOR—Is responsible for films used by television stations and oversees the work of film and video editors and photographers.

FLOOR MANAGER—Follows the television director-producer's instructions concerning the direction of performers.

PROGRAM ASSISTANT—Works under television's director-producers by helping with prop and cue card placement.

DRAMATIC ACTORS/ACTRESSES—Work on local productions or for network or independent producers.

PROMOTION MANAGER—Is responsible for publicity and ad and promotional work to promote the station to its audience.

CONTINUITY WRITERS—Are responsible for preparing commercial and public service announcements.

ENGINEERING

Radio and television engineering departments are responsible for the technical part of broadcasting.

CHIEF ENGINEER—Is in charge of the engineering department's technicians and equipment. Check with the FCC for licensing requirements.

BROADCAST TECHNICIANS—Are responsible for operating and maintaining electronic equipment. In television, some of them work as studio/field engineers, videotape engineers, audio control operators, camera operators, and technical directors.

SALES

Radio and television stations depend on revenues generated by their sales departments. There are three types of revenue stations receive: network, national, and regional and local. For example, some affiliated stations are paid by the network for airing its programs. Or stations hire national sales representative firms to tap advertisers who operate in faraway cities, but want to hit their market. Or local businessmen may buy air time which is handled by sales people.

SALES MANAGER—Is in charge of the sales department, establishing policy, overseeing selling activity, supervising the staff, and designing sales campaigns. Most sales managers move up from sales positions.

SALESPERSON—Gets advertisers or their advertising agencies to buy television or radio time. She must know the station's program schedules and times, personalities, audience, and special characteristics to sucessfully sell. Though some salespeople are not, being a college graduate with advertising, broadcasting, and marketing courses is advisable. Prior sales experience is also valuable.

TRAFFIC MANAGER—Is responsible for the daily activity logs of the station's programming, keeps track of the information concerning programs and commercials, and is valuable to the sales staff by supplying them with information on unsold time.

GENERAL ADMINISTRATION—As in all business, the administration of radio and television stations is performed by management and financial specialists.

GENERAL MANAGER—Is responsible for the day-to-day operations of radio or television stations. She sets policy, supervises station employees, and is liaison to the Federal Communications Commission. A good blend of financial and technical knowledge and creativity is recommended for this position.

BROADCAST JOURNALISM

This is the newswriting, reporting, editing, and production that takes place on network or national and local news. Beginning positions include desk assistant, newsroom secretary, and production assistant. After experience is gained, career pathing can move you to researcher, unit manager, or assistant producer.

Source: *Careers in Radio* and *Careers in Television,* The National Association of Broadcasters, 1771 N St., NW, Washington, D.C. 20036. Copyright © 1976. Reprinted with permission.

approves radio and television stations. The agency is located at 1919 M Street, NW, Washington, D.C. 20554.

You should also be interested in the area of cable television. People are needed in the area of development, maintenance, and operation. There are particularly good career opportunities in the technical area. There are several training programs that are emerging in the area.

PUBLISHING

If you love books, a publishing career can be exciting. You can explore career possibilities in one of the approximately 3,000 active publishing firms, educational and governmental units, and small private units. The main divisions of publishing are adult trade, children's, university press, religious and related, mass market paperbound, book club, professional and subscription books, mail order publications, and college, elementary, and high school textbooks. The hub of publishing is in New York City. Boston, Chicago, and Philadelphia follow suit.

Book-publishing jobs, like magazing-publishing jobs, were ways for Ivy League and Seven Sisters school graduates to have prestigious positions before marriage. Because these positions were "halfway" occupations, they tended to be low-paying. Today, the editorial side of publishing is still considered a labor of love profession and starting salaries are still low.

If you are interested in getting an editorial publishing job, you may qualify for secretary-to-the-editor/editorial assistant positions. Most publishing companies start beginners in these entry-level positions to learn the editorial process and to assist editors. Like magazines, book publishing houses advance employees only in the case of other employees getting promotions or leaving. The path to the top is therefore slow.

Noneditorial jobs are in design and production, marketing, and business administration. For a discussion of both editorial and noneditorial positions, see Table 27.

TABLE 27

RANGE OF JOBS IN BOOK PUBLISHING

EDITORIAL WORK

EDITOR-IN-CHIEF *(executive editor, editorial vice-president)*—Manages the department; makes most key decisions; heads planning and development of the editorial program of the company or division; organizes staff; sets budget.

SENIOR EDITOR *(sponsoring editor, project editor, acquisitions editor, associate editor)*—Takes part in developing authors and manuscripts; proposes and carries out editorial plans according to financial and policy goals; makes contracts; works with authors, agents, and sometimes with cooperating publishers, foreign and domestic.

MANAGING EDITOR—Coordinates all editorial functions to carry out plans for each book and project; keeps track of all schedules; manages traffic—for example, among editorial, art, and production departments.

ASSOCIATE EDITOR *(project editor)*—Screens and recommends manuscripts; handles rewriting and revision, working often with authors; works with production, art, and other personnel. As special editor, may direct projects in specialized fields.

COPY EDITOR—Examines accepted manuscripts line by line, not only making sure that style and grammar are correct, but considering the coherence, arrangement, and accuracy of the work (if other editors have not already completed this) and querying sources and author when necessary.

ASSISTANT EDITOR AND EDITORIAL ASSISTANT—Check, sort, and direct incoming manuscripts; give unsolicited ones a first (usually partial) reading, report findings, return rejected submissions; handle department's clerical work and filing.

DESIGN AND PRODUCTION

PRODUCTION DIRECTOR *(production manager, production vice-president)*—Directs the look and the manufacture of the books; maintains contact with editors and marketing people; has overall responsibility for purchase of materials and manufacturing services and for cost estimates; maintains budgets.

PRODUCTION ASSOCIATE *(supervisor)*—Does purchasing; oversees fulfillment of deliveries; sets up and supervises schedules.

COST ESTIMATOR—Computes all production costs or helps director or associate in doing so; may estimate break-even figures (how many copies must be sold to pay expenses) in relation to various cost estimates, quantities printed, and selling prices.

ART DIRECTOR *(design director)*—Responsible for the graphic aspects of books (art and typography, appropriate materials, appearance of book jackets or paperback covers); buys services from artists, illustrators, photographers, photo services.

DESIGNER *(artist, associate art director)*—Creates design, layout, use of art, typography, paper, and binding to make an integrated whole.

PRODUCTION ASSISTANT—Produces and maintains communications, purchase orders, production files, traffic control of reprints, follow-up with suppliers.

MARKETING

MARKETING DIRECTOR *(marketing vice-president)*—Plans and directs all marketing functions, coordinates efforts in sales promotion, advertising, publicity, and selling; coordinates marketing with editorial and other departments.

MARKET RESEARCH MANAGER—Provides data about new and established markets in order to expand them and to find markets for new products.

SALES MANAGER—Supervises sales; provides materials for sales personnel; draws up budgets and forecasts; works with sales promotion manager.

SALES REPRESENTATIVE *(traveler)*—Calls on bookstores, libraries, schools, etc., so as to take or stimulate orders; turns in market research data and editorial information from "the field."

SALES PROMOTION MANAGER *(may be same as sales manager)*—Directs selling by direct mail, provision of printed matter, point-of-purchase and display materials, circulars; directs selling by coupon and other direct-response advertising.

ADVERTISING MANAGER—Works with ad agencies or in-house staff; plans and directs advertising in printed or other media; coordinates with promotion and publicity departments.

PUBLICITY MANAGER *(publicist)*—Generates awareness of and interest in the firm's books through print, radio, television and through reviewers, booksellers, and others who influence buying. May be aided by associates assigned to radio, television, and reviewer liaison; directs writing and sending of press releases. Maintains close liaison with other departments, including subsidiary rights.

SUBSIDIARY RIGHTS MANAGER—Markets the licensing, to others, of rights to use the firm's published materials: rights including book club distribution, translations and foreign publishing, mass market reprints, publication in newspapers and periodicals, performance on radio, television, film, stage; quotation in anthologies or other publications. Copyright matters may be handled in the rights department, or in the editorial department or a separate department. Many of the aspects of rights may be handled by the author's own literary agent rather than by the publisher.

BUSINESS ADMINISTRATION

The job titles in this area are like those in many other industries. The functions are integral parts of the publishing process. Some of them are:

Setting financial goals and policies, in order to implement the firm's editorial and philosophical goals.

Analyzing financial results (costs, income, other matters).

Coordinating salary benefit policies.

Providing essential services within the firm—accounting, filing, payments, office housekeeping, and general order.

Supervising order fulfillment; filing orders, ensuring delivery.

Keeping all departments informed about their current and projected places in the company's financial picture.

Comparing the firm's performance quantitatively with that of others in similar areas and with the firm's own goals.

Personnel management: a division of management, involved with every department. It deals with salaries, benefits, hiring and termination

procedures, in-house communications, and various concerns of employees; arranging for in-house training programs or outside educational
opportunities.

Reprinted from *Getting into Book Publishing,* with permission of the R. R. Bowker
Company. Copyright © 1979 by Xerox Corporation.

PUBLIC RELATIONS

To career-path successfully in public relations, the bachelor's degree is fast becoming the prerequisite. A liberal arts background with a major in communications, journalism, or public relations will make you more marketable. The Public Relations Society of America (PRSA) reports that 140 colleges and 25 graduate schools offered degree programs or special curriculums in public relations.

In seeking a job, you should assess your skills to determine which are transferable to public relations. Many of us do public relations work for community projects, theater groups, women's organizations, and other volunteer endeavors. We rarely, however, look at this experience as marketable in public relations.

Public relations skills include programming; writing and editing reports, press releases, speeches, newsletters, and other printed material; disseminating information; arranging special events like news conferences; public speaking; research and evaluation; and production of brochures, special reports, and multi-media programs.

After assessing skills and tapping potential employers, remember that women tend to congregate in women-oriented areas within the public relations field.

Some of us have managed to get top positions, most often in community relations work for nonprofit organizations or public relations work in government agencies. Some have landed corporate positions in offices of community or social responsibility agencies. Blacks are likely to be found also in international public relations departments which have programs in third world countries, or with record companies in departments which handle Black artists. Some Blacks have started their own public relations firms.

What Will You Earn in Communications?

Salaries in the communications field vary. Some workers make lucrative six-figure salaries; others make a decent living. A National Association of Broadcasters survey states that weekly salaries of radio reporters range from $225 to $500, according to the Occupational Outlook Handbook. Reporters who are employed by daily newspapers and have contracts negotiated by the Newspaper Guild start with salaries ranging from $180 to more than $800 a week. Most start at salaries between $300 and $450.

According to a National Association of Broadcasters survey, salaries for television and radio announcers range from $12,800 to more than $182,000 a year.

Median weekly salaries of full-time broadcast technicians are about $330; some make more than $1,000 a week.

Median yearly salaries for public relations specialists who aren't self-employed are approximately $25,800; top earners make more than $52,000.

CAREER PROFILES

There are eleven women in this section. Judith Cummings of the New York *Times* is Bureau Chief. In magazine journalism, Marcia Gillespie is a free-lance writer. Susan Taylor is *Essence*'s editor-in-chief.

In the area of television and radio, only off-camera work is reviewed. Off-camera people rarely get coverage and are therefore emphasized in this section. There are several profiles. Darlene Hayes is a free-lance producer; Sherrie Carter is an engineer; Jessie Maple is a camerawoman; and Lois Fortune is a television producer.

Marie Brown is a literary agent.

Public relations specialists are Jewell Jackson McCabe and Victoria Lucas. Irene Gandy is a publicist.

Judith Cummings
Bureau Chief
New York Times
Los Angeles, California

Many aspiring journalists want to work for the New York *Times* because they consider it the best in the field. Future reporter Judith Cummings was no different. In her childhood days in Detroit, she grew up reading the New York *Times* and thought of becoming one of its reporters. Each of her educational accomplishments and job acceptances laid the groundwork for a career as a journalist.

The first step toward realizing the goal was enrolling at Howard University in Washington, D.C., and majoring in English. The summer before her senior year, Cummings participated in an internship at the Detroit *Free Press,* and the experience convinced her that her reporting dream was right on target.

After college, she began looking for a reporting job and in the interim took a writer's job at the Equal Employment Opportunity Commission. The position involved her in policy discussions of the top officials of the agency, from which she wrote reports to Congress, developed speeches, and conceived radio and television scripts.

When Cummings first approached the New York *Times,* she was told there were no openings. They were encouraging and told her to keep in touch. She did just that, and contacted the paper's Washington editors over the next two years. The payoff came when she landed a trainee position with the New York *Times* in its Washington bureau.

"The trainee position was actually a clerk's job, but it also allowed me to work as a beginning reporter," she recalls. "After a year, the paper could decide whether the trainee had what it took to be a staff reporter."

Cummings became a member of the Metropolitan News Staff at the *Times*'s home office in New York, where her experience included general assignment reporting, celebrity and entertainment column, and covering higher education and later transportation when both these systems were in crises. "One of the most instructive periods of my career was covering the dismantling of the right to tuition-free education at the City University of New York," she says. "And one of the most politically enlightening was the decline of the mass transit system."

In 1981, Cummings was promoted to the *Times*'s National Staff in Los Angeles, becoming the first Black woman at the paper to be a full-time national news correspondent in a regional bureau. As a correspondent, she was responsible for spotting and breaking news and features in her region of the Southwest. She is now the *Times*'s Los Angeles office Bureau Chief.

Cummings feels journalism is a good area to consider, but feels future reporters will need to specialize. "In coming years, reporters will need to specialize in areas like energy or the environment. Specialization will give you an added edge in the marketplace," she advises. "Select an area of expertise as soon as possible in college, and I strongly urge getting a graduate degree."

For Cummings, rising through the ranks to become bureau chief for a major organization has been challenging and fulfilling. It was competitive to get in and has been tough to advance. In a pressure-filled and demanding environment, she has had to perform at a high level and produce high-quality, stimulating pieces. She has accomplished these difficult tasks by hard work, integrity, and top-rate writing.

La Verne Powlis
Free-lance Beauty Writer/Consultant
and Author of
The Black Woman's Beauty Book *and* Beauty from the Inside Out:
A Guide for Black Women

After graduating from Hunter College in New York, La Verne Powlis encountered a tight job market and turned to the New York Urban Coalition for help. The staff of the Coalition's now defunct skills bank tested her and verified writing as a strong point. The Coalition referred her to *Family Circle* magazine and ultimately, she received the editorial assistant position.

Powlis's ability to "go the extra mile" made a lasting impression. When the secretary to the editor-in-chief resigned, Powlis's editor recommended her and she became the first Black in that position.

After eight months, the editor-in-chief realized Powlis's potential and promoted her to editor. As editor, Powlis wrote the "Living Black" column for two years, but began exploring other possibilities within the magazine. She eyed the fashion department, but there wasn't an opening. There was an opening in the beauty department and she transferred.

Powlis prospered in beauty, but soon wanted to expand her training in the area. Because *Family Circle* was not a beauty magazine, she job hunted at other magazines and cosmetic companies. Condé Nast, the magazine conglomerate that owns *Bride's, Vogue,* and other magazines, was interested, but had no immediate openings. Powlis gave up the search and settled into *Family Circle.* But two years later, Condé Nast called to offer Powlis an associate beauty editor position with *Bride's* magazine and she accepted it.

Powlis's efficiency and track record helped land the beauty editor position. "The beauty department focused on the bride's engagement period, the wedding day, and the year afterwards. As beauty editor, I was responsible for developing ideas for the beauty pages. Once they were developed, I presented them to the editor-in-chief for approval, and once they were accepted, I moved toward implementing them," she says. "Next, it was my responsibility to oversee the photographing of material to be used in the beauty pages. I interviewed and selected models, chose makeup and hair stylists, and ultimately brought together models, photographers, and the accessories editor to complete each issue's photography."

Powlis brought *Bride's* into prominence within the beauty industry. "*Bride's* is not known as a beauty magazine, but I worked very hard to make it visible within the industry. This was accomplished by requesting and receiving more beauty pages, which resulted in more advertising from the beauty industry and *Bride's* visibility being expanded," she recalls.

To further expand visibility, Powlis attended cosmetic companies' press functions where new products or seasonal introductions were previewed. "In a given week, there were three or four press functions to attend. Sometimes, there were three or four of these functions in one day," she recalls of the exhausting, glamorous schedule.

To best represent *Bride's* at these functions, Powlis felt it was her duty to look good and spent one day a week in beauty salons. Surprisingly, this job-related requirement led to another career: writing. Her search to get proper hair care was difficult and frustrating and she assumed other women were experiencing similar problems. From this difficulty, she developed an idea for *The Black Woman's Beauty Book*. Powlis juggled both her magazine- and book-writing tasks and completed the book, which was subsequently published by Doubleday in 1979. The book's success led to a consultant position with L'Oréal, and she left *Bride's* to travel around the country promoting the book and L'Oréal products. Powlis soon became a full-time free-lance writer, contributing to such magazines as *Vogue* and *Black Enterprise*.

This beauty specialist later relocated to Los Angeles. It was her volunteer work for the Coalition of 100 Black Women, Planned Parenthood, and the YWCA that landed her a job. "I don't think that Black women realize our volunteer work looks as good on a résumé as the ones we are paid for," says Powlis. "When I went to Los Angeles, my work with the Coalition, Planned Parenthood, and the YWCA is what I used to get an incredible job." That job was writing *The ABC Family Life Education Curriculum* for the State of California. For this assignment, she worked at the Redeemer Alternative School.

Afterward, she took another job with The Black American Response to the African Crises, working to help Ethiopian drought and famine victims. She ran the organization's office, helped promote its activities, and wrote press releases.

Powlis left this job, and after a brief hiatus wrote a new book, *Beauty from the Inside Out: A Guide for Black Women* (Doubleday). She was asked to help Audrey Smaltz write *Vogue*'s column for Black women, and she was also given an assignment as account manager, Field Promotions, for the Avon account with Uniworld Advertising Agency.

Marcia Ann Gillespie
Free-lance Writer
New York, New York

Marcia Ann Gillespie has enjoyed a brilliant journalism career and is still one of America's best-known Black women in the communications field.

After graduating from Lake Forest College in Illinois, Gillespie landed a job with Time-Life Books. While there, she approached the enterprising group of Blacks who were launching a new Black woman's magazine, *Essence*. They offered her the managing editor's job. Six months later, the editor-in-chief left, and Gillespie moved into the job.

In the following ten years, Gillespie made magazine history by pushing the magazine to worldwide prominence. Her editorial leadership has made *Essence* one of the top magazines in its field.

After ten years of nurturing the magazine, Gillespie followed another dream: free-lance writing. Today, she is a contributing editor at *Ms.* magazine, and writes a column that appears four times a year.

In addition, she is a consultant to publishing concerns that want to start magazines or publishing houses. She writes proposals and generally assists them in the "start up." Gillespie does this both in the United States and in the Caribbean. For example, she is helping a woman in Trinidad start a magazine there.

Gillespie fondly remembers her days in the hub of magazine publishing. Magazine publishing, like other publishing areas, is not initially a rewarding field in terms of salaries and advancement. "Editors must wait patiently for financial rewards. The beginning salaries are low, and real salary increases do not come until you move into the senior editor range. Movement into this range, however, can sometimes take six or ten years. It is not instant gratification," she says. "The mobility factor is also very slow, because magazine work is a very restricted hierarchy. It can take years to advance, because a job is not created for you. As one person moves, you then move. There also isn't a great turnover in this industry. The career span for editors is that most stay at one place for several years. If you're going to enter this field, I counsel patience."

Susan Taylor
Editor-in-Chief and
Executive Producer/Host
"Essence" *(the television show)*
New York, New York

Susan Taylor has carved out an impressive career in the beauty and fashion fields, but in winter of 1981, she reached a journalism height by becoming *Essence* magazine's editor-in-chief. Her climb to the top began with a success-oriented philosophy; she wanted to become a successful actress. She soon became a mother, and, feeling that she couldn't give her best to both roles, she looked for a more suitable career. Taylor became a cosmetologist, started a cosmetics company, and taught makeup and hairstyling at Ophelia DeVore's School of Charm. Beauty became her chief area of expertise. When *Essence* needed a beauty editor, she convinced them to hire her as a free-lancer.

Taylor free-lanced with the magazine until offered the permanent spot of beauty editor. Within the year, she also was asked to take over the fashion department. "At the time, I didn't have the fashion credentials, but it worked to our advantage," she remembers. "Since I was not locked into current fads and trends, I didn't feel the need to follow only what was hot. As a result, we developed our own unique fashion philosophy for Black women."

This trend setter developed a fashion and beauty approach that would endear her to *Essence*'s readers. She disregarded standard magazine fashion and beauty requirements and opened *Essence*'s covers and pages to a wide range of Black women. "We realize that most magazines require models to be five-seven or over, and wear size seven or eight, but

I think magazines are doing indelible damage to both Black and white American women's psyches by projecting certain unrealistic stereotypes," she stresses. "When I was fashion and beauty editor, any woman who was healthy could be on our cover. Our cover women sometimes have gaps in their teeth, full lips, black skin, broad noses, and are full-sized, too—in other words, they are real! As a result, you could and still can see women on the cover of *Essence* that you would not see on the cover of any other magazine. We tried to mirror the spectrum of Black women."

The innovative fashion and beauty editor reversed the standard method of securing models: agency referrals. Taylor instituted an "open door" policy allowing Black women all over the country to stop by and show their portfolios. She also selected people after spotting them in subways or supermarkets. Every Friday, she opened her door to aspiring models. Her blend of using professional and "ordinary people" has made *Essence*'s covers one of its chief selling powers and given the magazine uniqueness.

Taylor was satisfied with heading the fashion and beauty department. But after *Essence*'s fourth editor-in-chief left the magazine, *Essence* publisher Ed Lewis reasoned that Taylor's nine-and-one-half-year tenure would make her a likely candidate. The energetic fashion and beauty editor, who had traveled the world overseeing photo sessions, wondered about the primarily desk job of editor-in-chief. A special friend, however, convinced her to take the job.

The new editor-in-chief eased into the job with confidence. She had years of preparation for the job because of the many brainstorming sessions with former editor-in-chief Marcia Ann Gillespie. "Marcia and I had an incredible exchange during her tenure at *Essence*. We spent hours dissecting the book, thinking of what it should be and who the reader audience was," Taylor recalls. "My years of managing the fashion and beauty department also put me in touch with Black women and their needs."

Taylor's knowledge of the magazine and positive philosophy of life helped her pull together a dynamic first issue. The readership increased, and she says that "we picked up thirty-three thousand new readers in one issue.

"Being the editor-in-chief has given me an opportunity to put into practice things that I believe. Everyone who knows me realizes that my focus is really that of a spiritual nature. I think through spiritual awareness and growth, we can change this world. I know that I have changed mine," she stresses.

Taylor credits much of her success to her management style. "I developed a unique management style, and believe it is my strength. I believe in freestyle management, and I relate to the human side of people. When someone on our team does something that I am not particularly pleased with, we sit down and try to help them understand why an approach wasn't the best for us. I do this rather than be super critical," she says. "People are bringing their talents and work. Whether it's a secretary, art director, photographer, or writer, it's their art. I think that the way you critique someone is important. It should be done in a way that helps them expand, that helps them give the best of themselves, and grow."

Taylor's ideas and talents have paid off, but she has worked hard to achieve results. "The hours are long. But if you want to be successful, you must have a good idea, research it, and put energy behind it," she advises. "You have to be healthy, eat right, and exercise."

Susan Taylor qualifies as a first-rate fashion and beauty innovator. Her flare for fashion, understanding of Black beauty, and keen awareness of *Essence* readers' needs make her a successful editor-in-chief. After taking over, she used the same uniqueness and boldness in turning *Essence*'s look in a new and challenging direction. By everyone's estimation, she made the magazine into a uniquely different one. She's a winner, positive thinker, and by all predictions a survivor in the tough, competitive magazine industry. She is now also executive producer/host for "Essence" (the television show).

J. Darlene Hayes
Free-lance Producer
Former Senior Producer, "The Phil Donahue Show"
Los Angeles, California

J. Darlene Hayes started working as a secretary at the Dayton, Ohio, Urban League. When an inquiry came into the Urban League for a clerk/typist to work for "The Phil Donahue Show" at a television station, Hayes, who was divorced with two children, seized the opportunity. "I thought this would be interesting. It was 1969 and Black people in larger numbers had entered the communications field. At the time, the show had just two producers, a secretary, and myself, and it was only in three markets (Cincinnati, Dayton, and Columbus). A year after I joined the show, it was syndicated to Detroit and New York," she says.

Working for a television show whetted Hayes's appetite for more exposure. "The more I saw the show, the more I became interested in television production. Because it was a small market, I had the opportunity to do many things. In a larger market, union regulations would have prohibited me from doing these tasks," she remembers. "If someone asked me whether I could do something, I would say yes. But if I didn't know or understand something, I would ask. I moved into production by bringing in ideas and giving them to the producer. When some were used I knew I was on the right track."

Hayes was soon promoted to secretary, production assistant, and then producer. "To get promotions, I explained what I wanted to do. They said, 'Go ahead and try it.' I moved from position to position by listening and asking questions."

Hayes was the senior producer for "The Phil Donahue Show." Her job was finding ideas and guests. "Many publishers, public relations people, and others tried to promote someone or something and would call us. The unique thing, however, about the Donahue show is that we rarely used those sources. We tried to find guests, topics, and issues from magazines, newspapers, trends, or experiences in our own lives. I tried to take real life issues and formulate them into a format which fit our show. Most of the topics on the show are controversial; others are human- or news-oriented issues," she says.

Hayes's day was a long one. "I came into the office about nine. If it was my show, I went over the materials for the program. In most cases, I had previously researched the show's topic as much as two weeks or a month before. I just had to refresh my memory. I outlined things that I wanted Phil to cover or thought he should read. We went over the visuals, which are the name titles that show on the air, to make sure everything was spelled correctly. I looked over the tapes which were inserted in the interior of the program to make sure they were correctly placed," she says. "Phil came in about nine-thirty or a quarter to ten. I sat down with him and went over the materials. We discussed what I found interesting, things discovered by talking with the guests, and the direction the show should take. I left materials for him to read. By that time, the guests arrived. I went over the show with them briefly. Usually, Phil came in and talked to them about what he expected. Then the show went on the air. Because it was my show, I usually stayed in the studio, listened to the discussion, and determined if all the points were covered or it was going in the right direction. If a guest was a little weak or shy, I'd tell them to get their points across and not be intimidated."

When the show was over, Hayes returned to do what takes up a great deal of a producer's time: research. "The rest of the afternoon was spent thinking about or following up on other programs. For example, if I was interested in doing a show around a particular book, I read it and requested additional newspaper articles about it. Or sometimes, I spent a great deal of research time tracking down a person whom I was interested in."

Hayes, who was with "The Phil Donahue Show" for many years, feels those starting in entry-level positions can still move up, but feels a college internship will give you the edge in getting a job. "It's still possible for a secretary to move up. The competition, however, makes it more difficult," she says. "If you're in college, try getting an internship with a television station, which will help tremendously. Many people at our station started as interns. It's an inside track."

Hayes is now a free-lance producer who has worked on a number of projects, including a talk show with Geraldo Rivera, and a music video.

Sherrie Carter
Television Engineer
New York, New York

Sherrie Carter came to New York from Michigan, where she graduated from Michigan State University and worked at an educational television station. In New York, she worked for several television stations including NBC, ABC, and WOR-TV. She now works for WPIX-TV as a permanent television engineer.

"I have done a great deal of boom operating work. A boom operator stands on a platform holding a microphone on what looks like a fishing pole and follows guests or performers. I have done boom work for NBC: 'Another World,' the soap opera; 'Saturday Night Live,'" she says. "I have gained experience in patching microphones to the right systems in the studio to make sure they work properly. A boom operator also makes sure guests are miked when entering a set." She has also worked as a utility person, a technician who makes sure the television cables are out of the way which is particularly important since camera people are making awkward shots.

Although Carter's title says engineer, she is classified as a studio field operator. "A studio field operator's classification means I can work both in the studio and outside the studio on remotes like baseball games, news, or special events. I can do boom camera operation, sound, commercial carts, videotape editing, and camera operating," she says. "While employed by NBC, ABC, and WOR-TV, I was classified as a vacation relief. This meant I was hired on a temporary basis, and was able to work up to six months before being released. Sometimes I could get an extension and work nine months. In this industry, you are either permanently hired or work as a part of a vacation relief system. It has been hard for me to get a permanent job."

Carter feels getting FCC licensing helps in getting permanent jobs. "Although I worked as a technical engineer for an educational station, my experience would be enhanced by having an FCC license. If you can get that license, it will be a plus." She says, "I know people debate this. It's true that there has been an upward swing in terms of hiring minorities, but there is still a great deal to be done. I feel that with an FCC license, there will be a greater chance of finding permanent employment and not being transient."

Carter advises the woman who wants to make it in television's technical area to have a winning personality and persistence. "Personality has a great deal to do with movement in this industry. Without it, you can easily get lost in the shuffle. For example, in major cities like New York, most television engineers shift from network to network before achieving permanent status." She advises, "Persistence pays off in getting jobs, but once you have them you must be professional. You must be on time because television is a timely business. Many people have been heavily penalized because of being late."

Jessie Maple
Television Camerawoman
and Author of
How to Become a Union Camerawoman
New York, New York

Jessie Maple is the first Black woman to become a member of the International Photographers of the Motion Picture Industries, Local

644 IATSE. She moved into camera work after a career as a bacteriology technician and newspaper columnist. "I quit working as a bacteriology lab technician because I felt that I had accomplished all I could do in that area," she recalls. "I thought about a career in newspaper reporting and wanted to join a training program at the now defunct *Manhattan Tribune.* When the program was canceled, the publisher said I could stay and observe. I did, and soon began getting assignments. From there, I went to the New York *Courier,* where I developed my own column called 'Jessie's Grapevine.' "

After the *Courier* folded, Maple became interested in film. At the time, there were several training programs for minorities. "I enrolled in two: the Third World Cinema Program and WNET Television Training School. After graduating, I became a free-lance assistant film editor," she says. "I didn't like film editing. My husband, Leroy, was an assistant cameraman and I became interested in this aspect of film."

Maple's curiosity led her to apply for union membership. "I decided to take the test, studied six months, took it, and failed. But Leroy, who had observed the testing, said someone had tampered with the camera," she says. "We petitioned the board of directors and I was given another test. This time I passed and was given assistant camerawoman status."

There were hardly any waves made with Maple's admittance to the union, until she tried to upgrade her status. "Everything was fine until I asked the board of directors to change my status to camerawoman. They permitted me to work simultaneously as a camerawoman and assistant camerawoman, but my classification would remain the same," she remembers. "Working as a camerawoman, however, caused problems, and my ability to get jobs was threatened. As a result, I charged two of the major networks with discrimination because I couldn't get work." Her legal struggle to win the right to work is chronicled in *How to Become a Union Camerawoman,* which she wrote while out of work awaiting final decisions on the law suits. Ultimately, one of the networks settled out of court and one suit is still pending.

Maple soon began working as a free-lance camerawoman. "Being a camerawoman is not easy. The hours can be rough. Free-lance camera people's hours are particularly varied. There have been times when I was called at two in the morning and had to work all day. When there were jailbreaks and subsequent stakeouts, I was called to stay the duration. When the Pope came to New York, I had to be there at six-thirty in the morning and didn't get home until midnight," she says. "But the money is great. The year that I worked as a free-lancer, I averaged between $700 and $1,000 a week plus expenses."

Although the salaries are lucrative, there can be a great deal of competition for the camera person. "There's a great deal of competition and pressure. There are many free-lancers and the best ones get hired," Maple says. "If you're a camera person on staff, things are different and you can relax a little more."

Maple, who estimates that there are only two Black camerawomen who do field work in New York, says to compete, we should get the proper training and licensing. "To become a television camerawoman, you should get your FCC license. There are schools where you can prepare for it by attending classes for one year at night or six months during the day. After completing these courses, you can apply and take the tests. Or you can do like me and attend a twelve-day course which I took in Washington, D.C.," she advises. "But you have to be brave to do what I did. In fact, the instructor wasn't sure I could absorb that much material in twelve days. But I took the course, came home, and locked myself in my room for two weeks and passed the tests. FCC licenses are not needed for shooting cameras. They are, however, good to have because the FCC may ultimately demand that you have it to work with television electronic equipment."

Maple says prospective camerawomen should learn videotape. "After you get the FCC license, familiarize yourself with videotape. The stations have switched from film to video. With videotape, you can go out, shoot the news live, and know that you will get something presentable. Before you know what you have with film, you have to shoot, then go back to the station to develop and edit it," she says. "To learn video, I would suggest familiarizing yourself with video equipment at schools or community centers."

Maple, an activist who is interested in helping other Blacks get into the union, has opened a movie theater, 20 West Theatre, with her husband, Leroy Patton. She has completed two independent feature films, *Will* and *The McGee Twins*. She won a special merit award for *Will* at the 1981 Athens International Film festival in Athens, Ohio.

Lois Fortune
Executive Producer
Al Manahel
(Children's Television Workshop)
with Jordan Television
Jordan Company for Television, Radio
and Cinema Production LTD

Lois Fortune wanted to become a teacher of small children, but became interested in film while a student at Monteith College (part of Wayne State University) in Detroit. "I took a course in cinema and one of the options for a final project was to make a film. I made one and it was an enjoyable experience," she remembers. "I decided to put my interests in children and films together and work for children's television."

She took a course in television production and direction at New York University and also won placement in the competitive writer's training program at the Children's Television Workshop. At the end of the training program, she stayed on as a probationary writer. "Writing was my way into production. After my probationary period, I was made production assistant for 'The Electric Company.' I stayed in this position for two years and was promoted to animation coordinator," she says. "I believe in getting additional training and development, and in 1971, I went to the WNET TV Training School and trained for technical behind-the-scenes positions. From 1973 to 1975, I also worked as a trainee for the Directors Guild of America Producers Training Program and was involved in commercials and feature films." Concurrently she worked as an animation coordinator for the Children's Television Workshop's "The Electric Company," researcher for "The Best of Families," and production assistant for "Feeling Good." Later, she also became stage manager for "The Electric Company." Upon completion of the Directors Guild of America program, she became a second assistant director for feature films and commercials.

In 1976, Fortune became second assistant director for WNET's "Our Story: Jade Show," assistant to the director for Westinghouse's "Apollo" (shows one and two), and associate producer for WNET's "Watch Your Mouth." From 1976 to 1978, she worked as an associate executive producer for the New York State Education Department's "Vegetable Soup."

Afterward, she became associate producer in the International Department of the Children's Television Workshop and worked as a consulting liaison to foreign countries doing "Sesame Street." " 'Sesame Street' is seen in over forty countries and is translated into thirteen languages. My job was to give information and share skills and knowledge about making shows for preschool audiences to countries using 'Sesame Street,' without imposing our cultural considerations. We did script reviews from a research and content point of view. For example, we reviewed each script to see if it was frightening or confusing to children," she says. "I advised and taught countries some of the procedures that we had utilized at WNET to make 'Sesame Street' the unique show it is. There's a certain philosophy about the show which is not easy to convey. There's a certain understanding about the film's length and how to make it both appealing and comprehensive that comes after ten years of operation. Many people have produced films, but not for three-year-olds. We provided that type of expertise."

In November of 1979, Fortune became producer of the award-winning "Pinwheel," a cable TV show for preschool children airing on Nickelodeon, the Young People's Channel, (a programming service of Warner Amex Satellite Entertainment Company). In the summer of 1980, she became executive producer of the series of 260 one-hour shows.

Fortune is now the executive producer of the Arabic version of "The Electric Company." She is working in a consultant capacity to produce sixty-five half-hour shows for Jordan Television.

Fortune likes the production end of television work and advises others to consider it. "If you are interested in production, take any position to get your foot in the door. I have a master's degree in education, but worked as a production assistant which is basically 'gofer work,' " she says. "Once in, don't be too important for any task. If a task is humanly possible, do it. And don't play down any skill. I'm in communications, but typing, shorthand, telephone communications, spelling, and organizational skills are crucial and important ones."

Dorothy Brunson
President
Brunson Communications, Inc.
WEBB, Baltimore, Maryland, WIGO, Atlanta, Georgia

Dorothy Brunson is an excellent example of how a financial background can push you to the top. "In 1963, I started in radio with a company that purchased WWRL-AM in New York. I began in the accounting department, which is the heart of the operation, and I learned quickly what was happening throughout the organization," she remembers. "After a few months, the person who headed the department left and I took over. From there, I moved into more responsible positions."

One such position was assistant general manager for the station. "My job dealt with FCC regulations, mergers, acquisitions, consolidations of financial statements, and troubleshooting. I learned radio operations by assisting the general manager, whose background was primarily technical. We complemented each other. I taught him finance and he taught me the technical end. I did that for seven years," Brunson says.

While at WWRL, she met a Black salesman and joined him as a partner in a Madison Avenue advertising agency. In the early seventies, she sold her part of the business and began doing free-lance consultant work for advertising agencies and companies, while raising her children.

She joined Inner City Broadcasting in 1973. "Inner City Broadcasting, a Black-owned company, was in its formative stages and running into severe economic problems. I turned that around. I contacted banks and structured a company which was financially sound. I analyzed our growth potential by looking at other available stations and resources. I helped to acquire additional stations, set them up, hired the personnel, and did troubleshooting to ensure that people functioned within the Inner City concept."

Brunson's astute financial abilities won her respect. In her former position, as general manager, she was responsible for overseeing the management of Inner City's seven radio stations in New York, Detroit, Los Angeles, and San Francisco. "A general manager is responsible for the day-to-day operations including implementing policies which are formulated by the board of directors or president. A general manager is someone who oversees the entire organization and has the ability to gather, synthesize, and disseminate data that keeps things functioning smoothly. The position is the top of the line in terms of running a radio station. You can have a president who may or may not be involved in the day-to-day operations. I was a vice-president and corporate general manager with responsibilities for all of the stations. A general manager generally makes the final decisions about what money to spend and the direction the organization is to go. Of course, these decisions are made after input from the other people who report to us or from those to whom we report." This former general manager now owns two radio stations: WEBB in Baltimore and WIGO in Atlanta.

Brunson feels that career opportunities within radio stations are best at the entry level for those with knowledge of engineering or finance. For those who want top managerial slots, she suggests accounting or finance backgrounds: "Accounting and financial backgrounds lend themselves best to management rather than general management backgrounds. Financial people have more of a tendency to become aware of details and think in terms of checks and balances. This is important because managing is more than just being able to absorb data or look at something from a business point of view. It is being able to create a balance so that you can get a harmonic effect from your staff and from the people you work with on a one-to-one basis. It is being able to weigh the data so that you can make a decision. I have found that when I bring in people with an accounting, auditor, or controller's background, I get a more balanced person."

Marie Dutton Brown
Literary Agent
Editorial Consultant
New York, New York

Marie Brown majored in psychology at Pennsylvania State University. Because the psychology department was housed in the School of Education, she took several education courses and after graduation was permitted to teach. After teaching social studies in a Philadelphia junior high school, she became a coordinator of intergroup education for the school district of Philadelphia. "As coordinator, I was responsible for introducing multiethnic curriculum materials to teachers, administrators, and community groups. Since this concept was new to the school system, I conducted several human relations workshops," she remembers. To one of these workshops, she invited Loretta Barrett, an editor at Doubleday, to talk about multiethnic books.

When Brown visited New York, Barrett invited her to lunch and persuaded her to talk to some people at Doubleday about her work. Unknown to Brown, she was being interviewed and was offered a trainee position.

Brown took the trainee's job, which was to last ten weeks but stretched into ten months. She stayed for a year and a half, until marrying and moving to California. "While in California, I worked in a bookstore and did some free-lance editing. Subsequently, we moved to Washington, D.C., and I primarily took care of my daughter. During this period, I stayed in touch with the people at Doubleday. In 1972, I returned to Doubleday as an associate editor," she says. She was ultimately promoted to senior editor.

As a senior editor, Brown had a busy schedule. "I spent a great deal of time talking to people who wanted to get published. My days were also filled with considering proposals and submissions and working with authors or agents. I submitted these proposals or submissions to editorial meetings and sought approval for them there and from the publishing board. If they were approved, I negotiated the contract and worked with the author throughout the process," she says. "When the manuscript was completed, I read and edited it. I worked with the production and art departments, prepared information for the sales force, and developed marketing plans. I usually worked on eighteen books a year." Amid that busy schedule, she traveled to sales conferences around the country looking for trends that might inspire new book ideas.

As an authority on Blacks in the publishing world, Brown feels publishing offers good career opportunities for Black women. "To enter the field, I would suggest having a general liberal arts background. This is contrary to what people say, but I feel you should have as broad a background and cultural and intellectual experience as possible," she advises. "To become more familiar with the publishing industry, take one of the courses or degrees offered in publishing."

To advance your career in publishing, a great degree of patience is required. "While I was at Doubleday, there was a structured training program, although all entry-level editorial positions are secretarial. Now there are more men entering the field as secretaries than women. Prior to equal employment opportunities laws, men came into publishing at other levels such as research assistants or college travelers or salesmen. Now nearly everyone comes in on the same level." Brown says, "In the secretarial training program, you learn about the company. You can then move into editorial secretary, assistant to the editor, or editorial assistant positions. However, this takes anywhere from three to six years. For some, it takes four years; others take ten years. Some people fall in at the right time when an opening occurs because an editorial secretary or assistant leaves. It is a waiting game and the levels of frustration can be high. You must, therefore, be committed to publishing as a career."

Another possible frustration about publishing careers is the pay. "The salaries are low. If you are experienced, qualified, and have been exposed to a certain life-style, beginning in an entry-level job in the editorial end of publishing will be difficult," says Brown. "The most difficult thing for me was to balance my strong professional interests and the psychic benefits I received from my job with the wages I received."

Still, there are advantages to publishing careers if you love books. "I don't think anyone enters this field without loving books. The number one advantage for me was working in a job where I was happy. It was fulfilling," says Brown. "Another advantage was the diverse range of people to whom I was exposed and with whom I worked. One day I might to be working with a Black leader on a book of political significance. The next, I was working with a music personality or a psychologist or a poet."

Brown encourages other Black women to enter publishing. It is a field where we are needed. If Black writers are to continue to have their works published, we need the presence of Black editors in the publishing field.

Early in 1981, Brown left Doubleday to become editor at the now defunct *Élan*, a Black woman's magazine. She is now a literary agent and editorial consultant. Her clients include Ed Bradley, Quincy Troupe, Alexis DeVeaux, Audrey Edwards, Dr. Craig Polite, children's writer Eloise Greenfield, and others.

Jewell Jackson McCabe
President,
Jewell Jackson McCabe Associates
New York, New York

Jewell Jackson McCabe is at the helm of her own company. She was WNET/Thirteen's director of Government and Community Affairs Department, responsible for Thirteen's relations with federal, state, and city governments and with major community groups. "I was responsible for helping the network create a presence in the community by working with government, community groups, and civic groups," she says. "By communicating directly with these groups, I kept them informed of the types of cultural and public affairs programs and special interest projects."

While a child, McCabe learned effective communication. Her broadcast pioneer father, Hal Jackson, and mother, Julia Hawkins Jackson, provided an atmosphere where communicating was a family priority. McCabe thrived in this environment and grew up seeking a career to channel this energy through. After attending Bard College, she moved into the public relations arena as public relations officer for Special Services for Children. Later, at the New York Urban Coalition, she subsequently became director of public affairs and is best known for producing the popular monthly newsletter *Give a Damn.*

As a publicist, McCabe made a career change to associate director for public information, Women's Division, Office of the Governor of New York State. Under the tutelage of Mary Burke Nicholas, McCabe gained exposure to the art of lobbying. She also became exposed to a large number of business, civic, and political leaders. When WNET wanted to strengthen its federal, state, and city government ties, it sought someone who could effectively move within those circles. She became an easy choice.

McCabe's active job included audience development, which was accomplished through mass mailings, seminars, and public speaking engagements. A priority project was to help audiences become more intelligent viewers. "I wanted to sensitize people and make them aware of what they were watching. It was my hope that viewers would develop critical viewing skills to help them make better and more selective choices about what they watch," she says. Reaching audiences was particularly difficult because WNET's public broadcasting base does not have the advertising power of commercial television. She had to direct her staff toward making a concerted effort to reach potential viewers, and ultimately help them develop listening skills.

This dynamic communicator has a serious community commitment. Early in her career, she sought out community and civic groups. Her best-known work is as the president of the National Coalition of 100 Black Women, an organization of some of the country's most powerful Black women.

McCabe is affiliated with many other groups, including the prestigious Women's Forum; Women United for New York; Executive Committee, Association for a Better New York and EDGES; and she serves on the boards of Lenox Hill Hospital, New York Urban Coalition, Settlement Housing Fund, Inc., and Business Marketing Corporation. She also serves on David Rockefeller's NYC Partnership.

Jewell Jackson McCabe represents the growing breed of Black women careerists. She is committed to career, community, and civic groups. She is also president of Jewell Jackson McCabe Associates, a New York-based firm.

Victoria Lucas
President of Victoria Lucas Associates
New York, New York

Victoria Lucas is president of Victoria Lucas Associates, a New York-based public relations and market consultant firm. In addition to serving as consultant to major corporations, her firm has handled public relations for such clients as B. B. King, Melba Moore, Gladys Knight and the Pips, Roy Ayers, Ornette Coleman, the late Donny Hathaway, poet Nikki Giovanni, the Newport Jazz Festival–New York, the annual two-day "Mississippi Homecoming" festival cohosted by blues great B. B. King and Fayette, Mississippi, Mayor Charles Evers, and for "Vegetable Soup," a children's television series about racial diversity, airing on NBC and educational television stations across the country.

Prior to starting her company in 1969, Lucas was a newspaper reporter in her native Chicago, a copywriter for two major New York advertising agencies, Norman, Craig & Kummel, and Cannon Advertising Associates, as well as an account executive in the public relations firm of Rogers & Cowan.

Presently a member of the faculty of the New School for Social Research, she teaches a popular course entitled, "Introduction to the Basics of Public Relations" and is also an adjunct instructor in the Advertising/Communications department of the Fashion Institute of Technology.

In 1978 she and colleague Helen Kruger, award-winning advertising copywriter, created a series of highly successful, twice-a-year practical ten-week "Promotion on a Shoestring" workshops, which they continue to conduct. These reality-based sessions teach techniques of public relations, publicity, advertising, and direct mail to heads of small businesses, charitable and community organizations, and anyone who needs to "publicize, advertize, or dramatize on a very tight budget."

Lucas has served on the board of directors of the Publicity Club of New York, is a member of the Public Relations Society of America, the National Association of Media Women (and winner of their 1971 "Media Woman of the Year" Award), Women Executives in Public Relations, and is listed in *Who's Who in Black America* and the *Ebony Success Library.*

Irene Gandy
Entertainment Publicist
New York, New York

Interested in acting, Irene Gandy left her native Westbury, New York, to become an actress. While working at New York's Electric Circus and as an actress with a children's theater, she bumped into a high school classmate who asked if she would be interested in doing some public relations work with the Negro Ensemble Company (NEC), a theater group.

Gandy jumped at the opportunity and began to investigate. NEC had just received funding to train people in theater administration, management, company management, public relations, and lighting. She was told that an apprenticeship with NEC's press agent would be required. "I apprenticed for something like twelve dollars a week. The apprenticeship is, however, necessary to get into the union, the Association of Theatrical Press Agents and Managers," she says.

After her three-year apprenticeship, she became the first unionized Black woman press agent in the country. "There are about seven or eight women in the area of company management, but there are no other Black press agents."

As a full-fledged union press agent, Gandy works in the area of publicity. "Publicity is basically a behind-the-scenes job. A publicist is someone who represents her client, say a Broadway show, to the public and attempts to stimulate interest for that client," she says. "A publicist works on generating publicity for an event after it has happened. For example, after a show opens, I can arrange for the actors to be photographed so that the photos can be placed in a newspaper story. Or I may work with the show's advertising company on the best ways to advertise the show by deciding to buy ads in magazines or newspapers."

Gandy went on to specialize in theatrical publicity. "My first job was going on the road with *Purlie,* the Broadway musical. I was the advance person who preceded the company to a city about six weeks earlier to make arrangements and set up things for the show," she remembers. "I've since worked on shows like *Dames at Sea* with Bernadette Peters, *Front Page* with Helen Hayes, *Black Girl, Raisin,* and *Fifth of July* with Christopher Reeve." She has also worked with many of the top Black stars including Denise Nicholas, Richard Roundtree, and Rosalind Cash. And she has done publicity for *Sweet Charity, Arsenic and Old Lace, Me and My Girl* and *I'm Not Rappaport.*

For a time, Gandy ventured into the world of recording artists. "I worked with public relations specialist Vicky Lucas, who handled B. B. King and Gladys Knight. For a while I worked exclusively for La-Belle," she says. "I also worked as director of publicity in the special markets area at CBS Records. In special markets, Jon Lucian, Earth, Wind and Fire, Archie Bell and the Drells, and the late Minnie Ripperton were handled. It was my job to get reviews for the artists from both white and Black newspapers." After CBS, she returned to her first love, theatrical publicity.

"There's really no specified training required to become a publicist, but I recommend taking the apprenticeship and getting into the union. I do, however, understand why many Blacks can't see taking the apprenticeship. It's very hard for someone to apprentice for three years on those low wages and support a family," Gandy says. "It is also important for anyone coming into the field to understand that it is a behind-the-scenes job. My job is getting publicity for my clients, not myself.

The real joy comes in watching something come together and knowing that I was a part of it."

Gandy is also a columnist for *The Black American.*

Career Aids

Books and Pamphlets
JOURNALISM AND BROADCASTING

1. *Women on the Job: Careers in Broadcasting* (single copy free), available from:
   American Women in Radio and Television, Inc.
   1101 Connecticut Ave., NW
   Suite 700
   Washington, D.C. 20036
2. *Careers in Television* and *Careers in Radio* ($2.00 each), available from:
   The National Association of Broadcasters
   1771 N St., NW
   Washington, D.C. 20036
3. For information on colleges and universities that offer degree programs in journalism and scholarships, contact:
   The Dow Jones Newspaper Fund, Inc.
   P.O. Box 300
   Princeton, N.J. 08540
4. *Your Future in Newspapers* and *Facts about Newspapers,* available from:
   American Newspaper Publishers Association, The Newspaper
     Center
   P.O. Box 17407
   Dulles International Airport
   Washington, D.C. 20041
5. *How to Become a Union Camerawoman,* by Jessie Maple ($7.95; postage and handling included), available from:
   L.J. Film Production, Inc.
   1270 Fifth Ave.
   New York, N.Y. 10029

Professional Organizations

1. Women in Communications, Inc.
   P.O. Box 9561
   Austin, Tex. 78766
2. National Association of Media Women
   157 West 126th St.
   New York, N.Y. 10027
3. National Association of Black Journalists
   P.O. Box 17212
   Dulles Airport
   Washington, D.C. 20041
4. National Newspaper Publishers Association
   948 National Press Building
   Washington, D.C. 20045

PUBLIC RELATIONS

For career information, contact:
Public Relations Society of America, Inc.
845 Third Ave.
New York, N.Y. 10022
(Career information and a list of schools accredited by the Public Relations Society of America and the Accounting Council on Education in Journalism and Mass Communications are available for $1.00 from PRSA.)

All addresses and prices are subject to change.

8

An Attention-
Grabbing Career

ADVERTISING

Advertising conjures up images of glamour, cocktail parties, Madison Avenue slick: the easy, bewitching life. The reality is different: advertising is hard-driving, fast-paced, pressure-filled, and competitive. It's an industry hard to break into; tougher to stay in. Only skilled players win at advertising.

It is an industry that permeates every segment of society; it has rapidly become as American as apple pie. It has nearly replaced the door-to-door salesman because today's dollars are spent on media outlets capable of reaching millions of consumers at the least amount of dollars.

But what is advertising? Marketing theorist John E. Kennedy said

Parts of this chapter first appeared in the author's article "The Ad World," *Élan*, February 1982.

"advertising is salesmanship in print";[1] the definition now includes radio and television. Advertising's persuasive techniques make successive attempts to nudge consumers, through television, radio, magazines, newspapers, buses, trains, displays, billboards, and other outlets, to consider and purchase old and new products and services and keep abreast of new developments. Its wide-reaching effects have boosted the positive images of corporate America and helped retailers stay afloat. It is the most effective, least expensive way to reach potential consumers.

We are newcomers to the industry. Before the sixties, advertising eluded Black consumers. As in most industries, Blacks were excluded from plum positions and were conspicuously absent from television commercials and print ads. During the post-sixties era, America's consciousness grew and advertising agencies opened their doors. Blacks were encouraged to enter the industry; Black-oriented commercials were aired; the "billion-dollar Black consumer" was courted. But the road to advertising fame has been trod by few Blacks. For most, particularly women, the participation has been minimal.

The number of Black agency entrepreneurs is also small. Out of more than 6,000 agencies in the country, reportedly fewer than 20 are Black owned. The most notable are UniWorld Group and Mingo-Jones in New York and Burrell Advertising and Proctor and Gardner Advertising in Chicago. Though present, many Black agencies share small percentages of the advertising billions; low-paying "Black market" accounts are theirs almost exclusively.

But the battle for advertising dollars is not exclusively a Black concern. It exists across the board. With millions at stake, advertisers are choosy and demand perfection. If the agency is not top-notch, it is replaced. A great deal of agency manpower is directed to obtaining clients' approval.

To gain this approval, advertising strategies must be developed. To help in the process, most agencies have account management services, research, creative, and media departments. Larger agencies also have radio and television, broadcast operations, and print production departments; small and medium size agencies combine these functions with standard departments or hire outside firms.

Career Pathing in Advertising

Within the agency, the advertising process requires teamwork. First on the agenda for the team is to drum up business. Older, established agencies retain clients for years, but hope to eventually increase business volume with them, as well as generate new client business. Newer agencies lure clients by innovative advertising techniques.

Account Management Services Department

The account management services department is vital in generating this business and, once it is obtained, managing the accounts. Department members include assistant account executives, account executives, account supervisors, managers, and vice-presidents. But some account executives for large accounts are also vice-presidents.

The account executive plays an important departmental role. She is the go-between representing the agency to the client. She is his or her closest adviser. Her work includes investigating the client's product and sales patterns, sizing up the competition, and reviewing advertising problems. After completion, she recommends, in a written marketing plan, the best advertising program and supervises carrying it out.

Being an account executive means seldom having a boring day. You may spend one day in client meetings; the next previewing a storyboard with a copywriter; another on a commercial shooting; still another at television networks making sure copy is correct. Being a good account executive means having good management, organizational, communicative, persuasive, and follow-through skills.

The most marketable degree for account executive work is the bachelor's in business with a concentration in marketing or an M.B.A. But many account executives have diverse backgrounds.

Research Department

Advertising workers often rely on research to learn consumer responses about products; the creative and media departments also need research to properly do their jobs. The research department is an agency essential. It is vital to successful advertising in providing data on consumer responses to products or services. Using field surveys or existing studies, research workers determine what advertising works best. They may quiz consumers on product preferences, size up the competition, and discover new uses of products or ways to tap more consumers. They gain insight into consumer language that will be helpful to creative people.

Research workers may do field work or hire people to do it or use an outside research firm. Once the information is compiled, they study it and make recommendations to the account executives and the creative and media departments.

A bachelor's degree is the minimum requirement for entry into research, but some researchers have M.B.A.s and Ph.D.s. English, sociology, psychology, mathematics, and statistics are good backgrounds. Good organizational, writing, speaking, and analytical skills are key for research.

Creative Department

Researchers interact with the creative department by providing consumer information to help in the creative process. The creative department is headed by the creative director, who supervises copywriters and art directors in developing the written and visual components of advertisements. The creative process is done in several steps. First, a client's product must be announced by bringing it to the public's attention. At a small agency, for example, an account executive will meet the client to discuss the problems and forward this information to the agency. A meeting is set up between principal agency players: account executive, creative director, art director, copywriter. The account executive explains the client's needs, competition, and other problems. A comparison of existing advertising for the product is made. The initial creative direction is then established; budgetary concerns are raised.

Next, brainstorming sessions between the account executive, art director, and copywriter take place to establish a creative starting point. The account executive and copywriter sit down and begin to solve the problems. The art director or copywriter may come up with the visual, headline, or copy (ad text). They all hone their plans until satisfied and then seek approval of the rough from the creative director, who critiques it. Once accepted, the plan is passed along to the account executive, who is closest to the client and can tell the correct creative direction. If the account executive likes it, an appointment with the client is set up. If it is a major account or piece of work, the art director, creative director, and copywriter may accompany the account executive to the presentation. The client approves or disapproves. If there is disapproval, changes are made until approval is gained.

The next step is production. An illustration, photograph, or television or radio commercial may be used. If it is an illustration, the art director hires artists; photographs require photographers, models, shooting locations, props, wardrobe, et cetera.

Television commercials require visual and auditory images. The same brainstorming process used for print is applied to television commercials to gain client approval. The art director and copywriter then collaborate on a storyboard: a sequence of little pictures plotting the beginning, middle, and end of the commercial. The completed storyboard permits the client to almost visualize the action. After approval is gained, the production crew begins work. In larger agencies, there are in-house production departments, with producers in charge; smaller agencies hire production firms. The director of the production crew is the key person; he or she is reponsible when shooting commercials on location.

Radio spots require copywriting expertise. The initial direction must be agreed upon in a brainstorming meeting, but the copywriter will actually execute the plan.

The advertising creative team is responsible for turning out salable copy. The copywriter is the team player responsible for the written image.

Breaking into copywriting takes good writing, conceptual, creative, and communicative skills. A four-year degree is generally required, as well as a portfolio. Writing experience can complement a portfolio. Newspaper, yearbook, and public relations writing is a plus in getting copywriting jobs.

Another creative department team member is the art director, who is primarily responsible for the visual component of ads. It is the art director's responsibility to give input in the infancy stages of an advertisement's birth and, after approval, get the advertising to production. After determining budgetary considerations, he or she must select artists and illustrators.

Art directors should have business, conceptual, and visual skills. Completing course work at an art school is advisable but a college degree is not needed. A portfolio is required, but conceptual ideas are more important than artistic abilities. Once employed, future art directors must work in the agency's "bull pen," or training ground. From there, the survivors move into more responsible positions.

Media Workers

Once the advertisement has been developed, put through production by the creative department, and completed, it must reach the public. The media department's media director, assistant directors, planning supervisors, planners, buyers, and assistants help to place advertising in mass media outlets. Media people discover maximum exposure mass media outlets reaching the largest audiences at the best price.

Media workers have extensive knowledge of mass media outlets: their advantages, disadvantages, the best vehicles for reaching certain populations; best rates. Media workers are persuaders, negotiators, and barterers with good organizational, judgment, leadership, and communicative skills. A four-year degree is a must; marketing expertise is a plus. Some enter the field without marketing backgrounds.

Other Advertising Workers

Other advertising jobs at larger agencies are in radio and television departments, broadcast operations, and print production, but in medium and smaller agencies, one person may perform each duty. Radio and television departments specialize in purchasing time on network shows. For example, a client's products may appeal to housewives. To reach the largest number in this target population, the agency may contract for commercial time on a soap opera program.

The broadcast operations department supervises commercial making. It is a timely business and broadcast personnel make sure things go correctly within certain time restraints. Actors to appear on commercials must be hired; the broadcast operations department handles that. The departmental support team includes broadcast coordinators, business affairs personnel, casting people, and broadcast traffic operators.

Once the creative department completes the advertisements, the print production department steps into action and remains until the ad is distributed. It works collectively with printers, engravers, and others who can complete the ad's production. Department workers include print production manager, type director, proofreaders, and traffic controllers.

Although many advertising workers are employed by advertising agencies, many work in other industries. Some work for radio and television stations, magazines, newspapers, corporate advertising departments, graphic art studios, independent research firms, engraving companies, printing houses, recording studios, direct mail houses, mail order houses, display builder firms, outdoor advertising companies, broadcast buying services, media (radio and TV) representative firms, paper suppliers, sales promotion firms, typography companies, photostat houses, media associations, film laboratories and studios, manufacturers, retailers, tape studios, service organizations, fund-raising organizations, and in government. Related advertising positions include graphic artists, free-lance illustrators, free-lance artists and writers, actors, musicians, dancers, magazine account representatives, radio and television account executives, commercial retouchers, paper merchants, photoengravers, newspaper advertising department workers, typographers, printers, envelope makers, retailers, and others.

What Will You Earn in Advertising?

The Gallagher Report's recent salary survey states that top advertising personnel make salaries in the following ranges: chairman/president $156,818–$298,000; executive vice-president, $127,000–$192,143; vice-president/director of marketing, $41,885–$77,750; vice-president/ director sales, $65,000–$130,000; vice-president/director advertising, $40,250–$68,000; vice-president/director marketing services, $39,325– $67,777; product manager, $46,100–$52,000. Salaries are based on whether a person works for a manufacturing, nonmanufacturing, or diversified advertiser, and if the company is a consumer or industrial service or product marketer or retailer.

CAREER PROFILES

Caroline Jones and Lana Bingham are advertising's survivors. They have built successful careers in the field.

Caroline R. Jones
President, Caroline Jones Advertising, Inc.

Bright, attractive, highly competent, and good-humored are adjectives used to describe Caroline Jones, the president of her own agency. This career woman/mother has climbed the long distance from secretary to agency owner with tenacity, hard work, and a keen sense of politics. She is highly respected and one of advertising's most visible Black women.

Born in Benton Harbor, Michigan, Jones quickly became an achiever. By the time she entered the University of Michigan, she was firmly established on a fast career track. Success was not guaranteed but something she worked hard to achieve. Like many Black women college students, she received a teacher's certificate as a safeguard, but a chance meeting with a J. Walter Thompson Advertising Agency recruiter, who invited her to apply for a position, changed her career focus. The summer after graduation, she returned to Benton Harbor to work for a local newspaper, the *New Palladium* (now the *Herald Palladium),* and was subsequently given a week's vacation. She went to New York to look for a job and considered J. Walter Thompson's offer.

Jones was offered a secretarial position. She wanted to do more with a college degree, but friends persuaded her to take the job. In weeks, she sized up the agency and decided to move into copywriting. In those days, women were relegated to secretarial positions, but J. Walter Thompson offered Jones a unique opportunity—a place in its famous and competitive copywriter class. Jones applied, as did 300 other women, and was one of 18 selected. After the class ended, Jones spent a year in the newly developed consumer behavior group before junior copywriter assignments.

When J. Walter Thompson executives wanted to strengthen her consumer language experiences, she moved quickly to supervisor of the Consumer Research Group, a consumer behavior and creative guidance department. There, she held in-depth interviews to ask consumers about different products. Subsequently, Jones left the Consumer Research Group, after receiving a promotion to copywriter.

Jones values her copywriting training and work and considers it helpful to her present job. She feels it's an area for future advertising workers to consider. "A jack of all trades background is excellent for copywriting. A copywriter should have an ability to write good copy, but she should also have a basic interest in a variety of things. You can get on-the-job training, but a basic interest in just about everything is invaluable," she says. "A copywriter must write copy for a variety of subjects. For example, one day you could be writing about bread; the next day your topic could be panty hose; the following day it could be the airlines."

In 1969, Zebra Associates, the first full-service Black-owned advertising agency, was formed, and Jones was asked to join as a copywriter. She took the risk, left J. Walter Thompson, and began building a steady career. The risk taking paid off: she was promoted to co-creative director within a year and was made vice-president. Her responsibilities included overseeing the creative department, interacting with corporations and small businesses, and recruiting and training staff. She tried to delicately balance office and home responsibilities, but the weight of the work took its toll. She requested and was granted a leave of absence. While at home, she was called to take a senior copywriter position at Kenyon & Eckhardt and accepted it, since it gave her an opportunity to write for television. Simultaneously, she free-lanced as senior consultant and director of creative services of Kabon Consulting, a parent company of the Black Creative Group, a marketing creative project group. Ultimately, Jones left Kenyon & Eckhardt to become a partner/creative director for the Black Creative Group.

Jones, who has never gone job hunting, except for the J. Walter Thompson position, was called and asked to talk to Batten, Barton, Durstine & Osborn (BBDO) staffers. They offered her a creative supervisor position and soon she became a vice-president, the first Black woman so named in a major advertising agency.

Shortly afterward, Frank Mingo asked her to join him in a new agency. Another risk paid off. Mingo, Jones and Guilmenot began with two prestigious clients, Miller Brewing Company and L'Oréal International. They soon added Philip Morris and Uncle Ben's Converted Rice. They are perhaps best known for their "We Do Chicken Right" campaign for Kentucky Fried Chicken. Today, Richard Guilmenot has left the advertising world, and so has Jones.

Jones feels Blacks should be interested in the field. "Black consumers spend money for goods and services and should be interested in those messages that go to them," she says. "But it is not a traditional area for Blacks and very few of us are in it. There's a great deal of money to make in the industry and more of us should be interested in it for practical reasons. Once in the field, being Black is not necessarily an advantage, but our position is strengthening."

Breaking into the field is difficult. "It's very competitive to get an entry-level advertising position. There are probably a hundred people waiting for every job," Jones advises. "To give yourself an advantage and learn the business, you can do volunteer work. You may not be able to volunteer at a larger agency, but perhaps an art director or account executive at a smaller agency will be happy to give you some assignments."

To break into copywriting, she suggests, "Look at and analyze advertisements. Think of the concepts in each commercial. There's always a point to it. Understand what it is and how it works."

Once in the field, movement can be easier than entering. "This business is based on individual achievement. Once you get a reputation for doing good work, you can go far," Jones says. "But you must work very hard to get that reputation."

Jones moved up advertising's corporate ladder to success. She accomplished it with talent, hard work, and risk taking and by surrounding herself with a network of mentor-supporters. As a result, she is a mentor to others who want to enter and are presently in the field. She also has high visibility in the field, which has contributed to her success. She's a lecturer and sits on several boards including those of the One Club for Copywriters and Art Directors, the YWCA of the City of New York, and Edwin Gould Services for Children. She is a member of Advertising Women of New York, and National Association of Television Arts and Sciences. For her professional work she has received the following prestigious industry awards: Anny Award, Clio Award, and named as one of the "100 Outstanding Creative People in America" in 1976. Her awards for community work are Outstanding Young Women of America Award (1979); Who's Who in Advertising (1979); Who's Who Among Black Americans; National "Kizzy" Award (Womafest, Inc.); and National Association of Negro Business and Professional Women's Clubs Award. She is well respected and known in her industry and community. Caroline Jones is an achiever.

Lana Bingham
Creative Services Manager
Campbell and Wagman
Los Angeles, California

The world of advertising is tough, competitive, and fast-paced. Of its five major areas (account management, research, creative, media, and production), the creative aspect is perhaps the toughest. There's a great deal of money spent on creating and producing advertisements and they must be timely, appealing, and able to sell the product or service. If advertisements do not convince consumers to purchase or utilize your client's products or services, the client will become dissatisfied and change agencies. The agency loses and the creative staff people who are responsible for the ad's copy (text) and visuals (art work) may be replaced.

The creative director, art director, and copywriter are therefore constantly on the "hot seat." They must strategize, conceptualize, and develop the ad's visual and copy components and be right on target. The art director, along with the writer, is responsible for the ad's visual work. She is neither the artist nor the photographer, but is generally responsible for farming out illustrations and photographic work to outside artists or photographers. She is primarily a conceptualizer and businesswoman who gives initial input to the advertisement's development and later manages the visual component's budget and administrative workings.

Few Black women have moved into this position, but Lana Bingham of Campbell and Wagman managed to do so. After graduating from the Art Institute of Boston, Bingham wanted to pursue a technical illustrating career with specialization in engineering and architectural design, but instead she found a production artist position in a department store's advertising department. She did paste-ups and put ads together and longed for more challenging work.

She moved to the West Coast and became production artist for Ayer/ Jorgensen/Macdonald. For a year, she worked on their many accounts. Her work was good and people suggested that she consider an art director's job rather than a production artist position. When Foote, Cone & Belding/Honig was searching for an assistant art director, Bingham applied and was hired. A year later, she moved into the art director's slot.

"As an art director, I was responsible for the layout and design for print and television advertising. At Foote, Cone & Belding/Honig, we had teams of art directors and writers. Together, they worked on the ad's concept," she says. "My team took strategic direction from the account executive who knew the clients' wants and needs. We brainstormed and came up with a headline, visual, and graphics that best promoted the idea. Next, we showed it to our group head. If he approved and felt we hit the target properly, we would present it to the client. If approved, the idea went into production."

An art director has a budget with which to develop the visual's completion. She must decide the best ways to spend the clients' money by doing either illustrations, graphics, or photographs. She must decide how to achieve the best results in the most cost-efficient way. "I selected illustrators and photographers. For example, I worked on a car account. Initially, I selected a photographer and described the concept and type of models and background scenery needed," she says. Bingham was then responsible for negotiating and paying the photographers and talent. Afterward, she inspected the photographers' final work and was in charge of typesetting, color correcting, and making sure the ad was ready for printing.

Advertising is a timely business. Everything is done by deadlines, which can cause stress and pressure. But the final result often makes up for the tension. "It's great to see something created, born, in full bloom and selling your product," says Bingham. Tension is also relieved by the constant activity of advertisement preparation. "You can't get bored with art directing. One day, I was at the drafting table; the next on location where the ad was being shot."

Bingham has trained many students from the University of Southern California, University of California at Los Angeles, Long Beach State, and Art Center College of Design. "To become an art director, you should go to a school with a good advertising and design program. Taking an internship is also advisable and important. Many of our employees began as apprentices, and some have gone on to become art directors," Bingham says. "Next find an art director who is willing to coach and guide you. Making connections will facilitate entry into the field. Once in, you'll make a livable income, but the key to more money is constant job changing. It's hard to get substantial pay increases without gaining a title, or making a move."

Bingham feels art director positions are opening up for Black women. "It's not a visible field to us. But I feel that if you are qualified and can locate an agency to train you, then art directorship is a possibility."

Recently the agency considered Bingham's experience as an art director beneficial and suitable for managing the newly created in-house creative service department. As art director/creative service manager, she helped the other art directors with their ads. She hired free-lance production artists and designers to prepare each ad for print production and supervised them in preparing supers for television commercials. This agency service controls and executes the visual graphics for most of their accounts. That helps keep costs down for each client and helps eliminate the agency's dependence on outside studios.

It is tough entering and remaining in advertising. It is a matter of timing, contacts, luck, and politics, but it can be done. Lana Bingham has successfully surmounted obstacles and landed a creative services manager position with Campbell and Wagman. It has not been easy, but she's a survivor.

Career Aids

For career information, contact:
1. American Advertising Federation
   1400 K St., NW
   Washington, D.C. 20005
2. American Association of Advertising Agencies
   666 Third Ave.
   New York, N.Y. 10017

9

Fashionable and Beautiful Careers

FASHION AND BEAUTY

Fashion and beauty careers are synonymous with style and charm, and as Black women we may be attracted to these fields because they offer glamour and big bucks. But traditionally, we have looked narrowly at the fields, and we wanted to become designers, models, and beauticians. For years and, to a large extent, now, we have been channeled into these areas and kept away from other ones like management, production, engineering technology, interior design, photography, product marketing and packaging, sales, and finance.

In the area of fashion, we became visible because of the sixties' emphasis on "Black Is Beautiful." We have a flair for fashion. Many keen fashion observers watch us to pick up ideas for new styles. We are watched and copied. It was our cornrows which zoomed into the limelight as those *10* braids. It is the way that we flaunt our ethnicity which inspires some fashion designs. the dashiki dress, the African print designs, our headwrappings. It is the painstaking techniques of hand-stitching and embroidery passed down through the generations from our great-grandmother, grandmothers, and mothers which give us that special knack when it comes to garment construction.

But with all our flair and knack for fashion, we have not penetrated this multibillion-dollar industry. In the sixties and seventies, we were given exposure, but some predict the era of Black fashion has ended or is near death. Many of us knock at the "fashion door of success," but few gain admittance to the top slots in the fashion business. We can count those Blacks who have made it as top designers—the late Willi Smith, Stephen Burrows, Scott Barrie, and a few others. The same is true in the modeling field; there are very few of us who are top models —Beverly Johnson, Iman, Peggy Dillard, Sheila Johnson.

We have talent, but as in most businesses, talent is secondary to persistence, hard work, personality, the ability to get along with others —and more important, the ability to gain entrance to the inner sanctums where decisions are made. To do this, in the fashion world, we must have many contacts throughout the industry so that we can network. We must look the part and be able to penetrate the rarefied cliques where the powerful mingle—this is no easy feat. It is a very difficult one for the Black woman.

We must strategize our pursuit of careers in the fashion industry and be aware of areas other than modeling and fashion design. Some possibilities are: menswear, textile design, textile technology, patternmaking technology, management and engineering technology, fashion advertising and communications, advertising design, photography, illustration, display and exhibition design, and jewelry design.

We must also look toward the money management end of the fashion industry. So many of us explore fashion careers with just an eye on creativity. But successful creative people are also business people with an eye for finance. Some of us, therefore, should gain financial backgrounds to either help our own creative endeavors or those of our struggling sisters and brothers who want to remain creators. Money management, accounting, record keeping, and other financial matters are crucial to fashion-for-profit endeavors. Career pathing toward merchandise manager's positions can help us gain these valuable skills.

Fashion's sister career is beauty. If you choose the right career area, the billion-dollar beauty industry can be lucrative. In this world of cosmetics, toiletries, fragrances, and hair care, we can carve out good careers.

Black women can have lucrative careers in the beauty industry as hair stylists/beauty salon owners. We can also expand our career visions to include the many opportunities within the field. We can become marketing specialists, production personnel, laboratory technicians, production engineers, package designers, display designers, illustrators, and advertising specialists. We can become manicurists, makeup artists, nail sculptors, and scalp and skin specialists. We can seek free-lance employment with cosmetic and hair care companies, television stations, record companies, and photographers.

It is a business where looking good and projecting the beautiful and glamorous image of the product is foremost. Beauty is a career area that can be lucrative if we career-path creatively.

In both fashion and beauty, you can carve out careers with a little ingenuity, strategy, talent, and know-how.

Career Pathing in the Fashion Industry

The great thing about the fashion world is that you can, in nearly every instance, take an associate's degree in the area of your choice and be eligible for many positions in the industry. To improve your educational background further, you can go on to get a bachelor's degree in your chosen area or in fine arts. It is a good idea to locate in cities where fashion markets are located, i.e., Los Angeles, Chicago, New York. Most agree that New York is the best training ground, the heartbeat of the industry, and the base for a great majority of industry establishments. There are also many art museums, galleries, stores, and fashion-oriented schools in New York. A school like the Fashion Institute of Technology (F.I.T.), located in New York, is a good choice because it's situated in the hub of the garment industry.

Let's explore some of the major areas in which degrees are offered at F.I.T.

Menswear Design and Marketing: The menswear area is fast growing and offers more opportunities because it is a steady industry—and it pays very well. The menswear design and marketing major at F.I.T.

offers an opportunity to learn designing, buying, and selling techniques, while moving toward an associate or bachelor's degree.

Textile Design: Textile designers must know the weaving process. Coloring is also an integral part of the process and students learn screen dyeing, yarn dyeing, piece dyeing, and machine printing. After graduation, positions as designers, stylists, colorists, studio directors, or managers can be pursued.

Textile Technology: This is the scientific arm of the textile industry. Here, innovative fabrics and fibers and their uses are created. You can thank textile technology for its work in developing flame-retardant fabrics. Many textile technologists work in mills or in government testing research.

Patternmaking: Here you will learn how to take a designer's construction and create a pattern for it. This requires knowledge of garment sizing that corresponds to manufacturers' standards as well as a knowledge of garment construction. After graduation, you are qualified for patternmaker or pattern grader positions, from where you will be able to move into production supervision and management.

Management and Engineering Technology: The techniques of producing apparel are the major focus of this program. You will also learn how to keep production running smoothly and how to keep people and machines working to produce the finished product. After graduation, your career path will begin in positions such as a production engineer or administrator, then move on to management or consultant positions in this high-paying specialty.

Advertising and Communications: You will learn to write fashion copy for magazines or newspapers, ads for radio and television commercials, become fashion publicity specialists, or fashion writers for magazines or newspapers. An associate or bachelor's degree is offered in this area. This training prepares you for many areas of the industry; employment in retail stores, advertising agencies, public relations or publicity firms, publishing companies, and other communication organizations.

Advertising Design: Here you learn the techniques for designing advertisements, using graphic design procedures to produce camera-ready copy for printers. You can get an associate or bachelor's degree in this area. After training, you will be able to secure employment with retail and other stores, advertising agencies, newspapers, magazines, or you can free-lance or open your own business.

Fashion Photography: In this often lucrative field, you will learn to capture the beauty, sensuality, and other fine qualities of models with your camera. These photographs will then be used to sell products to the public. Photography is competitive and pressurized, and your work must be of top-notch professional quality. Only persistence and dogged determination will allow you to succeed in this field—even then success may be a long time in coming. For training in fashion photography you should acquire an associate's degree in the area or move on to the bachelor's degree.

Illustration: You will learn both general and fashion illustration and the sketching, drawing, and painting techniques used in different aspects of illustration. We see the work of the illustrator when we observe drawings or sketches in newspaper or magazine ads or columns, record album jackets, books, and brochures, just to name a few of the areas where illustrators are employed. Some schools offer the bachelor's degree in fine arts, or you can pursue an associate's degree in the discipline. At F.I.T., there is an optional one-year certificate program to enhance the associate's degree.

Display and Exhibition Design: The attractive store windows which lure us to buy are the work of display designers. These professionals also work in museums, galleries, showrooms, and manufacturer and trade show displays and exhibitions. In many instances, interior design, photography, and fashion design as well as mannequins, props, and lighting are incorporated in displays and exhibitions. After receiving the associate's degree, you may be able to secure positions like display designer or director.

Jewelry Design: Jewelry design majors learn casting, gem species, and fashion and marketing trends in the industry. Associate degree program graduates can become designers, then move into jewelry firm management, or establish their own jewelry design businesses.

Fashion Design: In this fast-paced and competitive area, you will learn to design contemporary apparel by studying fashion art, flat patternmaking, and draping techniques. An associate or bachelor of fine arts degree will provide you with excellent basic training in fashion design. After graduation, you can become assistant designers or patternmakers.

Interior Design: Interior designers are professionals whose work consists of fundamental design, design analysis, space planning, and programming. They design interior spaces and have an understanding of related aspects of environmental design. A full-time professional interior design school will award you a certificate or diploma after three years of training. Or you may graduate from a four-year college program which has degree programs in interior design.

After training in interior design, you should work for at least one to three years in the field before considering yourself to be a professional designer. You will then become eligible for associate membership in the American Society of Interior Designers (ASID).

Graphic Arts: If you are interested in pursuing a career in commercial art as a graphic artist, illustrator, or other art professional you can start your own business, work for advertising agencies or in other businesses which need the services of artists on staff, or as a free-lancer.

To train for a position in this area you can attend a trade school with a two- to four-year program, junior colleges which give associate degrees in various areas of commercial art, or four-year colleges or universities which offer degrees in art and related subjects.

Modeling: You can't pick up academic credentials to train in this area. You must be able to fit into a size 8 garment, on which designers base their samples. Your height must be between 5'7" and 5'10", and your measurements should be around 35-24-35. You must have flawless skin, long legs, radiant health, and a unique personality.

If you pass the scrutiny of modeling agency personnel, who see thousands of potential models but select very few, you will be expected to be professional, disciplined, and prompt for shootings. At home you must exercise, eat properly, and keep your weight down.

Your work will be grueling, both physically and emotionally, with long hours before the camera or on runways. You will also have to cope with being treated as an "item." Some models feel they are treated as "meat" rather than individuals, and you must prepare mentally for this. You will be well paid for your chores. Those who make it to the top receive three hundred to seven hundred dollars an hour. But your career will be short-lived because the modeling business is slanted toward youth and beauty.

If you do not possess the height and weight requirements, you may be able to enter other phases of modeling such as hand or leg modeling, and there are a limited number of modeling slots for large women. Or you may choose to go to Europe to work because there are areas of modeling that Black women may be able to enter there which are not available here.

However, in this country, your first step should be to contact a modeling agency for representation. They will slot you into the modeling area that is best for you.

Career Pathing in Beauty

In the beauty business, there are several career areas. In the areas of public relations, personnel, advertising, marketing, sales, and finance, you will need the traditional prerequisites for these positions. The Master of Business Administration degree (M.B.A.) is considered a plus in sales and finance.

Marketing directors and production managers will need the M.B.A. with an understanding of economics, though some have moved up through the retailing ranks from former salespersons, group managers, or buyers who handled cosmetic lines for a particular company. Some cosmetics companies have programs for qualified women who want to enter the field without business backgrounds, but these opportunities are limited and competition for these few slots is keen. Schools like the Fashion Institute of Technology and Parsons School of Design offer programs in cosmetics marketing.

For most positions in the scientific part of the cosmetics industry, where the product is developed, tested, and produced, a strong background in the sciences, particularly chemistry, is advisable, and some pharmacists find their way into this area. Laboratory technicians need strong chemistry backgrounds. Production engineers need solid engineering training because they design many items such as lipstick tubes.

On the creative side, there are package designers, display designers, illustrators, and advertising designers who work on marketing and presenting the final product. To become a package designer, you can enter one of the communications design programs which offer courses in package design.

Cosmetology is another area of the beauty business. You can own your own beauty salon, or work for beauty companies who employ cosmetologists to test their products by using them to color, wash, set, and style the hair of volunteers, or by demonstrating the effectiveness of the products in department stores, hotels, or barber shops. This field of course is not new to Blacks, but many neighborhood beauty parlors are being pushed out by franchises and white operators who have learned to work on Black hair.

Manicurists, makeup artists, nail sculptors, and scalp and skin specialists also work in this potentially lucrative area. To break into the field you must be licensed. This license is required by all states, which means you will usually attend state-approved cosmetology schools, and sometimes you must apprentice. After graduation, you must take state licensing examinations. Once you become licensed, you may go on to apprenticeship for a year or two. With the training and experience thus gained, you are qualified to free-lance for companies, magazines, television stations, record companies, and others who need hair stylists and make-up artists.

What Will You Earn in the Fashion Industry?

The Occupational Outlook Handbook states that median annual salaries of experienced full-time designers (including fashion designers) are about $21,900; top designers make more than $40,500.

Graphic artists (including fashion illustrators) earn median yearly salaries of $18,600; top earners make more than $26,000 a year.

What Will You Earn in the Beauty Business?

Beauty executives make very high salaries, some more than $50,000 a year.

Experienced cosmetologists earn between $250 and $400 a week. Beginning cosmetologists make between $120 and $160 a week, according to the Bureau of Labor Statistics (Department of Labor).

CAREER PROFILES

The fashion and beauty fields offer many career opportunities. Here are seven women who have successfully career-pathed in these areas: Audrey Smaltz, fashion consultant; Marion Holmes-Nadrich, a former merchandise manager, now owner of her own firm; Margaret Pazant, a former fashion editor at *Vogue* and now owner of her own firm; Lydia Hammond, a fashion photographer; Zelda Wynn, the supervisor of wardrobe/costume designer for the Dance Theatre of Harlem; Rita Falkener, an interior designer; Peggy Dillard, a top fashion model.

Audrey Smaltz
President of Audrey Smaltz Incorporated
Columnist for Vogue
New York, New York

Her bio says, "Even if she weren't six feet tall—which she is—you can't help but notice Audrey Smaltz." You do notice Audrey when she eases on stage to commentate a fashion show or as she strolls down New York streets decked out in Dior or Valentino garments, or when she high-steps in Dal Co pumps made and bought in Rome. Even in a simple dress draped with a Saint-Laurent scarf, Smaltz is smashing and all eyes turn her way. Named to the International Best Dressed List three times, she has come into her own and is strutting her stuff.

Born in New York, Audrey Smaltz attended New York's City College, graduating with a bachelor's degree in art. She took a job at Bloomingdale's New York store as a stockroom assistant but quickly advanced to assistant buyer. In love with fashion by then, she landed a dress and hosiery buyer's position at Lane Bryant and was ultimately named fashion coordinator for the Tall Division.

When the time came to select someone to coordinate and commentate the *Ebony* Fashion Fair, she was that magazine's natural choice. Smaltz set off for Europe to help in the selection of the clothing. Many of us still remember her smooth commentary and strikingly statuesque appearance during these shows. One fashion expert says of her, "Audrey Smaltz made fashion commentating a career."

Today she is owner of Audrey Smaltz Incorporated. Her clients, who are mostly designers and manufacturers, hire the company to produce or coordinate fashion shows. The company's client list has included Elizabeth Arden Salons, Crazy Horse, Bloomingdale's New York, the Congressional Black Caucus, Roberta di Camerino, American Fur Industry, *Vogue,* Neiman-Marcus, United Airlines, and many others.

"Our expertise is fashion shows. For example, we did a show for Sasson Industries, a company that started off making blue jeans. Today, they make a variety of clothing including men's, women's, children's, and maternity wear, sportswear, swimsuits, and fur coats. Sasson wanted to illustrate their new diversity in products to buyers and merchandise managers from across the country," Smaltz says. "They hired us to coordinate the show. My staff and I went around to their thirty-two licensees, selected merchandise, and pulled together an exciting fashion show." Audrey Smaltz Incorporated also does lighting, staging, music, commentary, and clothes and model selection for fashion shows.

Smaltz has steadily built her business. It now boasts a staff of thirty or more during peak seasons. She employs models, photographers, makeup artists, hair stylists, fashion coordinators, and others needed to pull together a show. Her employers either work collectively on producing or coordinating a show or are individually sent out to do assignments. For example, her makeup artist may be sent to a magazine or album cover photo session.

In her consultant and advisor capacity, Smaltz spends time on the road, traveling more than 25,000 miles a year.

Smaltz's career advice: "It's always good to have a retail background in the fashion industry. Work for at least two or three years at the retail level at a department or specialty store. Then work at a magazine. If you can work for *Ebony* or *Essence* that would be a good experience. After that, you might pick up experience at a patternmaking company —from there you can branch off and go anywhere."

Marion Holmes-Nadrich
Owner, Marion Holmes Enterprises, Inc.
New York, New York

Marion Holmes-Nadrich is one of the few Black women in the country who once sat in the powerful position of merchandise manager for a fashion mass merchandiser.

Holmes-Nadrich's climb to success began when she was a child. Talented and creative, she painted, sketched, and made her own clothes. By high school graduation, fashion plus painting was very much a part of her life and to perfect her painting skills, she pursued a fine arts degree at Cooper Union in New York. Simultaneously she took apparel design courses at Fashion Institute of Technology.

After college, she received a doll clothes designer position with Ideal Toy Corporation. The work was painstakingly difficult and the road to success was slow. Holmes-Nadrich turned to alma mater F.I.T.'s placement office for help and was sent in a new career direction. She was referred to a secretarial job at *Ladies' Home Journal.* In her year there, she researched editorial stories, assisted with the shopper's guide, and was subsequently exposed to several designers.

Striking out on her own, she left *Ladies' Home Journal* to help run an independent business. She ventured into small business ownership for three years but left for a brief rest in California. Upon returning to New York, she began free-lancing and looking for a permanent designer's position.

An employment agency counselor suggested that Holmes-Nadrich try the menswear industry. She had never considered the area but liked the idea. Soon she was hired as an assistant stylist at Van Heusen. A year of impressive work brought a promotion to stylist (designer).

Four years later, Holmes-Nadrich packed and relocated to Mann Manufacturing's El Paso, Texas, office. Metro Pants (a company that is now out of business) lured her back to New York to begin as merchandise manager of the contemporary division, which handled 10 percent of the overall volume. She was responsible for the company's entire line.

A merchandise manager is in a tough spot. Holmes-Nadrich was responsible for the bottom line: money. "I had full responsibility for what went into the line (the group of clothing to be sold within a given season). I participated in everything involving the line from its beginning to end. My responsibilities included sketching, producing prototype garments, and selecting fabric," she says. "After the prototype garments were made, I met with other management personnel, primarily the vice-president of sales and operations, and reviewed the line before buyers saw it. The line's marketability was discussed in these sessions."

Since a great deal of money was spent to complete the line, these discussions often meant changing original concepts. "A line could be changed a hundred times before it was ready to be shown to buyers. There were many alterations. For example, if the legs were too narrow, they were redone; or perhaps a vest was not right, it was redesigned," she says. "This constant revision was frustrating but necessary. If the line wasn't right, it didn't sell and the company suffered. So, it was my job to make sure it sold."

After the line was finalized, there were several stages the company completed before selling. One stage was to gather retail buyers and divisional managers to review it. At times, store presidents and vice-presidents and retail conglomerate groups previewed the line. Holmes-Nadrich's former job was to help them conceptualize the line. She was the expert who was with the line since its inception and teamed with sales people to convince retailers of its value.

If successful, this initial selling step led to purchasing the material for production. "After the line was sold, piece goods or fabrics were bought in thousands of yards. Because we often cut thousands of shirts or pants, we dealt with one to fifty thousand yards of material in a specific color or style. A typical order for piece goods or material could be eighty thousand dollars. I was responsible for signing the purchase order," she says. "That's why so much planning and discussion occurred before finalization of the line. We had to minimize risks. We didn't want half of the line ending up selling for less in a closeout sale or discount house. If that happened, the company lost money."

The finished product was taken on the road. Salespeople presented their wares to potential customers and made sales. From New York, Holmes-Nadrich monitored the activity. "I checked on the line's sales progress. There may have been adjustments. For example, I may have had to adjust the number we originally planned to make—or adjustments had to be made in the number of piece goods needed to make the items. Sometimes, there were mistakes in the way the cloth was cut, or the waist band was too narrow. Changes were constantly made throughout the season," she says. "In between, I worked on another season. I could be selling Fall, but planning and partially producing Spring, and planning next Fall."

Wedged in between planning and producing, Holmes-Nadrich traveled to Europe to attend fashion shows once or twice a year. She also shopped European fabric houses for piece goods and monitored people on the streets to gauge and pick up fashion trends. Back home, she duplicated what she saw. "I brought home samples and from them, developed my own color line. Usually, I sent a fabric swatch to a laboratory and had them formulate the color I wanted for that particular fabric or I sent some samples to a factory for remaking—removing belt loops or a pleat, or changed the silhouette. In this way, new ideas were formulated," she says. "I also got ideas from American markets by spotting trends in California or Florida. Buyers helped too. They gave me input about fashion trends in their states."

Moving to the top of the fashion industry was not easy but Holmes-Nadrich managed. Metro Pants has closed and she has opened her own company. But she still feels Black women should consider the field. "On the career path toward becoming a merchandise manager, you will start off as an assistant merchandiser or assistant product manager and have responsibility for follow-up work assigned by the merchandiser. The position will also allow you to give a great deal of creative input," she says. "The next step is merchandiser, who often works for the merchandise manager and is responsible for the styling, designing, coordinating, and selection of initial goods or fabrics. Afterwards, you can move into a merchandise manager's position."

As owner of her own company, Holmes-Nadrich has a position that affords a blend of creativity—designing and styling, administration and management. She's a creator and businesswoman delicately balancing both skills and encompassing two fashion world survival skills. She beckons you to follow her lead. "You should have a flair for fashion, but you must be well trained. There's a great deal of competition out there and sewing ability will not assure you a job," she suggests. "A combination of talent, training, and personality will get you noticed."

Margaret Pazant
President, Pazant Style, Inc.
Former Fashion Editor, Vogue
Upper Montclair, New Jersey

As a teenager, Margaret Pazant loved clothes and made many of her own. In the mid-sixties, fashion careers were not automatic career choices for Black females, and she went to the now closed Parsons College in Iowa to pursue speech therapy.

In college, she developed a sophisticated dress style. After a year at Parsons, she married and left school. She sought employment at the New York Telephone Company and was hired as a business representative. While she was working there, a neighbor spotted her good looks and fashion savvy and asked her to join his new company, Zuri Cosmetics.

Pazant jumped at the chance and soon began representing the cosmetic line. She traveled extensively across the country lecturing to Black women on skin and beauty care. She was so successful and popular that Zuri owners asked her to appear in their advertisements.

After some time, Pazant left Zuri to do free-lance modeling. One day, she noticed the work of fashion illustrator and photographer Lenny

Wooden and loved it. Wooden needed a photography representative to scout for work and negotiate contracts. He asked her and she agreed to handle him. The experience helped her develop an artistic "eye" and deeply appreciate the world of fashion. It helped mold a desire for her to further explore the fashion industry.

Pazant wanted and needed a fashion career that would pull together all of her experiences. She wanted a good training ground, a place where she could learn the basics. *Vogue* was a natural choice. She approached Condé Nast Publications, the owners of *Vogue,* and was told that there were no openings. They soon called to offer her a fabrics-assistant position, and she took it.

As a fabrics assistant, she covered the manufacturers and designers in the domestic fabric market. She learned about American and European market fabrics, projections, and forecasts.

After fourteen months as a fabrics assistant, Pazant wanted more. She wanted to move directly into fashion. She brought her career goals to the editor, was given a special assignment, and worked with fashion expert Audrey Smaltz on a special beauty piece for Black women. On-lookers recall that Pazant did a good job, and, more important, enthusiastically took on every job. No request was too difficult or too small.

Vogue's editors liked Pazant's work. As a result, she was given small assignments and was subsequently asked to give *Vogue*'s readers tips on good fashion finds. She was also asked to cover new designers. Later when a fashion editor left, a spot was created, and she moved into an assistant fashion editor's slot.

In one year and a half, she was promoted to fashion editor. The process usually takes longer, but Pazant had a rare combination that worked. "Becoming a fashion editor took a great deal of hard work and practical know-how. I never refused to do anything, and took on more responsibility. When I wanted to do certain assignments, I let it be known, and my instincts about things were usually on target," she says. "As a Black woman, I also gave the editorial department certain insights, and that helped tremendously. It was the first time that the fashion department had someone on staff with a Black point of view."

Her fashion editing responsibilities were varied. "I was a market editor. I covered the market instead of doing studio work like some editors. I covered about fifty designers and worked in the area of moderate to better sportswear. I worked with these designers by covering their collections to determine which ones warranted editorial coverage. I also helped get them in stores and generally gave them direction," she says. "At *Vogue,* everyone in the fashion department contributed information that went into a common pot. The fashion pages were the result of our collective thinking."

Vogue is considered by many fashion experts to be the best training ground. A career there can lead to many opportunities in the fashion world. Good training grounds, however, attract the best people. Competition for jobs is rough. "Anyone who wants to work in fashion journalism should have good writing skills and a good English background. If you have previous work experience in a related fashion or beauty field, that type of background can also be helpful," she says. "You should be highly motivated and a self-starter. You should be prepared to start at the bottom and work your way up. As you start from the bottom, you'll be learning from experienced staffers and building upon your fashion expertise. If you're talented and good, the chances are good that you'll succeed."

Once in the field, working for a magazine can be rough. It is a very high pressured, demanding field. "The pressure comes from having to have things completed on time—meeting deadlines," she says. "There's also the pressure to create new ideas, know how to spot the latest trends, and if necessary create them. You are required constantly to be on top of things."

Pazant feels that fashion journalism is a good field for Black women. "There are very few of us in the area, but we have a great deal to offer. Black women are naturals because of our individual style, flair, and uniqueness. Our fashion sense has always been respected," she says.

Margaret Pazant has built a good career in the fashion world. Recently, she left *Vogue* to start her own business, Pazant Style, Inc., a fashion consultant business. She produces fashion shows, benefits, and other shows. Her clients include TCB (Alberto Culver), the Jackie Robinson Foundation, the Bronner Brothers' Show, "America Cracks Down," etc. She is also editing the fashion pages of *Savvy Magazine.*

Lydia Hammond
Free-lance Fashion Photographer
New York, New York

Lydia Hammond treads a rare career path for Black women: fashion photography. Traditionally, this lucrative field has been closed to us, but Hammond has made some inroads. But like many Black creators, she was forced to relocate in Europe to get work. In Europe, she was nurtured and allowed to develop. "In America, there weren't enough Black women photographers for people to use as criteria. My work was odd to them," she recalls. "I showed my book around but all they saw was my potential. So I went to Paris to develop it."

Paris viewed Hammond in a different light. The Black woman fashion photographer was a curiosity but they wanted to see her work. "In Paris, I received breaks which made the difference," she says. "I received magazine assignments which developed my technique. Unlike American employers, the French allowed me to interpret ideas. Because they didn't give me layouts to follow, I wasn't a fashion technician like American photographers tend to be. European fashion photographers are expected to solve clients' problems by visually interpreting an idea. You must use creativity because they want beautifully personalized photos. The final product is a combination of instantaneous creativity coupled with the technical expertise to carry it out."

The European experience has given Hammond some American acceptance. "Clairol, CBS, *Flair, Cosmopolitan,* and *Vogue* magazines have used my work, but it's still difficult to break into advertising. It's still very hard to get through the door," she stresses. "But sometimes my European work experience hinders my progress. Since European style is different from American, I find resistance in acceptance of my work. It's too creative for this commercial market and they are not sure I can adapt to them."

Hammond became interested in photography in Spain. Her father, a member of the Foreign Science Diplomatic Corps, was assigned to the U.S. Embassy in Morocco. With his wife and ten children he relocated to North Africa. Nine years later, they were returning to the States and stopped over in Spain. The young Hammond was transfixed by Spanish art, especially the statues, and recorded them with a Brownie camera. "In a park, there were four statues: three were women sitting together, each reaching towards the statue of a dead poet. They were emoting and it was beautiful. I was transfixed and took pictures of them," she remembers. "But upon returning to the States, I submitted the film to a local drugstore for developing, and they lost the majority of my pictures. I decided this would never happen again. I would learn photography and how to develop my own film."

Her parents supported the photographic venture by updating Hammond's cameras yearly. By the time she went to Montclair State College, her interest in the field was firmly established. College became a training ground. An art major and photography minor permitted her technique to grow. She also consumed photographic knowledge by constantly querying teachers, reading about the field, and spending many lonely nights in the darkroom.

After college, she reluctantly interrupted the pursuit of a photography career to do substitute teaching. Her creativity was stifled and she quit to locate a photographer assistant's job in 1973. After locating a photographer in New York, she went to work to learn hands-on experience.

In 1974, Hammond met a writer and began concentrating on photojournalism. Afterward, she developed an interest in fashion photography. "My creativity was growing. I was putting a great deal of sensitivity in my work and fashion photography allowed me to explore this," she says. But breaking into the field was rough and in 1977, she moved to Paris.

Today, Hammond is actively pursuing the field and feels other Black women should. "To enter this field, you must work harder and be better. Start by reading everything you can about the technical end of photography. Go to school and learn techniques," she advises. "Afterwards, try to get a photographer's assistant position—to see firsthand what photography is all about. While there, perfect your darkroom techniques. I was able to get my foot in the door because I could develop and print."

Hammond also advises having a multiracial approach to fashion photography. "Any Black woman who wants to be a fashion photographer must deal with the concepts of white beauty," she stresses. "At first, I only saw beauty in Black women. As a result, my entire portfolio was of Black women. But those in a hiring position couldn't relate to or understand Black beauty. This also restricted my access to fashion jobs. So, you must come up with a firm belief in the beauty of all women."

Discipline is another virtue fashion photographers must have. Many are free-lancers or small business owners, and discipline and motivation are key to survival. "You must be self-disciplined because you're on your own," she says. "You must be able to get up early, call people, do your own public relations, and sell yourself. Or you must locate a good agent with solid contacts."

The hard work, discipline, and effort is ultimately worth it; fashion photography is lucrative. "The field is very lucrative. For example, a good photographer in New York can conceivably make as much as ten thousand a week. You can get from fifteen hundred to five thousand for one shot and a shot usually takes a day. If you're lucky and can get assignments, five days of shooting can bring in a great deal of money," she says. "If you can get photographic assignments from big clients like Bristol-Myers, Revlon, or Johnson Products, you can expect to be compensated richly."

Hammond hopes to reach a high-salaried peak but stresses that good things take time. With good technique, discipline, and stick-to-itiveness, you can land in the highly demanding but lucratively rewarding field of fashion photography.

Zelda Wynn
Supervisor of Wardrobe/Costume Designer
Dance Theatre of Harlem
New York, New York

Zelda Wynn began sewing at age three. "My mother made my clothes and I was very curious about sewing. Eventually she showed me how to make my doll's clothing." Wynn left her native Chambersburg, Pennsylvania, for Atlantic City, New Jersey, and ultimately went into the dressmaking business in New York. While in New York, she met entertainer Erskine Hawkins's wife and began to make clothes for her. Mrs. Hawkins was pleased with Wynn's designs and introduced her to other entertainers. Wynn went on to make clothes for some of the top stars, including Ella Fitzgerald, the late Dorothy Dandridge, Constance Bennett, and the late Mae West. "I made the first shirt Harry Belafonte wore on stage," says Wynn, who designed and made clothes in her shop, Chez Zelda.

In 1965, Wynn helped a Harlem-based arts and culture program set up twenty-three sewing centers in Harlem. A few years later, Arthur Mitchell was setting up the Dance Theatre of Harlem, the world's most celebrated Black ballet company, and needed costumes made. "Mr. Mitchell had brought me his nieces to teach them sewing. When he needed help with his company, which was going to Europe for the first time, he asked for my help," remembers Wynn, who has remained with the Dance Theatre of Harlem for many years.

"As supervisor of wardrobe, I make costumes for the company, ready them for travel when we tour, and supervise the dancers' dressing. When making a costume, sometimes I am given a picture or someone will draw some lines and I will interpret it. Or often I will be told what is expected and I will make it." Wynn also trains apprentices in the art of costume making at the Dance Theatre of Harlem's headquarters.

To become a costume designer, Wynn advises that you must be prepared, know dress construction well, and be a stickler for details. "Prepare yourself by learning patternmaking. Every ballet requires different costumes."

Rita Falkener
Interior Designer
Partner, Falkener-Stuetley Interiors, Ltd.
Brooklyn, New York

Rita Falkener followed in her interior designer mother's footsteps. After studying art design at Pratt Institute in Brooklyn, she journeyed to France to work as an illustrator and illustrated for magazines such as London's *Queen* magazine. A subsequent trip to Africa inspired a love for African art which would lead to a new career: interior design.

She returned to the United States to combine her artistic skills and African art love into the new career of interior design. The budding interior designer landed a free-lance position with *Essence* magazine and her highly stylized "before and after" rooms became one of the magazine's highlights.

A year with *Essence* increased Falkener's interior design expertise and prepared her for business ownership. "In 1976, I opened a home operated business. A year later, Stan Stuetley and I formed a partnership, Falkener-Stuetley Interiors, Ltd.," she recalls. "We now specialize in residential and commercial planning by using the ethics of fine design."

Interior designers like Falkener and Stuetley have more flexibility than interior decorators. She explains: "An interior designer designs interior spaces. Unlike an interior decorator who primarily deals with furniture arrangement, accessories, and colors, we are capable of space planning and design analysis. For example, if a room looks better without a wall, we are capable of removing it. Our capabilities also include the ability to work and interact with architects."

Clients who want help designing residential and commercial spaces seek Falkener's advice. Clients primarily come through two avenues: seeing Falkener and Stuetley's work at designer shows, or through word of mouth referrals. They are impressed by the well-regarded designer team's flair, and also their extensive media coverage in periodicals like the New York *Times*, New York *Post, House & Garden*, the Washington *Star, Interior Design, New York Magazine*, and *Black Enterprise*. Ultimately, the mostly upper-middle-class clients tend to be satisfied customers. The finished designs are sleek, elegant, and unusual, and many rooms bear the Falkener trademark of African sculpture.

The Falkener-Stuetley designing process begins with meeting clients, discussing ideas, and determining designing needs and wants. "We then give them a slide presentation of our work. We see their space and begin developing a plan and color scheme. We carry out the design plan by determining fabrics, style, and type of furniture," she says. "For each item a client purchases, we fill out a proposal sheet telling them exactly what they're getting and the cost."

Interior design salaries tend to be lucrative; top designers command top fees. It can also lead to hobnobbing with the well placed. But to reach this status, good training is essential. "You must go to school. In New York, schools like Parsons School of Design, Pratt, or Fashion Institute of Technology are good training grounds," advises Falkener. "Then you can do an apprenticeship or if you feel secure, go out on your own."

Becoming your own boss is one way to success in the field. But you will pay heavy dues. There are hard work, long hours, and disappointments along the way. Falkener has worked hard to succeed, and by all standards, she has made it to the top. It's not easy but "if you have a flair for interior design, you can do it," she says.

Peggy Dillard
Model/Owner, Turning Heads
New York, New York

Peggy Dillard's face has graced many magazine covers, including *Vogue*'s. Her classic beauty has prompted the competitive world of modeling to take notice, and by everyone's definition, she's a success.

While a junior at Pratt Institute, she accidentally moved into the field. In her spare time, she coordinated fashion shows and often approached major designers to borrow clothing. By chance, she met top designers Scott Barrie and Lester Hayatt, who persuaded her to model. She was intrigued by the idea, encouraged by her family, and began traveling the long road to the top of the modeling world.

Dillard found combining school and modeling difficult. Her priority was to complete school, but modeling was consuming a big chunk of her time. "Modeling was really difficult. I was doing runway shows from eight in the morning until six or seven at night. But I was determined not to drop out of school," she remembers. "My instructors suggested taking independent study courses and a program called University without Walls." The program saved her schooling by making both school and modeling manageable.

Soon, the pretty model's career picked up speed, but she found modeling wasn't as glamorous as projected. "I soon realized modeling wasn't as glamorous as people make it seem. It's hard work that requires a great deal of concentration," she says. "For example, on the set, you are dealing with ten to fifteen people. Everyone is giving orders and you must remember your purpose and reason for being there. You are there to do a job and perform a service."

The ability to do hard work and concentrate are requisites for becoming a model, but there are also other requirements. "The standard height requirement is from five-seven to five-ten and your weight should be under a hundred twenty-five pounds. The average clothing size is from five to twelve," Dillard says. "A model's age may range from four years old to twenty-five or forty, but the prime time is between sixteen and thirty." A healthy skin and good mental frame of mind are also important. Good eating habits and healthy living will help.

Most serious-minded models have agents. Selecting one requires planning. "Interview prospective agents and talk to other professionals about them. Get a good idea about the person you're dealing with. You will deal with your agent every day of your career. There should be a mutual excitement," she advises. "When you go to an agent, you should have at least five pictures, both black and white and color. They should be full face and body shots. If you have special assets, such as nice hands or feet, photograph them. You should also include a résumé showing acting courses, sports activities, or special skills. Acting or television division agents are especially interested in your special skills or sports."

After selecting an agent, it's time to talk money. "Beginning models usually make about a hundred fifty to two hundred dollars an hour.

Lingerie models can make four hundred an hour," Dillard says. "You should discuss a commission with your agent. First discuss how much money you can get per hour or day and then the agent's commission. Her commission can range from fifteen to twenty-five to thirty percent. A few agents have television divisions and you'll want to know the commission for television work. Next, ask if you're bound by contract, how long it is, and what the terms are. I read general business contracts and talked to other models."

Getting an agent, however, does not ensure employment. Models need good portfolios, a selection of pictures depicting different poses, and moods, and personalities. Building an impressive portfolio can be expensive, but it's an investment in the future. Be careful in selecting a photographer. Make sure the work is good by reviewing it or talking to others in the field. A picture reflects a great deal about you. Be sure to get the best available pictures, shot by a professional.

Models with good agents and portfolios can get work through "go sees." "After I acquired an agent, he sent me on a 'go see.' A 'go see' is when an agent sends you to see a client. At a 'go see,' a client looks at your portfolio. It's like a job interview with your portfolio being your résumé. You should try to look the part. Determine the type of model a client may be looking for or a particular designer's style," she advises. "Fashion shows become instant 'go sees.' All the magazines and designers came to see them. As a result, the photography world opened up for me, and people started calling for interviews."

There are other ways for models to gain employment. Some clients see their work in magazines; agents distribute head sheets to promote clients; some models have special personalities or skills. Dillard waterskis, swims, does bareback horse riding, sings, dances, and is often given assignments based on these skills.

To learn about outdoor or studio shooting, Dillard suggests contacting photographers who are "testing." "Testing means you give a photographer your time, energy, and talent. In return, you learn the basic mechanics of studio and outdoor shooting. Your agent can provide a list of those photographers who are testing. But be careful. Usually the best photographers aren't testing," she stresses. "Testing should not cost you anything. If the photographer gives you slides, you'll have to pay to have the slides enlarged into photographs."

After gaining studio and outdoor experience and passing "go see" interviews, it's time to take on an assignment. "On any modeling assignment, you should look neat and clean. You don't need a gimmick or have to wear expensive clothes. Just wear practical things, carry your own makeup base and makeup brushes, cleansers and other toiletries, body suits and undergarments, for cleanliness," she says. "Your reputation is built through word of mouth. People recommend you on the basis of your work."

Successful assignments lead to successful careers. Many strive for stardom, but only a few, like Dillard, succeed. It's a tough, competitive field boasting few survivors. But once successful in the field, you can begin to act or do still photography. Take it one step further and go into films. Working with magazines can lead to fashion writing or editing. You might open your own business. Or you can become a fashion and beauty consultant," she says. Modeling can also initiate other interests. Traveling to foreign countries can inspire you to learn a second language. Or improve your cultural development. Exposure to international cooking can enhance your culinary skills.

Entering the fascinating world of modeling can lead to money, success, and celebrity status, but its daily realities can produce discouragement and anxiety. "It's a field where only the strong survive. You have to be morally and spiritually strong to make it in this industry," she says. "But don't lose your self-respect or sense of Blackness, feeling for family or whatever is meaningful to you. These things will give you strength and buffer you during difficult times."

Recently, Dillard and her husband, Lloyd Toone, opened Turning Heads, a beauty salon in Harlem in New York City. The new salon has created quite a sensation and has been written about in *Essence, Vogue, The Amsterdam News,* and other periodicals. "Because in my work as a model, I have seen the work of the world's finest stylists, I've attempted to expose the average Black woman to the best professional hairstyling skills," says Dillard of why she opened Turning Heads. "We concentrate on teaching alternatives in Black hair care. First, we stress conditioning, then finding a style suitable for a particular hair type. We take this approach rather than selecting a style that is too stressful or damaging to hair on an everyday basis." Turning Heads services the needs of all Black women, whether they have permanents or "dread or African locks."

10

Money Careers

ACCOUNTING

The traditional view of accountants is that of three-piece-suited gentlemen bent over paper-strewn desks banging away at calculators on or before April 15—Income Tax Day. Rarely do we think of accountants as professionals who perform interesting tasks. Women are often thought of as nonmathematically oriented or reluctant financial problem solvers. But women, both white and Black, are making inroads into this once male-dominated field. And they are moving into positions of power as a result of their financial training and experience.

Accounting is a field that offers many opportunities. It offers competitive starting salaries for recent graduates. It is a career where top salaries, $125,000 or more, ensure economic independence and security. Accounting is giving women the clout awarded to financial professionals who can deal with the bottom line—money.

As women of social conscience, we rarely envision accounting as a field of social benefit or significance. But accounting is often the stepping-stone to positions of power which can have a significant and positive impact on our communities. An accountant who demonstrates financial astuteness can move into executive or administrative positions in government agencies and in the private sector. The financial overview that the accounting experience affords has been known to advance many individuals into influential positions which affect the economic policies of our society, cities, or states. Accounting careers *can* be socially significant.

Just imagine beginning in the accounting department of a nonprofit organization, gaining financial and management skills, and moving into top administrative levels based on your knowledge of the inner workings of the operation! Or imagine using your accounting training to boost you into an educational administration career! Or imagine using your accounting skills as a stepping-stone to a middle management position in the communications field!

Accounting can also give you the best of two career worlds. If you are interested in advertising, you can be an accountant in an advertising agency. If law is your preference, you can combine law and accounting. The combinations are as varied as you are innovative. There are few fields in which accounting and finance are not important.

Career Pathing in Accounting

Accounting offers many specialties: tax accounting, auditing, general accounting, controller, certified public accounting (CPA), management accounting, systems and procedure accounting, cost accounting, and budget and forecast accounting.

Tax Accounting: The tax accountant is most familiar to us when we prepare to beat the April 15 deadline for completing our income tax returns. Her calculating skills and constantly updated knowledge of income tax rules are a saving grace, relieving us of this dreaded task. The tax accountant also works for businesses, helping to determine the best tax advantages for corporations, large and small. If there are audits, she represents her clients before the Internal Revenue Service.

Auditing: Auditors are most familiar to those of us who work for nonprofit organizations that are scrutinized for possible improprieties by funding agencies. Auditors also work for businesses and organizations checking the accuracy of books. If improprieties are found, the auditor corrects them.

General Accounting: General accountants are responsible for day-to-day accounting tasks like record keeping, tax-related activities, and other duties.

Controller: The controller is in charge of the entire accounting department.

Certified Public Accounting (CPA): The CPA works with individuals and businesses offering many valuable accounting services.

Management Accounting: The management accountant is responsible for the company's financial and investment decisions.

Systems and Procedure Accounting: The systems and procedure accountant is a master planner who helps companies install effective accounting systems. Her knowledge of computer techniques is helpful in updating these systems.

Cost Accountant: The cost accountant helps company managers control costs by gathering necessary financial data.

Budget and Forecasting Accountant: The budget and forecasting accountant is a planning specialist who is concerned with budget preparation, market forecast projections, and other duties.

Every accounting career is built on the foundation of the bachelor's degree. To get the bachelor's, you must take a required number of credits in accounting, including basic, intermediate, advanced, asset, cost, government accounting, and auditing. Also recommended are courses in income tax accounting and financial statement analysis.

After completing your undergraduate degree, you must decide which accounting field interests you most. The bachelor's degree will give you the opportunity to land entry-level positions in private industry, private firms, educational institutions, local, state, or federal government agencies, or nonprofit organizations. But to build a career, you should pursue more advanced educational training.

A master's degree in accounting will specifically prepare you for professional accounting careers. Some programs will provide you with the educational requirements to take the Certified Public Accountant (CPA) examination; others will train you for controllership, financial management, professional accounting, and taxation careers. There are even some schools which have graduate programs designed for those with bachelor's degrees in disciplines other than accounting who want to enter business or accounting careers.

Master of Business Administration (M.B.A.) programs with specializations in accounting will prepare you for business careers.

If you are interested in public accounting, the CPA will provide you with optimum career leverage. A CPA is the top-of-the-line credential and a mark of professional achievement. To become certified, you must take the CPA examination administered by the American Institute of Certified Public Accountants. A college degree and at least two years of public accounting experience are the prerequisites required by most states. There are also professional programs designed to help you complete the educational requirements for the exam. To work as a CPA, you must have a certificate and license issued by a State Board of Accounting.

If internal auditing is the path you choose, you should consider acquiring the designation of Certified Internal Auditor (CIA), conferred by the Institute of Internal Auditors, Inc. Specified educational requirements, two years of work experience in internal auditing, and passing a four-part examination are the eligibility requirements.

If management accounting is your preference, businesses are increasingly accepting the Certificate in Management Accounting (CMA) as a mark of professional competence. This is issued by the National Association of Accountants. Eligibility requirements include meeting specified educational and work qualifications as well as passing a series of uniform examinations.

For those interested in teaching or other scholarly pursuits, you should pursue graduate studies necessary for a Ph.D. Or if you are interested in combining your business training with law, you may study toward a J.D.-M.B.A., which some schools offer.

What Will You Earn as an Accountant?

Your salary as an accountant can be very lucrative. In the beginning you can command good starting salaries. And as you move up, your earning power, depending on your career path, can be in the six-figure bracket. (see Table 28).

TABLE 28

ACCOUNTING STARTING SALARIES 1986

ACCOUNTANTS—INTERNAL—LARGE FIRMS	1986 SALARIES
(General, Audit, Cost)	
(c) 0–1 year experience	$17,000–$20,000
(c) 1–3 years experience	20,000– 27,500
(c) Senior	29,000– 33,000
(c) Manager	35,000– 50,000

ACCOUNTANTS—INTERNAL—MEDIUM FIRMS

(General, Audit, Cost)	
(c) 0–1 year experience	$17,000–$19,000
(c) 1–3 years experience	20,000– 25,000
(c) Senior	25,000– 31,000
(c) Manager	31,000– 36,000

ACCOUNTANTS—PUBLIC—LARGE FIRMS

(d) 0–1 year experience	$19,500–$22,000
(e) (f) Senior	26,000– 30,500
(f) Supervising Senior	30,000– 36,000
(g) Manager	38,000– 57,000

ACCOUNTANTS—PUBLIC—MEDIUM FIRMS

(Audit, Tax, Management Services)	
(d) 0–1 year experience	$18,000–$20,000
(e) (f) 1–3 ycars experience	19,500– 25,000
(f) Senior	25,000– 35,000
(g) Manager	35,000– 48,000

NOTE:

(c) Add 10% for a graduate degree; an additional 10% for a CPA; and an additional 5% for substantial travel.

(d) Add 10% for a graduate degree.

(e) Add 5% for a graduate degree.

(f) Add 10% for a CPA.

(g) Subtract 5% if not a CPA.

Source: *Robert Half's Prevailing Financial & Data Processing Starting Salaries 1986,* copyright © Robert Half International, Inc.

CAREER PROFILE

Paula Cholmondeley uses her accounting training at the Blue Cross.

Paula Cholmondeley, CPA
Senior Vice-President and Chief Financial Officer
Blue Cross of Greater Philadelphia
Philadelphia, Pennsylvania

One of the best-known Black women certified public accountants (CPAs) is Paula Cholmondeley. A Guyanan native, she journeyed to the United States to study business at Howard University in Washington, D.C. Specializing in accounting, she did not focus on a public accounting career. The time was not ripe for Black CPAs; she had no role models; it was a difficult goal. A chance meeting with a recruiter from Price Waterhouse & Company changed her mind. He challenged her interest and inspired her participation in an internship program at one of the large public accounting firms. "In the summer between my junior and senior years, I was accepted as an intern with Haskins & Sells. That experience convinced me to enter public accounting," she remembers. "Afterward, I discovered that my college accounting program geared us toward managerial accounting." If she wanted public accounting, she would have to augment her undergraduate work with graduate training.

Cholmondeley applied and was accepted to the University of Pennsylvania's Wharton School of Finance. While waiting to enter Wharton, she took another internship to strengthen her record. That summer she went to work for another public accounting big eight firm, Peat, Marwick, Mitchell and Company.

At Wharton, she pursued what seemed to be the best route, a master's degree in accounting. "I chose it over the M.B.A. program because the graduate accounting program suited my background. To pursue the M.B.A. would have meant repeating a number of courses I'd taken as an undergraduate." The accounting degree would provide a firm foundation for later career pursuits.

After graduation, Cholmondeley selected the public accounting firm of Arthur Andersen in New York. Some clever career pathing paved the way for an impressive start up the corporate ladder. "I started as a junior accountant in the small business division. Usually, a new employee spends a year on the general audit staff, then selects an area of specialization. But everyone told me the small business staff received more exposure and experience and allowed staffers to be generalists rather than specialists. So I worked out a deal," she recalls. "Depending on my ranking and evaluation after training, I asked to be put on the small business division. Since I did very well in training, I was placed on the staff. Later, I was transferred to consumer goods."

In the late sixties, opportunities for minorities were good and a few Blacks started the now defunct Zebra Associates, an advertising agency. Cholmondeley was offered the controller's position, a big jump up the ladder. With two and a half years of Arthur Andersen training, she left. "Zebra needed someone to institute an accounting system and bring it up to standard," she says. But after accomplishing the task, she wanted more than accounting. She longed for a position to broaden her background. After eighteen months, she left Zebra in pursuit of expanded duties.

The search for the "perfect" job was intense. She interviewed with many companies but chose a manager of cash operations position with International Paper Company. "My responsibilities included managing the accounting arm of the department. But in addition I was involved in the investment activities of the department—cash management systems, corporate finance, and several other areas," she remembers. "I stayed there for eighteen months and was promoted to another managerial position in international finance. There I was responsible for project analysis for all overseas investments and handled some bank financing in Latin America."

Another year and a half passed and she became manager of budgets and controls for a division of International Paper, with duties including preparing budgets, strategy plans, and monthly financial reporting. She was in a cherished line position, one that contributes directly to a company's profitability.

Yet Cholmondeley was clear on her long-term goals—to be a line manager with profit and loss responsibility. With this goal in mind, she joined Westinghouse Electric as vice-president of strategic planning and programs. This position broadened her background and gave her greater financial responsibilities in the nonfinance areas.

"If you have a good financial background, because every manager is responsible for a budget, it's twice as easy to move into other corporate departments. Managers' results are measured by the bottom line—money—and there is no decision made in a corporation—large or small—without a financial person being involved somewhere along the line. As an accountant, you are really in the mainstream of what goes on," she emphasizes. "Accounting is also good because traditionally you hear women have difficulty moving into management positions due to their uneasiness with numbers. Accounting provides the necessary familiarization with numbers. With an undergraduate degree in accounting coupled with an M.B.A. emphasizing marketing, you will have a broad background in preparation for moving up the corporate ladder in any area."

But if your goal is to stay in public accounting, you may want to pursue the top mark of professional competence, the CPA. "For Black women, I think it's good to have a graduate degree and the CPA designation. I think we still have to be more qualified than our white counterparts," she advises, but admits the difficulty of getting the CPA. "The CPA examination is very rigorous; it fails more people than it passes. It's a nationwide uniform examination but there are also work experience requirements. Check on your state's requirements because licensing and educational requirements vary from state to state."

Although the CPA is well respected and widely sought, the certified management accountant designation is fast becoming acceptable for those pursuing management accounting. "The Certified Management Accountant is designed for the person who has never worked in a CPA firm, doesn't want to, and is really interested in management accounting. This title is becoming comparable to the CPA and more corporations are accepting it," she says. "If you are serious about an accounting career, then get the CPA, CMA, or CIA (Certified Internal Auditor)."

Cholmondeley also advises women to become visible and active in professional associations. "Companies like visibility and professionalism, and they will support you," says Cholmondeley, who has been involved with the New York State Society of CPAs and the National Association of Black Accountants. "Involvement on this basis says you are capable of working and sharing information with your peers. It gives your employer a basis for encouraging promotion," she advises.

Believing in being visible with and active in one's career, Cholmondeley left Westinghouse Electric to become a White House Fellow. In that capacity she was special assistant to a U.S. Trade Representative for a year. When she returned to Westinghouse, she was manager, International Business Development and Latin American Operations. Afterward, she became regional manager for the Capital Cities Region, which included profit and loss responsibility for a tristate area.

Recently, she took her present position of senior vice-president of Finance and chief financial officer at Blue Cross of Greater Philadelphia.

Career Aids

The American Society of Women Accountants distributes *For Accounting . . . A Challenging and Rewarding Profession* (single copy free). Write to:
National Headquarters
35 East Wacker Dr., Suite 2250
Chicago, Ill. 60601

For career information, contact:

1. National Association of Accountants
   P.O. Box 433
   10 Paragon Drive
   Montvale, N.J. 07645
2. American Institute of Certified Public Accountants
   1211 Avenue of the Americas
   New York, N.Y. 10036
3. National Society of Public Accountants and Accreditation
      Council for Accountancy
   1010 North Fairfax
   Alexandria, Va. 22314
4. The National Association of Black Accountants, Inc.
   300 I St., NW
   Washington, D.C. 20002

BANKING

Although many of us may want banking careers, we must look realistically at the opportunities within this conservative industry. Traditionally, banks have not welcomed minorities with open arms. The Council on Economic Priorities' *Shortchanged/Update: Minorities and Women in Banking* states, "In 1940, of the 475,000 employees in banks, only 1.6% were minority group members."[1] It was not until the sixties that significant changes in employment opportunities occurred; even in the mid-seventies, improvements were at best modest.

Career Pathing in Banking

The majority of bank employees are employed by very large commercial banks but others work for mutual savings banks, the twelve Federal Reserve Banks, foreign exchange firms, clearinghouse associations, check cashing agencies, and other industry-related employers.

If you work in a bank, you may career-path in one of the most common areas:

Commercial Banking: is responsible for the profit of banks by lending to businesses. Commercial banking is regarded as the best place to career-path to the top.[2] If you career-path in a bank management program with an eye toward a commercial lending officer position, you'll be on the right track. Along the way, gaining expertise in credit analysis will make you more marketable.

Consumer Banking: is most familiar because it includes services such as checking and savings and installment loans for individuals and families.[3] Federal legislation like the Equal Credit Opportunity Act have opened opportunities for women in consumer banking. As an area where some women have successfully career-pathed, it can be the basis for moving into commercial banking.[4]

Trust Administration: is responsible for financial management of assets and estates for individuals as well as company benefit plans.[5] Trust administration can offer career advancement opportunities. Beginning as an administrative assistant, you may be promoted to an officer's slot. Specialization within the field can also boost your career.

Marketing: is in charge of promoting the bank's image and selling its services. Career pathing in marketing can place you in a position to interchange with many top banking officers.[6] Some of these interactions can become spin-offs to careers in other departments or advancement in marketing. But creative jobs in the area such as advertising, writing, art, or design are often not the basis for advancement within the department.

Operations: perform the bank's day-to-day activities. Operations careers can lead to advancement in and outside of the area and are considered one of the best advancement areas for women.[7]

Personnel Administration: handles the hiring, training, and promotion of bank employees and is also responsible for determining their salaries and benefits.[8]

The college degree is the minimum requirement for professional and managerial bank positions. Many prospective employees, however, have found the M.B.A. the most marketable degree.

If you are already a woman banker and interested in pursuing the college degree to advance to executive banking positions, there are several special programs cosponsored by the National Association of Bank Women (NABW) and a few institutions of higher education.

One is the *NABW/Simmons College Bachelor's Degree Program with a Concentration in Management,* which will prepare you for management jobs in banking. The program offers you the opportunity to complete your studies in three to five years, which is shorter than traditional night school. One advantage of the program is that you are required to attend six two-week, in-residence management institutes (two institutes per year for three years). Another NABW program is with Mundelein College in Chicago, Illinois.

What Will You Earn in Banking?

Salaries vary according to bank size, location, and your educational qualifications (see Table 29).

TABLE 29

BANKING STARTING SALARIES 1986

BANKING—LARGE ($300 MILLION AND HIGHER)

Senior Loan Officer	$36,000–$55,000
Commercial Lenders (Corporate/Middle Market/ABL)	29,000– 40,000
Consumer Lenders	25,000– 31,000
Mortgage Lenders (Commercial/Residential)	34,000– 45,000
Operations Officer/Branch Manager (Domestic/International)	26,000– 34,500
Loan or Operations Supervisor/Assistant Branch Manager (Domestic/International)	16,500– 25,000
Loan or Operations Staff (Domestic/International)	16,000– 23,000
Trust Officer (Corporate/Personal)	30,000– 40,000
Trust Staff (Corporate/Personal)	16,500– 25,000

BANKING—MEDIUM/SMALL (LESS THAN $300 MILLION)

Senior Loan Officer	$33,000–$44,000
Commercial Lenders (Corporate/Middle Market/ABL)	24,000– 37,000
Consumer Lenders	19,500– 29,500
Mortgage Lenders (Commercial/Residential)	24,500– 38,000
Operations Officer/Branch Manager (Domestic/International)	20,000– 32,000
Loan or Operations Supervisor/Assistant Branch Manager (Domestic/International)	16,500– 23,000
Loan or Operations Staff (Domestic/International)	13,000– 22,000
Trust Officer (Corporate/Personal)	24,000– 34,000
Trust Staff (Corporate/Personal)	17,000– 26,000

Source: *Robert Half's Prevailing Financial & Data Processing Starting Salaries 1986.* Copyright © Robert Half International, Inc.

CAREER PROFILE

Jean Smith sits in a responsible position at Chase Manhattan Bank. Her career advice is timely and on target.

Jean M. Gray Smith
Vice-President and Senior Banking Officer
Chase Manhattan Bank
New York, New York

There's a thirty-second commercial for Chase Manhattan Bank. It shows a Black girl who purchased a refrigerator for her mother, and later grew up to become a banker. That girl grew up to be Jean Smith, now senior banking officer at Chase Manhattan Bank's largest branch (the Flagship, as it is called). It's been a long and arduous climb for Smith from clerk through a myriad of clerical jobs to her present upper-middle management position.

Jean Smith began her banking career as a block or rack clerk running an IBM 360 Proof machine. Determined to achieve, she changed to bookkeeping and other clerical jobs until becoming a teller. A promotion to the commercial service supervisor started her on her way up the corporate ladder.

In her position as commercial service supervisor, she realized that her career was taking a wrong turn. Although she was teaching people who had completed the Chase Credit Training Program, and watching them become bank officials, her career wasn't leading to a bank official position. When she approached one of the trainees to ask for help, she was advised to learn the financial side of banking. She then turned to a bank official, who told her to get a college degree.

Believing in that advice, Smith enrolled at Fordham University as a business and economics major. At the time, she had two children to raise. With the help of her mother and two brothers, Smith, who is a widow, spent three and one half years taking twelve to eighteen credits at night to earn her bachelor's degree.

But barely into her senior year, she saw that her education and sacrifices were paying off. She was asked to join the bank's special program in Management Information Financial Control for the Community

Banking area. She developed several programs, one of which was a nonaccrual system. During the time of rapidly rising interest rates, the system was used to look at all the bank's loans by industry (a type of risk-management portfolio). She also built a file system that showed what every lending officer's authority was. This was something never done before, and one of Smith's first recognized accomplishments.

After she put the portfolio management program together, she was asked by the chief credit officer for Chase's Community Bank area to become his administrative assistant—an official position. She was responsible for all the reporting made to the chief credit officer—credit reviews, etc. Sometime later, she was given her biggest promotion, to assistant treasurer. Her boss then wanted her to go through the credit training program.

"Before entering the program, I had mixed emotions. Old colleagues cautioned that the program wouldn't be easy, and participants would be Ivy League graduates," Smith remembers. "But I had no choice. My boss had asked me to join. But going through the program was one of the finest opportunities that I've ever had. There were great people in it, and it was a great experience. It changed my career and lifestyle. It opened a new world."

After finishing the program, she received a promotion to second vice-president, and joined the jewelry-and-diamond team, lending money to the diamond industry. She then moved to the team that lent money to large nonprofit agencies such as the United Israel Appeal, United Negro College Fund, National Urban League, Ford Foundation, and Rockefeller Foundation.

In late 1983, she was asked to develop a sales and marketing plan for the South Bronx. Along with that move came another promotion to vice-president. At first, two heavy business branches reported to her. Eventually, she was asked to oversee twelve branches and one hundred people. "Someone in the bank called and asked me to work on a special project to investigate and develop a plan to address the commercial market in the south tier of the Bronx," says Smith. "We wanted to become a part of the community. Chase's mission and focus is to become the best there is in the communities it serves. So we're going toward a regional banking philosophy. As a regional bank, we try to be very attuned to the community's needs." Smith found herself involved in community activities such as the Boys and Girls Club, the Network Organization of Bronx Women, and the NAACP.

In November of 1986, this ambitious banker was asked to run the bank's largest branch, the Flagship. "We have close to $500 million in assets, which means that we could easily be a bank within itself. If you ranked us among banks, I think we would be ranked about forty-ninth in the country. So we're very large," says Smith. She supervises about one hundred people, and is still very active in that branch's community.

Smith advises women interested in climbing a bank's corporate ladder: "Don't isolate yourself. Don't think that hard work alone will do it. People have to know who you are. If two people have the same credentials, they will give it to whom they know. There are opportunities that come up on a daily basis—going to lunch or having drinks with those in the bank. I've noticed that some people don't take advantage of these opportunities to become known.

"Also, be personable. If someone asks you to do something, go the extra mile. It's great pounding away at your job, but you have to do something extra. Find that thin line that distinguishes you from the rest of the workers," says Smith. "Accept challenges and turn them into opportunities. For me, it was a tough road. Sometimes, I don't know how I made it. But I do know that I've never had to ask for a job. People have always thought of me as having a reputation of getting the job done."

Smith continuously upgrades her educational experiences. Recently, she completed a two-year professional program, the Smith Management Program, at Smith College.

She lives in the Bronx, New York, and is the proud mother of Charles and Kevin, and grandmother of Preston.

Career Aids

Books and Pamphlets

1. *NABW Fact Sheet* and *Careers Brochure* (each $1.50) and *Mundelein Brochure; Simmons Brochure* are available from:
   The National Association of Bank Women, Inc.
   500 North Michigan, Suite 1400
   Chicago, Ill. 60611

Professional Organizations

1. The National Bankers Association, Inc.
   499 South Capitol St., SW, Suite 520
   Washington, D.C. 20003
2. National Association of Urban Bankers
   111 East Wacher Drive, Suite 600
   Chicago, Ill. 60601

All addresses and prices are subject to change.

11

A Career of Your Own

STARTING YOUR OWN BUSINESS

Many of you may be interested in starting your own businesses because it offers a way out of dreary nine-to-five jobs. Business ownership may seem the path to independence, but a rocky road lies ahead.

Too many potential business owners feel that a simple wave of a magic wand can push them into the business arena. Too many feel a good business idea is all that's needed, but it takes much more. Candidates for entrepreneurship must engage in a series of complicated steps before opening their business doors. There is marketing research to see if ideas are viable, finding suitable locations, picking the right name, deciding the correct business form, raising operating capital, determining which licenses and permits are needed, developing good promotional techniques, and keeping the business afloat with expert management skills.

When you add to this list the forces of racism and sexism which consider women and Blacks bad business risks, the task of business ownership becomes more difficult. You may face difficulty in raising cash and getting credit extended for supplies or equipment. And in this period of harsh economic times, it is even more difficult for the Black business owner.

It will take an understanding of business ownership to prevent the failure that every one out of five businesses experience in their first five years of operation. You must cover all bases by planning for your business. There are nine basic steps to business ownership. The first step is coming up with the concept.

Step 1—Coming Up with a Marketable Business

A good idea is the foundation for a successful business. Good business ideas are generated every day. There's the woman who turned an ability to organize into a money-making venture, or the one who turned cooking skills into a prosperous catering service, and the ambitious public relations specialist who turned her flair for promoting into a lucrative public relations firm. A secretary may abandon her nine-to-five job to open a secretarial service. A teacher who's changing careers may help other career changers. And a steamstress may begin a dressmaking shop in her home.

If you look around you, there is an abundance of ideas for businesses. You can select a trend—a roller-skating boutique. Or you can zero in on one of your community's needs—a copy/duplicating office. The important thing is to pick an idea which is feasible for you to launch.

Step 2—Market Research: Do Others Think Your Idea Is Good?

After coming up with an idea, it is time to decide if others think it's as great as you do. If you are the only one who thinks your business is great, it won't stay afloat too long.

Many established businesses have marketing research staffs to evaluate their new ideas. Unfortuantely, the beginning entrepreneur often has limited capital which must be spent on other business needs. But you can achieve similar results to those made by marketing research workers. You can design and mail a questionnaire asking people whether they need or want your service, product, or talent. For example, a health food store may be a great idea, but are your neighbors more interested in a store that sells meat and potatoes? To gauge their opinions, you may spend one afternoon at your local shopping mall, asking others about their needs or wants. Or you can design and mail a questionnaire to a sample population in your neighborhood.

Some beginning business owners walk from door to door sampling opinions. Others send out brochures to potential customers and wait for responses. Others just plunge in and hope for positive responses.

Regardless of your marketing approach, you should give some consideration to analyzing your target population. A careful analysis will pay off when you are convincing others to invest in or lend money to your business.

Step 3—What Will Your Company's Name and Location/Image Be?

After discovering that marketable idea, you must now think about where the business will be located. In choosing a location you should consider the nature of your business, the image you want to project, and how much it will cost.

First, you should consider what location will be best for your type of business. For example, if you want to start a consulting business, can you begin it from home? Or if you want to manufacture tools, will you have to rent or purchase a factory?

You may find that it is more feasible to begin at home, which will cut down on operating expenses. Many businesses are started at home, expanded, and are then moved elsewhere. However, you should consider how your business will fit into your home life. Is there adequate space? Will clients need to come to you and are there facilities to keep them separated from the rest of the house? Do you have children and will your business interfere with their freedom to move throughout the house? Will your home business interfere with licensing procedures?

For example, if you have a cooking establishment in your home, will you be violating state health codes?

If your business requires that your client contact is through mail or telephone, perhaps you can get a post office box and a telephone answering machine.

Some beginning entrepreneurs share space with fellow business owners in professional office suites. Some rent space for one or two days to cut down on costs. Others use the services of companies which rent them office space, secretarial services, office equipment, conference rooms, and put their company's name on the lobby's roster for a monthly fee.

If your business must rent or buy commercial space, you should do comparison shopping. Remember the most prestigious location may be the costliest, and as a beginning business owner, you may find that your operating capital may be limited. Try to find the best location at the least cost. A good real estate agent who specializes in commercial space should be helpful.

Whether your business is at home or in an office or building, the location should reflect the image you wish to portray. Therefore, some of you may prefer prestigious locations if your potential clients are large conservative business organizations. Your office decor, business cards, and stationery can also help create the type of image you want.

In seeking a location for a new business, another consideration is whether it is convenient and safe. Is it located near public transportation or easily accessible by car? Will your potential clients feel safe in coming to your place of business? Is building security adequate?

In choosing a name, you should find one which is as appealing and practical as your location. Choose one which will present the image you want to portray. For example, if you have a consultant firm whose potential clients are conservative businesses, would a name like Folly's Funtime Consultants be appropriate? A name can also indicate the type of service your company will extend.

Name choices can be dictated by practical considerations. For example, if you want to incorporate your business in the future, using your own name will eliminate the required name search. If you use a name other than your own, in some states, including New York, you must file the "Certificate of Doing Business Under an Assumed Name," which will help creditors and others know the real names of business owners.

Step 4—What Type of Business Will You Have?

After location and names have been decided, you should determine what form your business will take: individual proprietorship, partnership, corporation.

If you choose the individual proprietorship, the main advantage is that you as the single owner will have complete freedom to make business decisions. Another advantage is that once the money rolls in, it is yours alone, minus the operating expenses.

The disadvantages of single proprietorships are more complex. First, you must shoulder the burden of the business alone. Second, until the business is financially solvent, you will have to shoulder the financial burden of the company and may not be compensated for several years. Without additional sources of income, you may personally go under financially. Third, if the business fails, you are personally liable for all debts. Fourth, you must pay all federal and state income taxes and social security deductions.

In partnerships, you can share the burden of running a business with one or more people. In these business marriages you may have a full or limited sharing depending on legal agreements which should be drawn up by your lawyer. In some states all the partners in a general partnership must pay federal and state personal income taxes, as well as taxes for unincorporated businesses. In limited partnerships, you can have partners who only put up the cash and are liable only for that amount of money.

The advantages of partnerships are that you, as an individual, may not be expert in all areas, and the contribution of another's expertise may be helpful. The disadvantages of partnerships are that sometimes too many cooks spoil the soup. As in all "marriages," unless there is harmony, breakups can be imminent.

Debts must be divided in general partnerships with the "partnership" taking the burden. If dissolution of the partnership or the death of one of the partners occurs, the partnership must be legally dissolved.

Unlike individual proprietorships or partnerships, corporations are entities unto themselves; they are created by the state as a privilege. Corporate liabilities are shouldered by the corporation instead of the owner or owners. The corporation is responsible for paying federal and state income taxes. The corporation must pay filing fees and organization taxes; it must also have a board of directors and draft by-laws.

Corporations may sell shares to stockholders to raise their beginning capital. But stockholders can invest in a corporation without having to be involved in the day-to-day business operations.

With all three of these business forms, you should get advice from your attorney to explore fully the best form for you.

Step 5—Getting the Money to Launch Your Business

Some of you may go through the preliminary steps of starting a business but stop in your tracks when it's time for financing. Since most of you may not be rich enough to pump thousands or hundreds of thousands of dollars into your business, you must seek financing from others.

Your first inclination may be to turn to your bank. You remember the thousands of dollars you've deposited in your bank over the years to support that lending institution, and you believe it will return your support by financing your new venture. Wrong. Banks rarely finance new ventures without track records. Contrary to what you may think, banks are very conservative in making loans to new businesses. To protect their interests, lending institutions want proof that your business will be profitable and their investments well spent and returned.

Lending institutions also generally require business owners who want loans to put up at least half of the needed capital in cash or assets. To many of you, this is baffling. But if you need $100,000 to start your business, a bank may require you to have at least $50,000 in cash, assets, or collateral. Many of you may not have this "up-front cash" and subsequently will be turned down for loans from many lending institutions.

Many of you may be rejected for bank loans because you have not developed a sound business proposal which establishes your thoroughness in approaching business ownership. Contrary to what many of you may think, business proposals are not simply affirmations of your desire to do business. They are very complex documents which can be one hundred pages or more in length. Proposals should include the following information: description of the company; the risks involved; the company's objectives; an analysis of the markets and competition; sales and marketing plans; the production process; distribution strategies; the facilities to be used plus costs; your management expertise; staff backgrounds, expertise, résumés; an organizational chart of staff, their responsibilities; the expenses including balance sheets and cash flow analysis; future trends for the company. If you are unfamiliar with business proposal writing, see Table 30.

Even with adequate and well-prepared business proposals, you may still be turned down for loans from lending institutions and have to seek assistance from private investors, friends, relatives, business associates, or in some cases, venture capital companies.

You may get help from the Small Business Administration (SBA). Or you can seek assistance from the Small Business Investment Companies (SBICs), which are licensed, regulated, and given financial assistance by the SBA to make "venture" or "risk" investments.

The Minority Enterprise Small Business Investment Companies (MESBICs) are authorized SBICs which specialize in providing sources of cash to minorities. The Department of Commerce's Minority Business Development Agency (MBDA) assists minorities in getting financing, drafting marketing plans, and managing their business operation. Its Business Development Offices are located throughout the country.

The SBA usually guarantees up to 90 percent of your bank loan values. To be eligible for an SBA loan guarantee, you must have been turned down by one or more banks and show an ability to repay the loan. In rare cases, the SBA will give direct loans to business owners who cannot establish credit with banks.

The SBA offers seminars on business ownership throughout the country and offers counseling through SCORE (Service Corps of Retired Executives) and ACE (Active Corps of Executives).

Step 6—Do You Need a License?

Once you are on your way to financing your venture, check on required licenses and certificates. Businesses like restaurants, stores, or lounges which sell beer and alcohol must be licensed in some states. Peddlers, employment agencies, locksmiths, cosmetologists, private investigators, notaries, taxi drivers, plumbers, electrical workers, and hotel/motel

TABLE 30

A SAMPLE PROPOSAL OUTLINE

1. Financing
   Amount requested
   Purpose and use of
     funds
   Structure of deal
   Capitalization
2. Description of the
   Company
     Name and location
     Nature of business
     Product
     Facilities
     Market and
       competition
     Competitive
       advantage
     Investment appeal
3. Rick Factors
   Management
     expertise
   Stage of product
     development
   Market trends
   Competition
4. Business Plan
   Objectives
   The product or
     service
5. The Market
   Description
   Competition
   Trends
6. Competition
   Size

Experience
Orientation
Changes
7. Sales and Marketing
   Strategy
   Method
   Pricing policy
8. Production Process
   Materials
   Supply sources
   Method
9. Distribution and Service
   Strategy
   Method
10. Facilities
    Location
    Size
    Age and condition
    Planned capital
      improvements
    Expansion
      opportunities
11. Management
    Organization and
    Personnel
      Management
        structure
    Description of
      directors
    Responsibility of
      officers
    Résumés of key
      members

Description of staff
organization
12. Expenses
Fixed overhead
Variable
Provisions for
increases
13. Financial Information
Balance sheets
Income statements
Cash flow analysis
Break-even analysis

Explanation of
projections
Earnings and
potential returns
to investors
Payback
14. Conclusions
Assessment of
opportunities
Status of the
company

owners must be licensed. Professionals including doctors, dentists, podiatrists, nurses, teachers in public schools, and engineers must be licensed. To determine which licenses are applicable in your state, contact local or state licensing agencies.

Step 7—Protecting Yourself!

Although, you may overlook it, insurance is a very important ingredient in business ownership. Think about it. What if fire destroyed your office, records, inventory, and equipment, how would you replace them? If burglars broke in and made off with all of your equipment and merchandise, or if vandals rendered your equipment inoperable, could you buy new equipment and merchandise? What if an automobile was vital to your business and it was involved in an accident where people were killed or injured, how would you pay for these losses? If a customer slipped and hurt herself on your property, could you afford her hospital bill? What if one of your employees was injured on the job or became ill, what if a tornado hit your town and destroyed your office? What if your business had to shut down temporarily, how would you keep it viable? What if you or your partner died, how would you protect your family and yourself from these losses?

Businesses must have insurance and you should discuss your business insurance needs with an insurance professional. An agent can help you determine whether fire, burglary, vandalism, automobile, workers' compensation (required for businesses for profit with more than one employee), property, natural disasters, and business life insurance are applicable.

Step 8—Promoting Your Business

Time invested in publicizing your business is a necessity, not a luxury. Although you can pay professionals to do this, many of you will have to do it yourselves. With practice, you may be able to paste up mechanicals for business cards, stationery, or other business needs. With a good eye, steady hand, and graphic materials like stick-on letters, you may be able to design presentable copies for printers to reproduce. If you are

not confident of your artistic ability, hire a qualified and competent
graphic artist to design logos and layouts for brochures, ads, and other
promotional materials.

Your promotional and advertising plans should also include press
release preparation. Releases should be sent to local newspapers, magazines, and radio and television stations. These press releases announce
to the general public the arrival of your new business. Many of the local
media outlets may be interested enough to do a feature story on your
business, if it is a particularly unusual one or provides a badly needed
community service. Read the copy used by other businesses and rede-
sign them to suit your own needs. In some cities, there are courses
available in press release writing techniques. Contact your local colleges
or universities, high school, or YWCA continuing education units.

Mass mailings are another means of promoting your business. In
some cities, there are "list brokers" who will sell you lists of various
groups such as housewives, doctors, teachers, and so forth. Once you
have these lists, you can send out brochures, flyers, or "individualized"
letters.

Step 9—Keeping Afloat

Smoothly running businesses are the results of good management. It is
said that many businesses fail partly because the owner or owners do
not have good management skills or have not hired or consulted with
those who can help them in this area.

Since many of you may not have been exposed to the world of business, you may know little about its inner workings. You may not be
familiar with purchase orders, inventories, record keeping, stock turn-
overs, overstocks, markdowns, and unit controls. Your background may
not have prepared you to understand or prepare a balance sheet, which
shows a picture of your business at a specific period of time, or a profit
and loss statement, which summarizes your business's activities for the
year. You need also to be capable of the successful management of the
day-to-day operations of the business and employees.

There are organizations that can help you obtain the skills to run
your business. Government agencies like SBA offer this service for
those companies under their loan programs. The MBDA will help train

you in management techniques. You might consider courses in small business management or taking a basic course in accounting. There are many books on the subject of business management and its many aspects. The astute small business owner will build her library diligently.

Franchising

If you do not want to begin a business from scratch, consider buying a franchise—an existing business. If you decide to start a business by this method, be sure to thoroughly investigate the prospective business. To get a good buying price and avoid mistakes, get good professional help from a lawyer or other knowledgeable source. And remember that purchasing a business is not always the most successful route to business ownership.

What Will You Earn as a Business Owner?

Do not expect to become an overnight success. Building a solid business takes time, hard work, and determination. Don't expect immediate financial gratification. It sometimes takes years to reap large financial rewards.

CAREER PROFILES

Yvonne Thompson, Frankie Jennings, Dorue Lin, Ruth Clark, Barbara DuMetz, and Rose Harris are Black women with successful businesses. Their career advice offers a great deal of information about business start-ups. For other business owners, see Carolyn Hughes, Muriel Petioni, Donna Mendes, Melba Wilson, Mildred Dixon, Adriane Murray, Nancy Boyd-Franklin, Lilia Abron-Robinson, Dorothy Brunson, Marie Brown, Jewell Jackson McCabe, Victoria Lucas, Caroline Jones, Audrey Smaltz, Marion Holmes-Nadrich, Margaret Pazant, Lydia Hammond, Rita Falkener, Peggy Dillard, Sheryl Warren-Carey, Judith Smith, Gloria Hartley.

Yvonne E. Thompson
Vice-President, Marketing
General Railroad Equipment & Services, Inc.
East St. Louis, Illinois

For many the thirties are turbulent career years; it is when most women are pushing their careers toward ultimate achievement. There is uncertainty and uneasiness about reaching success. Yvonne Thompson is the exception rather than the rule. She has reached a career pinnacle by having and successfully operating several businesses. She began her first business by founding The Venture Group, a financing company that primarily served minority business owners.

The Venture Group was successful. "My company provided 'short term secure lending' to companies, typically in the form of accounts receivable financing. The company generally provided lines of credit to businesses secured by their assets," she says.

Step-by-step Thompson made a difficult but steady climb to entrepreneurship. She plodded through Fisk University in anticipation of a business career and M.B.A. She interrupted the dream to get married and entered retailing via Alexander's, a New York department store. When Thompson's marriage dissolved, she decided to pursue her dream—getting the M.B.A. Moving to California, she studied for and received her M.B.A. degree at the University of California at Berkeley.

With newly acquired financial clout from her business school training, Thompson captured a plum job as investment analyst for Opportunity Capital Corporation in San Francisco. This new work changed her life and put her in line for business ownership. Ambitious and competent, the young analyst absorbed the business operations and moved quickly to head up the company's financial and management services subsidiary company, a provider of management consulting services and commercial financing to portfolio companies. This experience was a springboard to business ownership.

When Thompson wanted to start a business, the Opportunity Capital Corporation backed the project financially and emotionally. "To a large extent, my former employer assisted me in the company's initial financing. I did a good job for them and they believed in me. With their contacts and those I had made over the years, I was able to secure financing," she reveals. "I had very few problems in starting the company. In retrospect, it's almost inconceivable that everything went so well." But Thompson learned a great deal during the training period with the Opportunity Capital Corporation. Long hours, hard work, mastering financial expertise, and going beyond required duties set the stage for easy adaptation to entrepreneurship.

Thompson then steadily built an impressive company: The Venture Group. Clients were referred to her by her former employer and similar companies across the country, banks and other financial institutions, trade associations, and customers she'd cultivated.

Thompson credits prior business training and hands-on experience as the key prerequisites to The Venture Group's success. "Lack of experience and expertise is a major problem for beginning businesswomen. As women, we usually come from backgrounds with little or no business experience, but have great plans for doing fantastic things in the business world. It just can't be done that way. You must pay your dues somewhere along the line," she stresses. "If you want to start a company, you should get exposure in some aspect of the business area you plan to enter. For example, if you want to open a boutique, to gain experience, work in a boutique or department store. I've found that this type of firsthand experience is invaluable."

Developing hands-on experience is half the battle; financial managements skills are a must to keep the ship afloat. But going to business school is not a requirement. "Anyone without a business background who is considering ownership should take an accounting course. It will give you a very good business overview. For example, you'll learn about balance sheets, profit and losses, and cash flow statements, and how they work. You don't need to come out of an accounting course knowing how to audit books but it will give you an opportunity to learn business mechanics," she says. "Another good course is finance. But if you can't attend school, there are good books on these subjects."

Thompson also suggests having a good attitude: "Don't go into business thinking that someone owes you something. If you have that feeling, you are bound to fail." Instead, she says, get as much experience and expertise beforehand and your road to business ownership will be somewhat smoother.

Recently, Thompson joined her brother at General Railroad Equipment & Services, Inc., a family-owned business. She is vice-president, Marketing. The company designs and manufactures freight railroad cars. In addition, the company produces large metal fabrications. General Railroad has two plant locations in the State of Illinois and employs 260 people.

Frankie Jennings
Owner and President,
Frankie Jennings Cosmetics, Inc.
Atlanta, Georgia

After her college days at Albany State College, Frankie Jennings became a nurse. It was a satisfying career but a modestly paying one. To augment her take-home pay, she sold Vivian Woodward Cosmetics part-time, and enjoyed selling thoroughly. When her sales climbed, she took the risk of leaving nursing to sell cosmetics full-time. The risk paid off; she sold her way to a distributorship and the company's 1971 "President Pacesetter Award" for excellence in marketing and the 1975 "Eastern Regional Countess Award" for top Eastern recruiter. Selling was satisfying, but selling for another was limiting.

"After Vivian Woodward was phased out, I had the choice of returning to nursing or opening my own company. I chose the latter. I wanted to develop a line of oils and lotions which would be distributed through home demonstrations," she remembers. "My first step was to contact New York-based companies that mass produce huge volumes of skin care products. These products can be purchased and marketed under any individual, group, or company name. Although the availability of these products was ample, I was looking for a superior product. I by-passed these companies and developed my own line from scratch."

It wasn't easy for Jennings to develop a cosmetic line. It meant plenty of footwork, hours of research and testing, and picking salable products. "I had to select my own fragrance and other ingredients. I went to perfume houses to sample and test about a hundred essences. Finally, I selected five essences which would be the basis for my seventeen products," she recalls. "Some people thought seventeen products were too many to begin with, but I reasoned that we needed enough merchandise to display at home demonstrations. I ended up with three body care kits for women, each containing five items including bath solution, perfumed body oil, cream massage lotion, eau de cologne, and creme perfume. We also have two items for men including after shave lotion."

Jennings's careful selection of products was only stage one to realizing her goals. "Many of us have great ideas but don't get past the idea stage because of financing. I went to three different banks and was turned down by each. They felt the cosmetic business was too risky. I then took my proposal to an investor who also wasn't interested," she recalls. "So I turned to my five thousand dollars savings and got a second mortgage of seven thousand on my house. With this twelve thousand, I made my initial investment."

Her life savings and home were at stake, but Jennings believed in her company. Would others? Testing the idea was the key. "I went door to door, asking people if they liked the products, prices, and asking for suggestions on getting people to come to demonstration shows. My husband Roy was also invaluable in helping with market research," she says. People loved the product. In February of 1978, it all came together. Jennings began recruiting and training consultants.

Today, Frankie Jennings Cosmetics, Inc., has grown into a thriving business. Its success is partly based on a unique philosophy. "My product's name is Murl, which is a line of body care and relaxation kits for women and men. Our oils, lotions, and other products are designed to stimulate relaxation and assist in total body care," she beams. "My idea is that the average person cannot go away often for a relaxing weekend or to a spa. So I said, 'Let's create a relaxation experience around the daily bath time. Why not turn the bath time into a ritual by creating a mood?'" Jennings reasoned that the average person takes the shower or bath for granted and the bath's beautiful potential has been dampened by quick showers and fast baths. Murl Products, she says, are created specifically to enhance the ritual of the bath.

Jennings's relaxation experience, "The Murl Interlude," centers around a forty-minute luxurious bath. She invites customers to devote this time exclusively to themselves and consider it a special time of day. "We tell customers to select a big fluffy towel to use only for 'interludes,' a beautiful gown, a candle, and soft music for the background. To go on your 'interlude,' light the candle, prepare your water, and step in. Now go on a mental trip by visualizing yourself on a beach or in an open green field. Think of it mentally until you feel the water or grass, which will create a perfect moment of rest," she says. "Participation in this ritual will help you require less sleep, think more clearly, and make more precise decisions. When relaxation is an ongoing daily process, you'll relax, cool out, and create a space for yourself. Many customers say they feel better and are more effective as a result."

Jennings's unusual approach to cosmetics comes in a period of "body and mental consciousness." Many want to reduce stress and live more productive lives. Her tapping of this steadily growing group contributes to the company's success. Now Murl is displayed in hundreds of homes because more than fifty consultants sell the products in Atlanta, Louisville, Cincinnati, Rockford (Illinois), New Orleans, Milwaukee, Charlotte, and Detroit. The company's growth is expanding. With the help of a Small Business Administration loan, the company now manufactures in house all thirty of its products and does private label packaging for other companies.

Dorue Lin
Owner, Dorue et Enfants
Pittsburgh, Pennsylvania*

Dorue et Enfants (Dorue and Children), a made-to-order clothing salon in Pittsburgh, Pennsylvania, is a business which was born at home. Dorue Lin prides herself on having a unique business in the Pittsburgh area. A customer can bring in a sketch or an idea, and the family will design and produce a custom-made garment.

Dorue had dreamed of owning her own salon since childhood. To pursue that dream she attended the Art Institute of Pittsburgh and the La Grande Chic School of Fashion Design in Detroit. After school Dorue worked at a variety of jobs, including factory assembly-line worker, millinery designer, and designer for a small fashion house in Pittsburgh.

In the fifties, while her children were young, she began to design and make clothes and hats for customers at home. She opened a millinery shop in 1963, but was forced to close.

Dorue closed her shop, but soon after resumed her home-sewing business. "People said that creating custom-made garments was a dying art," she said. "But I was determined to be a success!" As the business grew she began to sponsor fashion shows and as a result customers began beating a path to her door. Forced to expand, she opened her clothing salon eleven years ago. Today, she employs other workers and trains volunteers. She also travels throughout the United States and Europe to promote her business.

Dorue urges women who have talent or an idea to test it at home

---

* This profile is excerpted from the author's article "Home Grown Businesses," *Essence,* November 1978.

first, and if a skill is involved, to get some professional training to hone any rough edges. She says it is wise to separate family demands from business, although this can be extremely difficult if you have young children.

Recently, Dorue married. Her husband is a T'ai Chi Ch'uan teacher. To incorporate their two loves, Dorue has expanded her business to include a fitness center.

Ruth Clark
President
Clark Unlimited Personnel, Inc.
New York, New York

Ruth Clark was the first Black woman to start a temporary personnel agency in New York City, and today Clark Unlimited Personnel (CUP) is reportedly the largest Black company of its type on the East Coast. She is the recipient of numerous industry awards and currently sits on the Board of Directors of the New York Association of Temporary Services (CUP is also a member of the group).

Ruth Clark ventured into business ownership because she had an extremely strong desire to go into her own business, as well as do something for the Black community. "In March of 1974, I took thirty-nine hundred dollars of my savings and incorporated Clark Unlimited Personnel," she remembers. "In the beginning, it was bleak, but I never gave up. Every morning, I arrived at the office at eight or eight-thirty, stayed until ten at night, and had Saturday off. I went to sleep on Friday nights, slept straight through, and went back to the office Sunday mornings. In those days, I worked six days a week. But for the first six or seven months of the business, I didn't take a salary. When I did take a salary, it was only a hundred fifty a week."

Clark's dedication paid off. She is aggressively pursuing the lion's share of the temporary industry against established competition like Kelly Services. Her clientele now includes over 300 Fortune 500 companies such as CBS, Chase Manhattan Bank, General Electric, and the New York Telephone Company. "At the close of 1980, we grossed two million dollars," she says of the rapidly growing business. "In January of 1977, we founded Clark Unlimited Placement, to place permanent employees. Since its incorporation, the agency has been a great success. We have placed applicants in all phases of the corporate structure."

Five and a half years after starting Clark Unlimited Personnel, Clark opened a Wall Street office to accommodate her downtown accounts. "We are now the only Black agency to have two locations in the greater metropolitan area. We have plans of expanding our offices around the country," she says.

Part of Clark's success is counseling her applicants on job-hunting techniques. "We counsel women to exude confidence and look the part of the desired job during a job interview. I tell them that many people who do not necessarily have all the qualifications get jobs because they show the right attitude, ability to learn, and have the right appearance," she says. "We also advise them to write a good résumé."

For the woman who wants to start a temporary personnel agency, Clark advises, "Although it may be difficult in the beginning, you have to stick to it. Never lose sight of your goal, particularly when success doesn't come quickly enough," she advises. "Setting realistic goals is very important. But, more than that, always be honest with yourself and your clients when filling contracts. This will establish a track record of reliability that is essential to any service industry. Start small and slowly build your business. Sometimes we start off on a grand scale and six months later we're out of business."

A woman who began a business with limited savings but a great deal of drive and persistence, Ruth Clark has shown that it can be done. Her success is a lesson to us all.

Barbara DuMetz
Photographer and Owner of Photography Business
Los Angeles, California

Barbara DuMetz is owner of her own photography business and relies on advertising agencies for free-lance assignments. Her list of clients include Toyota, Kraft, and Proline; and her photographs have appeared in *Essence, Black Enterprise,* and *Ebony.*

A career changer, she left the security of retailing to strike out on her own in photography. "When I realized that photography was something that I could do, I became interested in it as a career. It was easy for me to see photography as a way to make money because my grandfather was a photographer," recalls DuMetz. "I feel a job should be a way of expressing yourself."

Moving to Los Angeles from the East Coast, DuMetz enrolled in Art

Center College of Design, where she majored in photography. Afterward she opened her business and began showing her work. In a competitive field, she is slowly etching out a lucrative career. "Photography is relatively hard to break into because of the limited amount of work available, and the large number of photographers."

DuMetz's photography assignments are varied. "I am really good at still life food shots, and shots for commercial advertisements. I ultimately hope to complete a portfolio on just food. Food photography is a specialty."

Being a photographer is rough because the business is highly competitive. "Maintain some professionalism," DuMetz says. "Don't take jobs which are over your head—you might not have the equipment or personnel to handle some of the larger jobs. If you mess up, your reputation gets soiled."

Her career advice: "Make sure you have the right kind of information, schooling, technique, and training. After school, apprentice with a professional who knows the business," she advises. "Or if you're not a hustler or go-getter, you can find a job as a staff photographer. There are many photographic specialties you can pursue. If you like journalism and traveling, there's travel photography and fashion photography."

Rose McQueen Harris
Owner, Park Avenue Children's Place,
Formerly the Children's Factory
Piscataway, New Jersey

Rose McQueen Harris epitomizes the dedicated educator. For two years, she taught school at Roosevelt Elementary School, and after school she became the administrator, curriculum designer, and evaluator for a preschool, the Children's Factory, located in her home. She soon left teaching to run the Children's Factory full-time.

Harris's humanitarian drive began when she was a freshman at the State University of New York at Stony Brook buckling down to begin premedical studies. She finished with a B.S. in biology and wanted to attend medical school but chose marriage instead. Redirecting her original goals, she applied and was accepted to a master's program in education at New York University and received an M.A. in elementary education.

Armed with her master's degree, Harris began working at Hillcrest School in Somerset, New Jersey, but her old desire to work in the health field reappeared. Combining her two loves, health and education, she accepted a position as a health educator at a neighborhood clinic in Plainfield, New Jersey, and remained there five years. Afterward, she moved to the Newark Health Department in the same role, for two years.

The demands of being a health educator conflicted with home pressures. Harris needed a job closer to home because her children were young. Traveling from her home in Piscataway to Newark became burdensome. When a position opened in Roosevelt Elementary School, she decided to take it.

So, impressed with the results of teaching several years, she began thinking of ways to independently expand upon career development in the field. Unexpectedly her baby-sitter instigated a career breakthrough by announcing to Harris her intention to marry and her need of a better-paying job. Harris, who did not want to lose this valuable employee, toyed with ideas to keep and pay her. The Children's Factory had its beginning. She decided to start a preschool for a small group of two to five children and to develop a curriculum for her baby-sitter to implement. She wanted to start on a small scale and the first year she worked on applications, health forms, educational units, and trips for the four to five children the school accommodated.

Harris developed her school with planning, implementation, and careful follow-through. First, she wrote to the State Department of Education and asked for applications for a day care license. Then she went to the municipal government to determine zoning information. Fortunately, in New Jersey, if a school has less than five children, there is no licensing needed. She chose a name because the school had to be registered with the state. She also had to register with the State Bureau of Taxation and look into unemployment and disability insurance for her employee. The Internal Revenue Service was also contacted for tax purposes.

All schools need insurance coverage. Harris selected a good insurance policy to insure the children, her house, and employee. Because she planned to serve meals, she contacted the Health Department to determine if the school's meals were in compliance. The Health Department was also helpful in giving information on immunization and health records.

The Children's Factory opened its doors slowly after Harris advertised in a local paper to attract parents. Her advertising was concise and professional so that a parent could gain insight into the school's services. After she advertised, people called and appointments were made with both parents. She encouraged parents to attend interviews while school was in session so that their children could play and see how they fit in. Once parents and their children were accepted into the program, she held an open house so the children could meet the teachers and lessen the anxiety of separation from their parents.

The Children's Factory's name has recently been changed to the Park Avenue Children's Place.

Career Aids

Books and Pamphlets

1. *A Woman's Guide to Starting a Business,* by Genie Chipps and Claudia Jessup ($6.70 paper), Henry Holt and Company.
2. *Minority Capital Resource Handbook: A Guide to Raising Capital for Minority Entrepreneurs* ($5.00) from:
   The Securities Industry Association
   120 Broadway
   New York, N.Y. 10271

Government and Other Organizations

1. The Small Business Administration
   1441 L St., NW
   Washington, D.C. 20416
2. The Minority Business Development Agency (MBDA)
   Department of Commerce
   Main Commerce Building
   14th and Constitution Ave., NW
   Washington, D.C. 20230
3. American Women's Economic Development Corporation
   60 East 42nd St.
   New York, N.Y. 10065

Professional Organizations

1. The National Association of Negro Business and Professional
   Women's Clubs
   1806 New Hampshire Ave., NW
   Washington, D.C. 20009
2. National Association of Minority Contractors
   1250 I St. NW
   Suite 505
   Washington, D.C. 20005
3. The National Association of Women Business Owners
   1722 Connecticut Ave.
   Washington, D.C. 20009
4. National Association of Black Women Entrepreneurs
   P.O. Box 1375
   Detroit, Mich. 963-8766
5. American Association of Black Women Entrepreneurs
   2300 South Elm/Eugene Street
   Greensboro, N.C. 27406

All addresses are subject to change.

12

Soft-Sell Careers

SALES

Many of you may shy away from sales because you feel it is a field which doesn't fit your personality. You may think of salespeople as aggressive hard-sellers who push their intentions on others in order to close a deal. But sales isn't really like that.

Sales is an organized method of persuading others to purchase. It involves pinpointing potential customers' needs and wants, creating and carrying out a convincing sales presentation, and after the deal is closed, delivering the goods or services as the need occurs. It takes heavy research, long hours, time management, record keeping, and persuasion techniques to close the deal.

As a salesperson, you will be in an important position in the company, because you will contribute directly to its profits. Sales can often lead to management or upper-echelon positions, since you can prove your worth tangibly through sales. You will in most instances have flexible hours, field work, and supervisors who don't breathe down your neck. Travel might be included in your job duties. If you receive a commission, you can bring home fat paychecks. And if you want to switch careers, sales is one area of business which doesn't require a Master of Business Administration degree (M.B.A.).

Sales also offers the opportunity to rectify some of the conditions complained about in other careers. For example, in sales, working hard and spending extra time on the job can often lead to fat commissions, vacations, product or cash bonuses, and other incentives.

Career Pathing in Sales

Sales has many opportunities in many different areas: consumer products, industrial, office equipment, radio and television time, direct sales, pharmaceuticals, print advertising space, securities, medical supplies and equipment, real estate, insurance, new technology, and other areas.

Manufacturer salespeople and wholesale salespeople are two general categories of sales workers. Manufacturer sales workers usually sell nontechnical products for one manufacturer, by visiting firms in their territory.[1] But some may work in the highly technical electronic equipment field. Wholesale salespeople work for a wholesaler who can handle hundreds of similar products, which must be successfully moved from factories to customers.[2]

To become a manufacturer salesperson, you don't necessarily need a college degree, but it is becoming, increasingly, a must in the selling of some products.[3] For example, if you want to sell pharmaceutical products, you will probably need a knowledge of pharmaceuticals and the human body. If you are going to work with electrical equipment, you may need special training in the area.

For wholesale sales work, educational requirements will also depend on the product, but some of these workers have worked their way up from entry-level positions in wholesale firms.[4] Along with training, you will also need good communication skills, both verbal and written.

To get hired, sales experience is a plus, but not always necessary. In addition, you must be able to sell yourself in the interview situation. Attend seminars that will help you prepare résumés and gain tips on how to obtain entry-level sales positions.

When hired, you will probably be placed in a training program that will familiarize you with the company, product, customer population, and competition. On-the-job training will follow.

From sales you may be able to work your way up to sales management, first on the district, then regional level, and then your responsibilities will include supervising other salespeople. To gain additional training at this level, Sales and Marketing Executives International, Inc. sponsors the Graduate School of Sales Management and Marketing at Syracuse University.

What Will You Earn as a Salesperson?

Sales salaries are as varied as the field itself. Full-time manufacturers' salespeople have median annual earnings of $23,400. Top earners make more than $44,200 a year.[5]

Full-time wholesale trade sales workers' median weekly salaries are about $450; top earners make more than $850 a week.[6]

CAREER PROFILE

Rose TenEyck is in radio sales. Her career story will be helpful to prospective saleswomen.

Rose TenEyck
National Sales Manager
KGO NewsTalk Radio
San Francisco, California

Rose TenEyck attended Nassau Community College and was working on a degree at Hofstra University but postponed its completion to work. A personnel agency directed her to Dancer, Fitzgerald, Sample, an advertising agency, and she started work in the media research department. A good supervisor and other staffers taught her research mechanics and she augmented on-the-job training with courses at Bernard Baruch College.

She was in constant contact with media research and broadcast sales workers. Through those experiences, TenEyck became interested in sales. "While in media research, I became familiar with people in the

broadcast sales department, who bought time in the buying end of advertising. I found broadcast sales challenging and lucrative and decided
to move into the area," she remembers. "But I couldn't jump from
media research into sales. I therefore developed a career plan to accomplish this. My first strategy was to move to a higher level of research. I
applied and was accepted as research director for a small radio representative firm."

Work as research director broadened TenEyck's experience. "I managed to get the job because of my knowledge of the advertising business
and research," she said. "Work at the rep firm was good experience. A
radio representative firm nationally represents a station. For example, a
San Francisco radio station may hire a rep firm to get advertising agencies in New York, Chicago, and Los Angeles to buy time on the station.
But generally, a representative firm can handle upwards of seventy-five
to a hundred stations nationwide."

Her research directorship bridged the experience gap between research at a representative firm and a radio station. "Once I had the
research director experience, I was able to apply that to a similar job at
a radio station. That experience landed me a job as research director at
KGO Radio, an ABC-owned station in San Francisco," she says. "In
research, we provided information salespeople needed for client
presentations. My ultimate goal was sales, but in research I would work
closely with salespeople. Sometimes, I actually went out on client calls
with them."

The career planning and strategizing paid off. Two years later,
TenEyck moved into sales but not with KGO. The station had no immediate sales openings. There was, however, another division of ABC,
ABC Radio Spot Sales, the in-house national representative for ABC-
FM stations. "A national radio representative firm represents four of
the seven ABC-owned stations, but the in-house representative firm
handled the ABC-FM stations and about thirty independently owned
stations. I worked there for a year until ABC phased out the division,"
she remembers. "Luckily, KGO asked me to return and join their local
sales staff."

As an account executive, TenEyck landed her dream job. "I serviced
assigned advertising agencies and their clients. If they wanted to buy
radio air time for a commercial or have a particular advertising campaign which needs extensive radio coverage, it was my responsibility to
help them come up with a time schedule," she says. "But my job wasn't

simply helping them decide the best times the commercials should air. First, I prepared presentations to convince them to retain our station. There's tough competition in San Francisco because there are about sixty-four stations. My presentation included giving a summary of the station, listing our unique features, presenting our personalities, giving them statistics on the listening audience, and convincing them of reasons to choose us. For new clients, I used similar methods to drum up business." Recently, she was promoted to National Sales Manager.

Primarily TenEyck uses speaking and writing skills. "There's a great deal of letter writing, particularly when preparing a new pitch. There's verbal communication when I'm doing a presentation," she stresses. "Because of the importance of presentations to clients, the best preparation for radio sales is some experience in marketing, sales, or public speaking. Also, writing courses will be beneficial when preparing written presentations."

But acquiring these requisites will not assure landing a radio sales position. The competition is keen and astute career planning is necessary. "It's very difficult to walk in and get a radio sales job without previous experience. First, you may have to go to a small market and work up to a larger one," TenEyck advises. "For example, a friend had to go to a smaller town and sell for a small radio station to gain radio selling experience. Or if you can gain access to another broadcast position, it's then easier to move into sales."

Also, TenEyck feels the M.B.A. may not necessarily be a substitution for sales experience. "The M.B.A. may give you an edge in getting a radio sales position but that depends on the station," she suggests. "The M.B.A. is probably more marketable in moving up through the corporate ranks of broadcast sales and operations," she says. "In considering a career in time sales, it's probably easier to break into radio than television. There are more radio stations per market than television stations, which results in more opportunities to apply for available positions."

TenEyck challenges Black women to consider radio sales because it's rewarding and lucrative. "At our station, we get a salary plus commission. I would say the average salary is about $35,000 a year," she says.

To break into this exciting, lucrative field, you must develop a firm career plan, talk to those in the field, and move deliberately toward your goal. TenEyck decided early to embark upon a radio sales career, set her sights on it, and plotted each move. Today, she is reaping the handsome rewards.

INSURANCE

When many of you think about careers in insurance, you picture the aggressive salesperson calling or visiting people in an effort to sell life insurance policies. Many of you may not totally understand the valuable role insurance plays in our lives and as a result do not pursue careers in the field. Many see insurance as focusing on death and may simply wish to avoid a career which stresses the hereafter. However, insurance is a multifaceted business which touches us as we live, as well as after we're gone.

How would you pay for escalating hospital costs without insurance? If you died, could your family survive without your income? If your home or apartment was burglarized or destroyed by fire, could you replace your losses? Could you pay for injuries or the deaths of others in the event of an accident in your car? How would you rebuild your home if a tornado destroyed it? If you own a business, how would you replace supplies, records, and other valuables in cases of fire, vandalism, or robbery at your place of business?

Insurance protects you and your loved ones in the event of these and other potential disasters. It is a billion-dollar industry with an increasing growth potential as more people, homes, transportation vehicles, and businesses require additional protection.[1]

The key is to move into positions that will have ultimate impact on the lives of those in your community: sales, underwriting, and management. For example, an estate sales agent can help a family gain protection in the event of the death of the breadwinner.

Career Pathing in Insurance

Two important insurance areas are life and property/liability (fire and casualty) insurance. Three of the industry's occupations are underwriters, agents and brokers.

Underwriters

Underwriters determine which risks insurance companies will take by scrutinizing applications carefully, and approving or denying them based on their own judgments and the company's past experiences. Most specialize in a particular insurance area: life, property and liability, or health. Or they can specialize in individual or group policies. Some, called commercial account underwriters, specialize in business insurance. Others specialize by type of risk insured like fire, automobile, marine, or workers' compensation.[2]

A college degree is increasingly important for entry-level underwriter positions. A liberal arts and business administration background are marketable for an underwriter trainee position.

To advance, you should continue your education. Once you have experience, you can pursue additional educational opportunities for which many insurance companies will pay tuition costs.

Agents and Brokers

Agents and brokers are the industry's salespeople who sell policies to individuals and businesses. They can sell one or more types of insurance: life, property/liability (casualty), and health.[3]

Life insurance agents, also known as life underwriters, primarily sell policies that pay survivors after deaths. These policies can also be designed for retirement income or to finance educational costs for a policyholder's children.

Casualty insurance agents offer policies that protect policyholders from financial losses resulting from fires, theft, automobile accidents, or other losses. They also work in the industrial or commercial lines—product liability, medical malpractice insurance, or workers' compensation areas.[4]

Underwriters who work in the health area, sell policies to help policyholders combat escalating hospital and medical care or income loss from illness or injury.[5]

Agents may work as salaried or salary plus commission employees for a company, or as independent brokers who can represent one or more companies. Brokers do not work exclusively for any company, but place policies with companies which best serve their clients' needs.

The college degree will qualify you best to become an agent or broker, but many agents and brokers are not college graduates. You must also be licensed by the state where you work and licensing requirements include passing a written examination.

Once on the job, you will get a great deal of on-the-job training. Your hours will be flexible, but many evenings and weekends may be spent in meeting with clients.

You will be encouraged to gain additional life insurance knowledge and several insurance industry organizations provide this. You may want to get a diploma from the Life Underwriter Training Council (LUTC), which is awarded after successfully completing a two year life insurance program. Once experienced, you may want to pursue the Chartered Life Underwriter (CLU) designation, which requires passing a series of examinations given by the American College of Bryn Mawr, Pennsylvania. As a property/liability agent, you can earn the designation Chartered Property and Casualty Underwriter (CPCU) conferred by the American Institute of Property and Liability Underwriters.

What Will You Earn as an Insurance Professional?

A survey of property and liability insurance companies reveals that noncommercial underwriters make median salaries of $21,500 a year; commercial lines underwriters make $21,200 a year; senior personal lines underwriters make $27,000; underwriting supervisors earn approximately $31,000; underwriting managers make about $37,000 a year.[6]

Many large companies pay insurance agents approximately $1,200 a month during training, according to the Department of Labor, Bureau of Labor Statistics. Life insurance workers with five to ten years' experience have a median salary of $35,000; those with ten or more years make $55,000; and many make more than $100,000.[7]

CAREER PROFILES

LaVerne I. Stephens and Joyce Johnson work in insurance. Each has an unusual and helpful career story.

LaVerne I. Stephens
Claims Consultant
Group Insurance
Metropolitan Life Insurance Company
New York, New York

Thirty-seven years ago, LaVerne Stephens was both a night student at City College of the City University of New York and an employee of Metropolitan Life Insurance Company. She began her career at Metropolitan Life as a mail distributor in the Personal Life Division. At the time it was difficult for Black women with only high school diplomas to get substantial positions. But Stephens persevered and moved quickly from mail distributor to various clerical jobs.

Since she wanted to remain in insurance, she transferred to the College of Insurance, the industry's only college, and Metropolitan's tuition reimbursement program helped finance her education.

After beginning her college career, she was transferred to the Group Department. During her second year in the department, she began taking computer courses in a school in Orange, New Jersey, and continued to pursue College of Insurance studies. She used the computer training to assist in setting up a computer program in the billing system of Group Accounts.

From there, she was transferred into Group Life's death claims. She moved rapidly from assistant claims approver to senior claims approver and ultimately supervisor of the claims unit. As assistant claims approver, she did correspondence; as a claims approver, she approved death claims. As senior claims approver, she was responsible for claims which presented problems. For example, if more than one person claims to be beneficiary, a senior claims approver may step in. Or there may be foreign beneficiaries or accidental deaths. Her unit dealt primarily with company groups. If a company's employee died, the employer let them know and they determined the beneficiaries and processed the claim.

While an approver, Stephens received her bachelor's degree from the College of Insurance. But competition was keen. Claim approvers were hired with college degrees. To advance, Stephens needed an M.B.A. She received one at Fordham University.

With M.B.A. in hand, Stephens was offered the position of group representative in the newly created sales office at Metropolitan. Her responsibilities included drumming up sales to new customers and serving existing ones.

Stephens feels that group insurance sales offers vast opportunities for women. "Being in my present job means having a career; my supervisor's position was just a job," she says. Her drive, ambition, and hard work have eased this courageous woman up the corporate ladder. She recently made a lateral move to the position of claims consultant. She writes guidelines and procedures according to changes in law or company policy.

Joyce Johnson
Insurance/Financial Planning
New York, New York

After attending Howard University, Joyce Johnson began a teaching career, in Montessori Schools. She became a head teacher at one in Washington, D.C., but relocated to New York. In New York she remained in the field of education and became an early-childhood specialist for the Day Care Council of New York. She worked at City College of the City University of New York on a study concerning discrimination in children and was also on the staffs of the NAACP and WNET's children's workshop.

Her career pathing into insurance was accidental. "I was trying to get a friend a job and my district manager recruited me," she remembers. Although Johnson was not sure how well she'd do in this new field of insurance, contacts that she'd made through previous employment helped. "In my first four months, I sold 1.4 million dollars in insurance. When I started, my friends were very supportive and helpful. I knew a great many people in a variety of fields, which was also helpful," Johnson says. "Selling insurance is not an easy job, but it's not hard either. It depends on your outlook and number of contacts. It's a job where you must go out, get your own clients and often educate them about insurance—that can be difficult."

Although the novice may experience problems in making contacts, Johnson says contacts are essential. "This is a referral business. If you have one friend, she must also have a friend. Or her friend must have a neighbor or know someone who is getting married, buying a house, getting divorced, having a child, or starting a business," she advises. "I tell trainees to ask for at least ten names from one friend or referral. If they get five, they are fortunate. From these five names, none might be interested, but they will refer them to someone who might be." A good agent should expand her business to include other markets and cities. Johnson has clients in Washington, D.C., Maryland, Virginia, New Jersey, New York, and Connecticut.

This astute businesswoman says the key to success is to prepare yourself for all types of markets. "It's very important to have a supervisor who can swing you into a variety of markets. When many Blacks come in, they rely primarily on their friends. Today, however, there are Black businesses that we can now tap. Black businesses are a viable market. You should not rely solely on the 'across the kitchen table' approach, but also hit the professional/business market," she advises.

Having credentials within the insurance field is also important. "Everyone in life insurance should get the Chartered Life Underwriter (CLU) designation, which I am studying for now. It gives you the opportunity to learn the insurance business," Johnson says. "It's fine to sell $10,000 or $100,000 in insurance, but the CLU can put you solidly in the business market. The CLU will enable you to understand the jargon of business people, for instance. You will have the knowledge to advise potential business clients. 'If your business value is this, you should have this amount of coverage to protect your estate, family, et cetera.' The CLU will put you on the level of one of their professional representatives. Of course, you can establish this type of expertise without the additional credential, but the CLU helps tremendously."

Making contacts and obtaining credentials contribute to success in the insurance field, but the number of sales is important and newcomers should give some thought to their companies' compensation policies. "As an agent, you may be either a company's employee or a broker who is an independent business person. Compensation depends on the company. Some have straight salary arrangements, but you get a portion of the commission. Others come in on straight commission, particularly those transferring from other companies.

"I came in on the salary plus commission arrangement, which was a guarantee that my bills would be paid," Johnson says. "Now, I'm basically a broker. I am not salaried but an independent business person. It's similar to having an agency within an agency. I have the right to sell insurance for different companies."

Johnson advises that when selling insurance, you should have your customers consider all the aspects of insurance besides death benefits. "I don't sell insurance to people primarily for their beneficiaries' use after death. If I am selling whole life insurance, I want my customers to use it for a variety of purposes like investments, real estate, or whatever they desire," she says. "I think you should be able to sell everything in your portfolio. But before you can do this, you must understand everything, and you should get as much information about the different offerings as possible. Then practice and develop your skills as you are learning the business."

Recently, Ms. Johnson added financial planning services for her clients.

REAL ESTATE

The real estate professional's work is multifaceted. She must locate suitable housing for tenants as well as potential homeowners. She might also manage rental properties. She can help in the rehabilitation of old properties and may handle conversion from rental to condominiums. She may help business people who want to remain in urban areas and find suitable space for others who want to relocate.

In the past, many of us have viewed real estate from only one perspective: residential. We are now exploring the many other opportunities that the field can offer. Women are slowly moving into commercial leasing—handling apartment units, office buildings, complexes, and shopping centers. We are engaging in property management—overseeing rentals, maintenance, and handling tenant relocations. We have moved into real estate appraisal—working as appraisers who determine property values for government agencies such as the Federal Housing Administration (FHA).

Real estate careerists have moved in limited numbers into the area of sales and mortgage banking—facilitating the financing of investment properties. Some are involved in real estate securities and syndication, which brings property investors together in partnerships to purchase large properties.[1]

But there are other real estate specialties, like land development— revitalizing unused land for marketable ventures like shopping centers —which remain largely untapped. Nor are many involved in real estate research, where forecasts and trends of the field are analyzed and disseminated. Real estate counseling is another area.[2] (For real estate specialties, see Table 31.)

Career Pathing in Real Estate

Real estate careers usually begin with sales. To become an agent, you must be licensed. Qualifying requirements for licensing include, in addition to a high school diploma, passing a written examination. Most states require thirty hours of classroom instruction. You may, however, feel more comfortable taking real estate courses to help prepare you for the examination. These courses can be taken at junior colleges, colleges, universities, adult education programs, or courses sponsored by many local real estate boards that are National Association of Realtors® members. Some schools offer the bachelor's degree in real estate.[3]

After passing the examination, you will generally become affiliated with a real estate firm involved in residential sales. Your work will involve learning about the neighborhood in which you will be selling. You must assess those neighborhood characteristics that will interest potential homeowners.

When buying homes, people are concerned with good schools for their children, churches in proximity to their homes, convenient transportation networks, good stores nearby, and proper maintenance of the neighborhood through efficient sanitation services. A real estate agent must scan neighborhoods, noting their advantages and disadvantages. Then you will match your clients effectively with the kinds of neighborhoods that they want to live in.

After you've acquired sales experience, you may want to become a broker. You must be licensed. To do this, you will be required to take the qualifying examination for which you will have to be sponsored by a broker; and you will need at least ninety hours of formal training and usually one to three years of selling experience. In some states, a bachelor's degree in real estate can be used in lieu of work experience.

As a broker, you will be an independent business owner who can close real estate deals. As your business grows you will employ salespeople to work for you.

If you are interested in commercial leasing, using your sales license and work experience as a base, you can approach commercial leasing

TABLE 31

REAL ESTATE SPECIALTIES*

RESIDENTIAL BROKERAGE
Largest single field of real estate activity.
> Good opportunities for rapid advancement and increasing income.
> Requires broad knowledge of community and neighborhoods, economics, real estate law, finance, and the money market.

COMMERCIAL BROKERAGE
Specializing in income-producing properties (for example: apartment and office buildings, retail stores, warehouses).

INDUSTRIAL BROKERAGE
Developing, selling, or leasing properties for industry or manufacturing.

FARM AND LAND BROKERAGE
Not necessarily limited to farm land. Cities often require rural land for expansion; farm management for absentee owners also a possibility.
> On-the-job training a must; formal agricultural training an advantage.

REAL ESTATE APPRAISING
Gathering and evaluating all facts affecting property's value, and rendering an opinion of that value.
> Many different types—assessed value; insured value; loan value; market value.
> Some appraising knowledge required for any real estate work.

PROPERTY MANAGEMENT
Supervising every aspect of the property's operation to produce the highest possible financial return over the longest period of time.
> Includes renting, tenant relations, building maintenance and repair, supervising personnel and tradesmen, accounting, and advertising.

LAND DEVELOPMENT
Turning raw land into marketable, profitable subdivisions, shopping centers, industrial parks, etc.

Includes selecting sites, analyzing costs, securing financing, contracting for physical buildings, supervising construction, and promoting finished development to prospects.

URBAN PLANNING
Anticipating city's future growth, and proposing productive, economical ways of using land and water resources to accommodate this growth.

REAL ESTATE SECURITIES AND SYNDICATION
Developing and offering limited partnership in real estate for investment purposes.

Generates capital for expanding the real estate industry.

Gives individuals the opportunity to invest in large properties without becoming involved in management or exposed to unlimited liability.

REAL ESTATE COUNSELING
Giving advice about property, frequently on productive uses for different kinds, or income opportunities.

REAL ESTATE RESEARCH
Providing precise information on land use, urban environmental patterns, and market trends.

Physical—finding ways to improve buildings.

Economic—compiling data for future planning—probable demand for new homes, percentage of substandard housing, changes in financing and interest rates, effects of urban planning programs, etc.

* Source: *Careers in Real Estate,* published by the National Association of Realtors®. Reprinted with permission.

brokers. You should take courses in commercial leasing at colleges and universities which offer them. This will enhance your knowledge of this area of the real estate industry.

If you have an interest in property management, it is best to affiliate with a firm which specializes in this area. You may begin as a management assistant and move into a manager's slot after acquiring experience. If you want to improve your professionalism, you can take courses offered by organizations like the National Association of Realtors® local boards or sponsored by the Real Estate Management Brokers Institute (REMBI), an affiliate of the National Association of Real Estate Brokers, Inc., the minority professional real estate organization.

If you want to become an appraiser, you will determine property values for insurance companies, private agencies, attorneys who need appraisal work for their clients, government agencies, and individuals who need appraisal information.[4] The work is detailed, exacting, and requires an aptitude for figures.

Appraisal courses are available through some National Association of Realtors® affiliates, or through the National Society of Real Estate Appraisers (NSREA).

You can also move into sales and mortgage brokerage, industrial brokerage, land development, real estate securities, and syndication. Farm and land brokerage may be particularly interesting considering the issues arising around Black farm and land ownership in the South.

What Will You Earn as a Real Estate Professional?

The Bureau of Labor Statistics reports that full-time real estate agents make average salaries of $19,000 a year; real estate brokers make approximately $31,600 a year.[5]

CAREER PROFILES

Sheryl Warren-Carey is an investment consultant; Judith Smith is a co-partner of a real estate property management firm.

Sheryl Warren-Carey
Investment Consultant
Beverly Hills, California

After graduation from Fisk University in Nashville, Sheryl Warren-Carey settled into a teaching career but found it unsuitable. She had reached a high salary level, had a master's degree, and was working on a doctorate in educational supervision but thought teaching was limiting. As a sideline, she joined two friends in a career consulting firm. Counseling others on career changing sparked her own interest in leaving teaching.

Real estate always fascinated her. Moving into the field would require taking a course, an examination, and finding employment. Warren-Carey withdrew her retirement monies and took the plunge into the unknown. "Real estate had been in the back of my mind for three or four years. But I kept saying I would get around to it. Teaching was very comfortable, secure, and I was making $20,000 a year," she reveals. "Yet if I remained a teacher, I'd only make $30,000 maximally. After giving it some thought, I enrolled in a real estate class, got my license, and stopped teaching. I drew out my retirement money and said 'This is it.' That money provided a necessary cushion, because real estate salespeople have to work on commission."

Warren-Carey convinced Red Carpet Realtors, a group of California franchised real estate agencies, to hire her for residential sales. Two years later, she had established experience and expertise in the area. Using residential sales as a foundation, she moved into position as senior investment consultant at H. Bruce Hanes. "I dealt strictly with apartment buildings by acquiring property for apartment owners. I was a finder who either sold for clients or put them into exchange situations where they were trading up for larger or more expensive units," she says.

In her primarily desk job, she spent work time securing potential clients from sources like an apartment owners' directory and making cold calls and asking to be of service. She then arranged for sales or exchanges. To upgrade services and move from strict buyer/seller relationships, Warren-Carey set her sights on establishing long-term client relationships; she was not content with one-time transactions.

Warren-Carey's work has netted large rewards. In her first six months in the investment area, she says, her $20,000 teaching salary tripled. There are big stakes: apartment buildings sales net large commissions.

Warren-Carey is now a broker. She has her own company and works with a select group of clients. She is presently dealing with rehabilitation projects and working with developers.

Warren-Carey thinks real estate offers great opportunities. "My area is very lucrative because I deal with more expensive property. Traditionally, it's not an area many Black women enter. For example, I was the first Black woman hired to join a fleet of two hundred agents," she says. "But more Black women should become interested in the investment area, and in real estate in general. Most of us have been taught to surround ourselves with security but what really is security?"

Sheryl Warren-Carey has shown that skills learned in traditionally secure areas like teaching can be transferred into more lucrative careers. She gambled and took a risk which has paid off handsomely.

Judith Smith
Vice President
Myers, Smith and Granady
New York, New York

Judith Smith left social work, became a real estate salesperson and after a few years an appraiser, and eventually a broker. Subsequently, she and two other real estate brokers joined to establish a property management firm. Myers, Smith and Granady, Inc., manages thousands of housing units in the New York area. "My firm is essentially a property management firm, but we do some sales and leasing in the midtown area. We manage thousands of housing units which are basically high-rise federally assisted housing developments. We're responsible for the day-to-day physical maintenance, rent collection, accounting and bookkeeping procedures. In addition, we supervise all staff, both administrative and maintenance. We report monthly to the owners of the project, as well as to supervisory government agencies," she points out.

Smith's twenty-year-old company began as a merger of three real estate professionals. "Each of us were individual brokers with a brokerage firm. But we recognized that the one-person brokerage outfit was really obsolete," recalls Smith. When the three merged, HUD had set guidelines encouraging minority participation on all housing levels. "Prior to that, minorities had primarily been involved in the management of run-down tenements. Blacks were given the crumbs; white firms were involved in more sophisticated type buildings. So HUD's mandate laid the foundation for our involvement. But we realized that if we were going to be involved, and meet the criteria, we would have to pool our resources," she says.

Smith, Granady, and Myers formed a strong team; each brought impressive skills. "One partner has the national and international professional designation of Certified Property Manager. The other has the Certified Resident Manager, a companion type designation from the National Association of Real Estate Brokers, Inc.," she says. "I had a real estate and social work background which is needed particularly in today's housing market. It is very important in the tenant relations role we play. As a property manager, you literally become involved in the daily lives of tenants. You are not only servicing apartments, providing heat, hot water, and clean lobbies, but we also make referrals to social agencies and provide recreational activities and senior citizen activities." The three partners' skills made the firm confident and competitive.

Smith's involvement in real estate has been rewarding. She has found career happiness and success. But she cautions prospective real estate professionals to rid themselves of myths about the field. "Sure, real estate is lucrative, and as one of my professors said, 'You can't help but make money in the field.' But there's a direct correlation between making money and putting in many hours," she advises. "You won't make money by thinking real estate is glamorous—where brokers or salespeople drive around showing clients houses all day and at the end of each week making x amount of sales. It just doesn't happen that way.

"You may have to call someone at six in the morning because it's the only time he or she is available. Or you might have an appointment at seven or eight in the evening. You can also expect to have weekend appointments fairly regularly. The name of the game is to please the client and you must make yourself available," Smith advises. "And if you're in property management, you have no control over emergencies. You may have to go to a site at any hour of the night or day. Being in real estate involves a great deal more time than an ordinary nine-to-five job. Frequently, we work all hours and certainly all hours of the weekend."

Lucrative salaries can happen but do not come to beginners. "What makes many Blacks reluctant to enter the field of real estate sales is that six months can elapse before making any money. It's strictly commission. But in some cases, you can enter an agreement with a broker. You may get some type of draw until a contract is signed which can take two or three months," she stresses. "So you really should have some other income or savings during that initial period. The financial problem keeps many Blacks out of the field."

Surviving initial financial and time hardships are real estate realities. But Smith suggests that you talk to people in the field about expectations versus realities. "Learn about the field from an insider. You may have certain images of the field, but a person in the field can help you decide whether those images are based on reality," she says.

Career Aids

For career information and a list of colleges and universities offering courses on real estate, contact:

1. The National Association of Realtors
   430 North Michigan Ave.
   Chicago, Ill. 60611
2. The National Association of Real Estate Brokers, Inc.
   1101 14th St., NW
   Suite 1000
   Washington, D.C. 20005
3. The National Society of Real Estate Appraisers, Inc.
   c/o The National Association of Real Estate Brokers, Inc.
   (Address same as above)

All addresses are subject to change.

RETAILING

When we think of retailing, we focus on the buying and selling of glamorous clothing, the hustle and bustle of crowded department stores, and the fun of being surrounded by beautiful things. We envision ourselves ultimately becoming buyers, traveling around the world, responsible for the purchase of a variety of marketable goods. Or we see ourselves climbing corporate ladders—from sales to management—and influencing this billion dollar industry.

Regardless of our retailing career fantasies, this field has not been good to Blacks. Until recently, Blacks, for the most part, have been relegated to blue-collar and service jobs. In recent years more of us held clerical than sales positions. In a pioneer report by the Council on Economic Priorities, *Help Wanted: Minorities and Women in the Retail Industry,* it was stated that "minorities held the lowest paid and dirtiest jobs" in the retail industry.[1] Now, things are somewhat better.

Today, Blacks are moving into retailing, trusting that it will provide a springboard to management positions and other careers in cosmetics, fashion, magazine publishing, advertising, public relations, personnel, or business ownership. The economy has taken a toll on the industry, but it remains an area that women want to enter and is therefore discussed here.

Career Pathing in Retailing

Retailing has several major areas including merchandising, sales promotion, and store operations. Other areas are personnel, control, and electronic data processing, but they are not discussed.

Merchandising: This is the largest and most familiar area of retailing. If your career objectives fall in the management area and your educational qualifications are sufficient, you should begin in executive training programs, setting your sights on ultimately becoming a buyer, or divisional merchandise manager.[2]

The buyer is the pivotal person from whom many merchandising activities—the buying and selling of goods—flow. Her selection of goods will determine the success or failure of a department store or specialty shop. The buyer's ingenuity and creativity in displaying goods or arranging her department will determine the volume of sales for her department. For example, she may suggest livening up junior sportswear by putting in disco music or mirrored walls. The buyer must also keep in touch with what competitors are doing and improve on their ideas. And in her pressure-filled work, she must travel constantly to the

New York, Chicago, Los Angeles, Dallas, and Philadelphia markets, hunting new finds.

An associate degree in a two-year or community college whose curriculum includes course work in retailing, fashion buying, or merchandising is one method of preparation for this work. But in today's competitive job market, you may need a bachelor's degree. In both instances, your college training should be augmented with internships in retailing establishments.

After being hired, you may be placed in executive training programs and, in many instances, given the title of assistant buyer. You will probably spend time in classroom situations and you will often be sent to branch stores to perform your tasks as an assistant buyer. Larger chains may place you in their central buying offices where you will have on-the-job training as well as classroom instruction.

After several years as an assistant buyer, which often involve relocation to different branch outlets, you may be able to move into a buyer's position. The length of time it takes to become a buyer depends on many factors, including the type of store, available buyer slots, job performance, the ability to increase sales, and how well you are perceived by management. Afterward, you may move into buying for several related departments as a divisional merchandise manager.

Sales Promotion: When we hear announcements of sales on the radio or see such advertisements on television, in newspapers, or magazines, sales promotion professionals are partly responsible for these efforts.[3] Copywriting is a vital component of the sales promotion area, and this field may be approached by attending a two-year college program that specializes in advertising and communications or getting a four-year degree. (For more information on the field, see the careers in "Advertising," chapter 8.)

When you are hired for your first job you will probably begin as a copy runner. From there you can move on to junior copywriter, then copywriter, and ultimately—you might become a chief copywriter.[4]

For those interested in art directorships via illustrator's positions, an associate degree or four-year college degree in fine arts is recommended. (For more information, see "Advertising" in chapter 8.) You can become a layout worker or artist, using lettering, photos, design, and painting to get the store's message across. From there you can advance to art director.[5]

For the future display specialist, an associate degree in display and exhibit design will train you in lighting techniques and mannequin and prop use, and give you exposure to photography, fashion design, and interior design. You will begin as an assistant display designer or window trimmer, and from that point move into display designer or display director positions.[6] Window and display people create attractive and appealing displays that attract the attention and patronage of prospective customers.

Public relations is another facet of sales promotion. As a public relations specialist, your goal will be to present and promote the company's best image to the public. In these positions, you may plan special promotional events like fashion shows, lunchtime career seminars, or special events for children. (For more information, see "Communications," chapter 7.)

Store Operations: These managers are responsible for accurate and timely store deliveries, providing customer services, and making sure the store's physical plant is maintained. You could begin in sales positions and move into service manager positions on the selling floor, or supervisor in areas like receiving or delivery. You can move up in managing several departments—ultimately moving into the position of merchandising supervisor.[7]

What Will You Earn in Retailing?

The median yearly salary is $19,500; most buyers make between $15,100 and $28,500 a year.[8]

CAREER PROFILE

As one of the few Black women buyers at Bloomingdale's, a New York department store, Gloria Hartley reached an important career plateau from her beginning as a stock clerk. She has since gone on to start her own business.

Gloria Hartley
President, CIDDA
New York, New York

Many women are attracted to retailing. Its glitter and glamour are appealing. Few realize the hard work and dedication needed to push to the top. "The road to becoming a buyer is long and difficult. There's a great deal of pressure, hard work, and long hours," says Gloria Hartley, who was a buyer for Bloomingdale's in New York and now owns a retail service business, CIDDA. At the buyer's level, the job pays quite well, and the work is rewarding, but you must be able to survive to reach that level.

Hartley has made a phenomenal climb from stock clerk to buyer to business owner in this competitive, high-pressured industry. In the early sixties, she was limited because the selection of retailing jobs available to Black women was limited. "I took a summer job as stock clerk in a Fifth Avenue retail establishment because they would not hire me for sales. After a week, I was convinced the field was for me," she recalls. "Everyone I talked to thought a Black woman pursuing a retailing career was a joke, since retailing was and to a great degree still is a difficult field for minorities to advance in. My mother encouraged me to believe I could do anything in life, so I started out with that premise."

After the stock clerk job, Hartley wanted to advance and left for a merchandiser distributor position with Franklin Simon, at the time a New York-based department store chain. Through hard work and determination, she moved into an assistant buyer's position in cocktail and better bridal dresses, where she stayed for a year and a half. She then went to work for Allied Stores Marketing Corporation International, a nationwide conglomerate of 146 stores. She felt a move to Allied would offer better career possibilities, but she had to start on the bottom in the clerical staff.

To further improve her career chances, she enrolled at Bronx Community College in the Bronx to pursue an associate's degree. At the same time, she was placed on Allied's executive training squad. As a member of the training squad, she was able to move out of the clerical job to become merchandise distributor. "In this position, I did distributing for Allied's different stores which were located throughout the country."

Merchandise selections were based on the different stores' needs, taking into account the climate and cultural needs in each area. For example, Miami is a resort area. "We planned, bought, and sent resort-oriented clothes there," Hartley remembers. "Some of the merchandise planners and distributors primarily planned and specialized in specific classifications." From merchandise planner and distributor, she was made assistant buyer in junior dresses, and subsequently buyer in the junior dress department.

After Allied, she went to Alexander's "Experiment One" as buyer. Experiment One was a small specialty chain owned by Alexander's. A year later, she went into the parent store. In the nine years there, Hartley was buyer in junior dresses, bathing suits, half-size dresses, and budget sportswear.

Taking advantage of a real career boost, Hartley accepted a buying position at New York's chic Bloomingdale's. As the store's first Black female buyer, she bought for a multimillion-dollar department in the junior sportswear division. "I was responsible for the day-to-day running of the department, as well as shortages, customer service, product development, planning and controls, buying of merchandise, scheduling of stock and sales staff, floor presentations, markdowns, advertising, the selection of merchandise for displays, et cetera," she says. "My responsibilities included everything that happened in the department including shortages caused by shoplifting, and returns."

Hartley supervised a large staff including those in Bloomingdale's branches. Her substantial responsibility meant hard work and long hours. "Working fifty hours a week was moderate. Then there was the work I had to take home. This homework included scanning magazines like *Vogue, Essence,* and *Glamour* and monitoring ads from other stores," she says.

Traveling was also another big responsibility for Hartley. A successful buyer must scan the country and foreign countries. For unusual "finds" she went to places like China, Singapore, and Uruguay. Hartley traveled constantly, spending about 50 to 60 percent of the time away from the New York store, including overseas and branch visits. Hartley thinks traveling was one of the job's great advantages. "I've traveled all over the world, and as a result have acquired exposure to cultures I may not otherwise have been exposed to," she says. "Although I enjoyed the traveling, there are disadvantages to that type of constant traveling. Being out of the country a great deal interfered with my personal life.

Working nights and holidays also has its effects. For most of my professional life, I had to put my personal life on the back burner."

After working for others for more than twenty years, Hartley left Bloomingdale's to start her own business, CIDDA (Creative Investment Developmental Dressing Alternatives, Inc.). CIDDA's services include investment dressing services and retail services. In the investment dressing services, Hartley helps clients coordinate their favorite pieces with quality separates in natural and blended fibers, buy customized suits and blouses from a Hong Kong tailor, and purchase ready-made and custom-tailored furs. In the retail services, she does planning (sales, and stocks, markups, markdowns, and gross margins), private label development, fashion newsletters, and overseas buying of open market goods.

Hartley also teaches at Fashion Institute of Technology in New York City.

Hartley feels retailing is a rewarding career. She feels a bachelor's degree will help you gain employment and later advancement. "Although it is not specifically required, the majority of the candidates hired for the training program do have bachelor degrees, two-year associate degrees, and some even have M.B.A.s. Some people are also hired into this business without a college degree. However, they generally have a significant amount of work experience to compensate for the lack of formal college training."

One of retailing's drawbacks is a low starting salary. It also takes a long time to move up in the ranks. "It generally takes three to four years to move to the level of buyer, if you are really good," Hartley says. "It is, however, more difficult for Blacks to advance in retailing. Let's face it, most Blacks in retailing are concentrated in the receiving area, sales, personnel, training, stock, and other nonmerchandising areas. Rarely are Blacks found in the merchandising areas. The picture has changed somewhat during the last decade as more Blacks have sought careers in retailing. The number of Blacks in buying positions, however, is still relatively low in comparison to Blacks in the nonmerchandising selling areas."

13

People-Watching Careers

PERSONNEL

If qualified, talented, and capable employees did not exist, how could today's private businesses or nonprofit, public sector, and government agencies survive? Employees are the precious commodities, the heart and soul of companies, organizations, and agencies. Companies are only as good as their employees. Personnel workers are needed to recruit, train, place, promote, and negotiate for the best possible employees available.

We have all come in contact with personnel workers. We have been lured to their companies by ads they've placed in newspapers. They are the first to screen us and arrange the interview processes. Or you may have first come into contact with personnel workers when they came to your college as recruiters.

Personnel staffers determine placement—where you will best fit in an organization. They write job descriptions after determining management's needs. They determine salaries, benefit costs, and arrange transfers to other departments if necessary.

Personnel workers also mediate employee-management disputes, negotiate contracts, research and develop plans to implement affirmative action/Equal Employment Opportunity guidelines, and establish and implement health, safety, and security policies for the plants we work in. Many are drawn to this field because they enjoy working with people, and they may choose employment and placement initially. There are other areas—training and development, compensation and benefits, employee and labor relations, health, safety, and security—in which you can career path depending on the size and type of organization you work for. The many areas of personnel work in which you can career path include personnel executive, Affirmative Action/Equal Employment Opportunity, testing, counseling, career planning, placement, training, and office and clerical supervision. Also included are the areas of research, benefits, personnel administration, wage and salary administration, job evaluation, employment, employee services/communications, recruiting, running your own personnel agency, and labor relations.

Career Pathing in Personnel

The bachelor's degree is rapidly becoming the educational requisite for personnel workers. In some instances, the Master of Business Administration (M.B.A.) with a specialization in organizational development will give you an added advantage in private industry.

After you complete your educational training, depending on the size and type of company you choose to work for, you may move into one of several areas: employment and placement, compensation and benefits, training and development, or employee and labor relations.

Employment and Placement: Employment interviewers, equal employment opportunity specialists, college recruiters, and employee orientation specialists—these personnel workers are most familiar to us.[1] They handle employment, placement, and recruit prospective employees from colleges. They interview and process job applications, handle affirmative action concerns, and familiarize us with the company we work for.

Compensation and Benefits: These workers develop job duties and descriptions, do compensation surveys, and analyze benefit programs.[2] Entry-level positions are wage/salary administrators, benefit planning analysts, and benefit administrators.[3]

Training and Development: They work with new employees who must often be trained in company procedures and policies or may need training in a specific area in which they will work.[4] They also govern on-the-job training programs. The training specialist is an entry-level position in this area.[5]

Employee and Labor Relations: These workers gather information, establish guidelines, and help management to negotiate labor contracts.[6] Once the contract is accepted, these workers will aid supervisors in interpreting and implementing the conditions of the contract. Entry-level positions in the employee and labor relations area are labor relations representative, plant personnel assistant, and employee relations specialist.[7]

Health, Safety, and Security: In this division of the personnel field, you will be responsible for helping your organization interpret and implement health and safety programs, keep records of accidents, submit government reports concerning health and safety policies in your organization, and develop and administer security programs. You might begin as a plant safety specialist in this increasingly important area of workers' health and safety.[8]

What Will You Earn as a Personnel Worker?

A recent survey by Abbott, Langer and Associates reported that the median salary for compensation analysts was $25,150; for benefits planning analysts, $23,890; for employee counselors, $26,712; for recruiters (professional/managerial), $26,460; for personnel information specialists, $24,300; for E.E.O./affirmative action managers, $35,000; for compensation and benefits managers, $33,417; for training and organizational development managers, $37,682; and for labor relations managers, $37,500.[9]

A recent Bureau of Labor Statistics survey reported that average

annual salaries of personnel directors in private industry ranged from
$35,444 to $65,874.[10]

New graduates who work for the federal government have starting
salaries of approximately $13,800 a year; those with a master's degree
start at approximately $21,000 a year.[11]

CAREER PROFILE

Charlene Taylor-Hill[*]
Assistant Vice-President/Training Manager
Southeast Bank, N.A.
Miami, Florida

A bachelor's degree in business administration from Bethune-Cook-
man College prepared Charlene Taylor-Hill for work in the training
and management development department in Southeast First National
Bank of Miami. As a training coordinator, she was responsible for developing and implementing instruction programs in the areas of supervisory and management skills, customer relations, performance evaluation, and time management. In addition, she has worked in the areas of
employment and the interviewing of management trainees for the
bank's corporate, retail, and international banking training program.

When an opening for personnel officer appeared in the trust department, the bank looked internally to fill it. Hill was selected. The trust
company is chartered as a separate affiliate of Southeast Banking Corporation and handles the financial management of trust estates and
investments for individual and corporate customers. "I was responsible
for managing the personnel function for the Trust Company, which
included everything from recruiting, interviewing, hiring, and salary
administration to the writing of position descriptions," says Hill.
"While I was the immediate supervisor for two people, I was responsible for the personnel matters of about two hundred forty-five employees
throughout the state."

Believing that additional training and education could help her advance, Hill earned a certificate in personnel administration from Florida
International University.

---

[*] Parts of this profile first appeared in the author's "Women in Banking," *Essence,*
November 1978.

Charlene Taylor-Hill feels her work in training has led to good advancement opportunities and afforded her a good opportunity to get on-the-job exposure to banking. "Training is an area of personnel I wish a lot more Black women were involved in. Women who have backgrounds in psychology and education would be particularly interested," she says.

A few years ago, Hill was promoted to assistant vice-president/training manager, and is no longer in the trust company of the bank. She is responsible for nineteen people statewide, and a half-million-dollar budget. Her department handles training, education, and development.

Career Aids

For career information, contact:

1. The American Society for Personnel Administration
   606 N. Washington St.
   Alexandria, Va. 22314

2. For the *Careers in Training and Development* booklet, contact:
   American Society for Training and Development
   1630 Duke St., P.O. Box 1443
   Alexandria, Va. 22313

All addresses are subject to change.

14

Government Careers

FEDERAL, STATE, AND LOCAL GOVERNMENTS

The federal government is the country's largest employer, and many of us are drawn to federal employment. Uncle Sam has provided a comfortable niche for many of us with its traditional job security, good fringe benefits, and retirement plan. Many feel the government offers the golden employment opportunity. Women, however, are still relegated to the lowest-paying and lowest-status positions and, as in private industry, we are lowest in the hierarchy.

Today, the government, like other employers, has recognized the inequities for women and minorities and is attempting to rectify some past injustices through programs like the Federal Women's Program. Attempts have also been made to pressure the government through legal action to prohibit the use of the Professional and Administrative Career Examination (PACE), which many feel bars minorities and women from access to professional positions. But women still face obstacles to career advancement and equal employment opportunities.

Now, and in the future, federal jobs are competitive to get and the present Administration's policy on government hiring freezes and layoffs will make getting employment tough. This presents a particular problem for the many Blacks who rely on federal employment. Many Blacks were forced to leave good government jobs at the end of the last Administration and reports indicate that many of these slots have not been refilled by us. The government, however, remains this country's largest employer and its existence as a career option is something to be considered.

Career Pathing in Federal, State, and Local Governments

Although Washington, D.C., is the federal government's headquarters, only about 12 percent of all federal employees work there. Many work in federal agencies around the country and abroad.

Requirements for most federal white-collar positions vary. To become a trainee in administrative and managerial occupations, you should show potential, but specialized knowledge of the field is not required.

Most professional and nonprofessional jobs are covered by a merit system. The civil service system covers about six out of every ten federal jobs. Under the system, there are competitive examinations and applicant selection. However, some agencies, like the Federal Bureau of Investigation, have their own merit systems.

To become competitive for civil service examinations, you must be a United States citizen, eligible for appointment, and meet minimum age, training, and work-experience requirements. After taking the examination, you will be notified of eligibility. If you are eligible, you will be placed on a list according to your test score. Veterans are given a ten-point preference.

After being placed on the list, you must then go through a selection process. The top three scorers' names are sent to agencies, which select one of the three. With this system, getting a job with Uncle Sam can be a lengthy process.

If you are selected, there are several types of appointments: temporary, term, career-conditional, career. Temporary appointments usually last not longer than a year and you cannot be transferred or promoted or put under the retirement system. A term appointee works on a special project which lasts more than a year but less than four and is also ineligible for the retirement system. However, a term appointee can be transferred or promoted within the project. A career-conditional appointee is put on probation for a year, but has promotional and transfer privileges and after the probation period, cannot be removed without cause or layoffs. After serving as a career-conditional for three years, a career-conditional can become a career appointee. The appointment brings promotional and transfer privileges, and these employees are among the last group to be laid off.

There are various career possibilities within state and local governments which many of us may overlook. For example, teaching positions with a local government may be doubtful, but employment with the state department of education may be available.

To find employment, you must have the best qualifications. Job qualifications tend to vary from state to state, but the majority of jobs are held by state and local government-district residents.

Since most state and local government jobs will fall within basic career occupations, you can find general educational requirements for these fields in other sections of the book.

What Will You Earn as a Federal, State, or Local Government Employee?

More than half of all government employees are paid under the General Schedule (GS); others are paid by the Postal Service Schedule and the wage system. Check with federal government agencies and city, state, and county agencies for exact salaries.

CAREER PROFILES

Beverly McAfee has worked her way up to a responsible position in the federal government. Mary Kate Bush started in banking and is now with the International Monetary Fund. Lillian Roberts worked for the

New York State Department of Labor. Sherry Suttles is Assistant County Manager for Mecklenburg County, Charlotte, North Carolina. R. Joyce Whitley is an urban planner and co-partner of Whitley/ Whitley, Inc., an architectural and urban planning firm. Although she doesn't work directly for a city, her company is employed to perform urban planning structurings for many cities. She represents one of the career options that urban planners can choose: business ownership. Juliet Blackburn-Beamon oversees advertising operations for a government transit system.

Beverly McAfee
Supply Systems Analyst
Defense Construction Supply Center
Columbus, Ohio

Beverly McAfee rose from clerk/typist to her present position. Her federal jobs included receptionist and supply clerk before she took and passed the Professional and Administrative Career Examination (PACE). After PACE, she was upgraded to inventory management intern. She was noncompetitively promoted to inventory manager and remained there about six years. When the government wanted to cut back the work force, she was realigned, taken out of her career field, and placed into another career: supply cataloging.

During her stint in supply cataloging, she became active with the Junior Executive Advisory Council (JEAC), an organization of junior executive interns that identified problems and came up with solutions. As the result of a JEAC project, she was loaned to the personnel department. There she received experience in formulating and analyzing surveys and giving presentations to management about attitudes on equal employment opportunities.

After six months, McAfee went back to cataloging but soon a position for EEO (Equal Employment Opportunity) specialist opened in the EEO office. She qualified as a trainee and in a year was promoted and moved to EEO specialist. She was finally assigned to the Federal Women's Program.

"The Federal Women's Program is an umbrella program under the Equal Employment Opportunity Commission. It is available primarily because women have been treated as minorities and denied access to the same career opportunities and career paths. In the government, we occupy some of the lowest paying jobs. We tried to provide programs to help remove these barriers," says McAfee. "Basically my approach was to provide women with information, to be accessible and to help them get beneficial training. We ran seminars on 'assertive training,' 'successful professional appearance,' 'goal setting,' and 'making responsible decisions.'" She used a variety of methods to reach large numbers of women: brown-bag sessions at lunch, after-work groups, Saturday workshops, three-day seminars.

McAfee is on leave from her job with the Federal Women's Program, and is working as a supply systems analyst. "The federal government is now computerized. I help make sure the systems are working correctly," she says. "I write procedures on how to use the system, train employees, and am a trouble shooter."

A busy career woman, she combines family and job with the help of her husband, Dr. Oliver McAfee.

Mary Kate Bush
Alternative United States Executive Director
International Monetary Fund
Washington, D.C.

Mary Kate Bush graduated from Fisk University with a double major in economics and political science. After graduation, she attended the University of Chicago and received her M.B.A. "As an economics major, I had taken a few business-oriented courses. Although I liked economics, I thought of it then as more an intellectual pursuit. Business seemed to offer more opportunities for hands-on practical experience," she says.

After graduating from the University of Chicago, Bush obtained a credit analyst position at Chase Manhattan Bank in New York. "At Chase, I went through the commercial lending training program, which focused on accounting and corporate finance, with some marketing and management. I felt it was a good supplement to the Chicago M.B.A. program. It was geared toward developing financial skills needed in evaluating companies and in making judgments about lending to those companies," she recalls. "It was similar in its rigor to my M.B.A. studies. The first six or seven months involved classroom work with case assignments. The second half was spent putting the acquired skills to use—analyzing live credit situations. Those who did not perform well for the training program quite likely did not remain with the bank or were transferred to other areas of the bank."

Bush completed the training program but decided to move to Citibank. She was given a lending job and handled large corporate clients. Shortly afterward, she was promoted to assistant treasurer—the first level officer position. She remained in that position for two years and then moved to Bankers Trust Company as an assistant treasurer. Nine months later she was promoted to assistant vice-president. She feels her promotion to assistant vice-president was because of her bringing in new accounts. "I managed accounts of some of the bank's major corporate relationships and brought in new profitable business."

Her financial astuteness paid off again and Bush was promoted to vice-president in the World Corporate Department.

As vice-president, Bush had great responsibility. "I managed ten major multinational accounts by taking care of some of their commercial and corporate financial needs," she says. "I managed a team of three people: two assistant treasurers and an assistant vice-president."

Bush left Bankers Trust to become executive assistant to the deputy Secretary of the Treasury at the Department of the Treasury. She since has become alternative United States executive director for the International Monetary Fund.

Lillian Roberts
Former Commissioner,
New York State Department of Labor

In the spring of 1981 Lillian Roberts was raised up one career notch. Former New York State Governor Hugh L. Carey appointed her the state's first Black Commissioner of the New York State Department of Labor. Roberts, who built an impressive labor career at District Council 37 (American Federation of State, County and Municipal Employees), reluctantly left her family of 110,000 Council members and approximately 600 staffers.

Roberts began climbing to the powerful position of New York State Labor Commissioner. As a youngster, in her native Chicago, Illinois, she saw her family forced onto welfare and she witnessed a great deal of suffering. The experience helped develop a humanitarian and caring attitude for fellow welfare recipients and others.

Like many, she wanted to improve her life-style, but also be of benefit to others. Her mother had stressed education and wanted her children to complete high school. Roberts wanted more and in 1944 won a scholarship to the University of Illinois. Unfortunately, the scholarship covered tuition only, but a brother contributed to her room and board. When he was drafted, there were no other financial resources and she was forced to drop out.

The reality of dropping out of school was painful to Roberts, but she was a survivor. Leaving school meant finding a job and the process was difficult. She applied for and took a $23-a-week nurse's aide position at the University of Chicago's Lying-In Hospital. It was there she had the first brush with unions. "I was the first Black nurse's aide they hired. After my appointment, they hired a former army sergeant as the director of nursing. She wanted fewer workers and more work out of them. She literally punished the best workers," she remembers. "The increased work load forced me to work the operating room, nursery, and the floor to help out. Ten aides left and were not replaced. We became very upset, tried to talk to the director, but were ignored. The shop steward was timid and did nothing. I called the union office, and was told we had a legitimate complaint and that if our shop steward didn't handle it, then we should elect another one."

The strong-willed Roberts was elected shop steward. "As shop steward, I gathered all the information on the number of aides who had left, the length of time that they were gone, and the number of people being exploited because of the personnel shortage. I presented the complaint to the nursing director and told her there were five days to respond. She became upset, screamed, and resented my presence," she recalls. "Two days later, she demanded an apology. I refused and she threatened to fire me, but I told her there were three days left for her response to the grievances. In the end, she hired ten people. It was a gratifying experience and I felt the union really worked."

The union intrigued Roberts and she began working to support it. Her reputation for hard work and accomplishments grew and she became secretary of the local. She cared about workers and respected their rights.

Victor Gotbaum, former executive director of District Council 37, was sent to Chicago to build up the hospital branch, and he became impressed with Roberts's work. Shortly afterward, she became an organizer for Districts 19 and 34 (State Mental Health Employees and Volunteer Employees) and was sent to work throughout Chicago. Her most difficult challenge was to organize white mental health workers to strengthen their rights. She considers their ultimate support one of her career's highlights. Soon, she moved into the national union's vice-president slot.

The late sixties was a time of turmoil. DC 37 and the Teamsters were pitted against each other trying to organize New York City's hospital workers. Gotbaum asked Roberts to come to New York to help. "I became involved in what became the largest single election between the AFL-CIO and the Teamsters. I set out to build the organization and requested the rank and file's help. We drafted a program that identified hospital workers' needs, and we presented it to hospital workers across the city. We beat the Teamsters by approximately eight hundred votes. On recount, a couple more hundred votes were added. The AFL-CIO was quite pleased," she says. "Originally, I came to New York for four months, but decided to stay longer. I had made a great many commitments to people. I promised the members upgrading programs to take them from nurses' aides to LPNs and nurses, educational programs, and legal and medical benefits." She has delivered those promises.

Moving up the ranks, Roberts progressively gained responsibility. One assignment led to a jailing. While she was on loan to organize state mental health workers, the late Nelson Rockefeller, then governor, used the Taylor Law to jail Roberts. She prompted strikes at several hospitals because the state refused to recognize the union. The sentence was stiff and she received thirty days and a $2,500 fine. Public support intervened and shortly thereafter, she was released.

In 1967, this dynamic woman became associate director of District Council 37. "As associate director, I was responsible for a hundred and fifty field people. My former staff handles grievances and does a fair share of negotiating. If there was a problem, I was called in," she says. "I was a strategy person. During New York City's fiscal crisis, I was able to get a substantial number of people rehired."

Often called the "First Lady of Labor," Roberts combines career and civic work and is active on many boards and in community groups. She has received numerous awards including the NAACP, New York Branch, "Woman of the Year"; Ebony Exclusive, Inc.'s "First Annual Scholarship Award"; "Woman of the Year Sojourner Truth Loyalty Award," Coalition of Black Trade Unionists (CBTU); and the Crown Heights Jaycees' "Service to the Community Award." She also has an honorary degree of Doctor of Humane Letters from the College of New Rochelle.

Roberts's rise to New York State's Labor Commissioner proves intelligence, tenacity, skill, and support can help lift one up. Lillian Roberts has always given. First, to her family by raising her deceased sister's three sons. Next, to the workers who have benefited by her existence.

Roberts's phenomenal career proves that perseverance pays off. It was her love for humanity and workers that pushed her up the ladder of success. If it hadn't been for the outstanding work that she did at District Council 37, she would have never caught the attention of former Governor Carey. She has taken that love for others and done a commendable job as Labor Commissioner. Her work in that position has benefited countless workers.

Roberts, who recently resigned her position as Commissioner, continues to shine in the Black community. She is still our "First Lady of Labor."

Sherry A. Suttles
Assistant County Manager
Mecklenburg County, Charlotte, North Carolina

Sherry Suttles set career goals and followed them. She has careerpathed to the top and became the only Black female city manager in the country. In her former position, she managed the day-to-day activities of Oberlin, Ohio, and was responsible for annual budget planning, tax collection and disbursement, law enforcement, and public works.

A city manager's position requires at least a bachelor's degree in a related area like political science or government. The degree is a qualifier for entry-level government positions, but a master's degree in public administration (M.P.A.) or in public policy is needed for advancement in the field.

Suttles prepared thoroughly for city management. Specializing in local government at Barnard College in New York, she graduated, did an impressive internship in New York City's Urban Fellowship Program, and received a master's degree in public policy from the University of Michigan.

Unlike many novice city managers who begin as assistant city managers, administrative assistants, or department head assistants, Suttles worked first as assistant director of the management development center at the International City Management Association's (ICMA) Washington, D.C., headquarters. She got that job after contacting the organization for a list of job openings. At ICMA, she met many people in the field. As a result, she met the city manager of Menlo Park, who persuaded her to consider a position as assistant city manager of Menlo Park, California.

Leaving Washington and heading for California, Suttles began her challenging job. "In Menlo Park, I was one of two assistant city managers with responsibilities for personnel and assisting with the budget. In my second year, I was responsible for housing rehabilitation, physical services planning, and public works," she remembers. "I stayed there for three years but then moved to Long Beach, California, to head a productivity improvement project. After a year and a half, I learned through an advertisement in an ICMA publication, and communication with people in the field, that the city manager position in Oberlin, Ohio, was available. I applied, interviewed, and was hired by the City Council."

Like most in the city management field, Suttles realized that frequent relocation is an occupational reality. She relocated for the third time in her career, to Ohio, and approached the challenge of managing the town which houses Oberlin College. The city's population was approximately 8,600 and Suttles explained its population when she was there: "It was an integrated town with about twenty-five to thirty percent Black and about twelve to fifteen percent elderly. So, it's very diverse."

Her responsibilities as city manager were varied. "I implemented policies set by the City Council, which set goals for the city. I then assisted them in implementing these goals. My job also included giving direction to city personnel, and directing, planning, coordinating, and supervising the police, public works, utilities, recreation, senior citizens, and fire departments. I also prepared and implemented budgets for each department," she says.

Sitting at the helm of city management can be tough: the job's demands can be difficult. "My job was very pressured because there were many deadlines to meet. It also meant constantly interacting with other government agencies and people in the community. At times, being city manager was a twenty-four-hour-a-day job. You can literally spend every waking hour on the job."

Suttles feels that city management offers exciting opportunities for Black women but advises that setting goals is important. "I've been successful in career pathing because I've set and followed my goals. You have to determine what you want to do. Even if you make a very general goal, like wanting to work in local government, it's important to set that goal," she says. "The professional association, ICMA, was my access to the field of city management and for other Black women, I feel it will also be the best route."

Although Suttles left the city management field briefly, and became government relations director for United Way Services in Cleveland, Ohio, she is now again in the field. "I came back into local government after a three-year stint in the nonprofit arena. My subsequent move into county government is part of a long-term career plan," she says. "I am back as an assistant primarily to help reentry into public life again."

In addition to her career in county management, Suttles is also the author of *Fielding's Africa: South of the Sahara*, which encourages people to know about, visit, and do business with Africa. She is also the mother of Kamau Ademola.

R. Joyce Whitley
Urban Planner/Vice-President
Whitley/Whitley, Inc.
Architects and Urban Planners
Shaker Heights, Ohio

R. Joyce Whitley is an urban planner with thirty-three years of professional planning experience. Urban planners, sometimes called city planners, most frequently work in city, county, or regional planning agencies or for agencies of the state or federal government. Some own their own businesses and work as consultants.

R. Joyce Whitley prepared for urban planning by getting a master's degree in City and Regional Planning from the University of Chicago. In addition, she has done course work in architecture at Illinois Institute of Technology. She also holds a master's degree in sociology from Western Reserve University, now Case–Western Reserve University. She received her bachelor's degree in English from Fisk University.

Choosing a career field which was new, Whitley picked urban planning primarily because of an interest in anthropology. "While studying for a master's in sociology," Whitley says, "I became interested in anthropology. When I discovered a planning program at the University of

Chicago, which had planning concerns for underdeveloped countries, I saw how I could relate that program to my interest in anthropology."

She enrolled in the city and regional planning program at the University of Chicago and began mapping her career plans. Before completing the master's, she received a position at the South East Chicago Commission's Planning Unit, which was the group doing the planning for the Hyde Park Community, the initial urban renewal project in the country. "It was the best project to be working on at the time," she says.

She subsequently was the director of community relations at the Community Conservation Board in Chicago (now incorporated in the Department of Development and Planning). From there, she worked as planner-in-charge with Jack Meltzer Associates, a prestigious city planning firm in Chicago. While with Meltzer, she established a reputation as a hard worker and cultivated a mentor relationship with her boss.

Her mentor proved to be very helpful to her career. She later moved with Jack Meltzer as a research associate to the Center for Urban Studies at the University of Chicago, one of the first such centers in the country. In 1967, Whitley became Chief Planning Advisor for the Model Cities Administration, Department of Housing and Urban Development, in Washington, D.C. After remaining in this position for a year, she joined her brothers James and William, who are architects in Whitley/Whitley, Inc., to combine her abilities with their architectural and planning skills.

As a planner, Whitley must develop plans for the revitalization of cities and communities. "A planner is concerned with the growth and revitalization of cities or communities by defining the guidelines architects work within. We specify where certain kinds of buildings can be developed, or if certain areas can be devoted to housing as opposed to commercial or industrial use; or if an area can be developed for high-rise buildings as opposed to low-rise. The objective is to develop a physical framework that will accommodate the people who live there and provide for them the necessary facilities like schools and transportation," Whitley says.

In thirty-three years, Whitley has seen many changes in the field. "Traditionally, the planner was concerned primarily with the 'ideal' community concept, which dealt primarily with physical elements. The planner sought to encourage development of the ideal physical form," she says. "Today, those issues may still be of concern but the overriding problem is how to keep people living in the cities. One of the projects I worked on in a midwestern city had a large proportion of abandoned buildings. In effect, people had written off living in this area, accounting for a population loss of over a hundred thousand people or one fifth of the city. My challenge was to develop plans to reestablish and revitalize this area so that people could and would want to live there again. Planners and the cities which hire them must plan communities and cities as places where people will want to live, or cities will continue to die."

Whitley knows that planners must be keenly aware of the prevailing economic situation. In view of the limited resources available today, cities and communities have to build in such a way that what is built today isn't negated tomorrow. They have to plan for future desires and needs as well as for what is to be implemented now.

As vice-president of Whitley/Whitley, Inc., Whitley is in a unique position of being associated with architects. "There is a direct relationship between planning and architecture. Planners develop plans which architects help implement. Our firm attempts to get planning jobs at the community level that will lead immediately to a development project. We then stay and provide architectural services for the development," she says. "Nationally, we have an edge because of our combined capabilities. Few of the Black architectural firms have recognized planning capabilities." Whitley and her firm have helped to plan and revitalize the Midtown Community in Gary, Indiana; Hough, Central, and Kinsman in Cleveland; and Woodlawn in Chicago. The firm has also helped plan communities in Saginaw, Michigan; St. Louis, Missouri; Indianapolis, Indiana; Buffalo, New York; and Washington, D.C.

Whitley's fine work has made her well known in planning circles. She has been on the Board of Governors of the American Institute of Planners (AIP), the Board of Directors for the Society of Consulting Planners, and a director of the National Organization of Minority Architects. She has toured several countries in Africa for the U. S. State Department's American Specialist Program, giving lectures and providing general consultation in planning and housing development, and participated in the White House Conference on Balanced National Growth and Economic Development and in the late Vice-President Humphrey's Task Force on Ethnic Minorities and Urban Problems.

She has also been a lecturer at the Center for Urban Studies, University of Chicago; visiting associate professor for the Department of Planning, Howard University; visiting professor, Department of Architecture and Planning at Cornell University; and on the visiting committee at the Graduate School of Design, Harvard University.

Because the focus of urban planning in the last decades has involved Black communities, Whitley feels the field is an area which should interest Blacks. "For the last thirty years, the major focus of urban planning in the U.S. has been on the segments of the city in which Blacks are concentrated. After the sixties, there was a push to increase the number of Blacks in the field," she says. "Because planning dealt so directly with Black communities and Black community people became involved in the planning process, Black professionals have been welcomed.

"Planning is primarily a graduate degree program and you will do better with the advanced degree. There are, however, a few good undergraduate programs like the one at the University of Cincinnati, which produces graduates who can successfully compete in the job market," she advises. After graduation, Whitley says employment will likely be in the public sector.

If you do not enter one of the planning undergraduate programs, you can prepare for graduate work by taking a liberal arts program. Although majors in architecture and engineering were once favored by future urban planners, now political science, sociology, economics, geography, and English are considered good foundations for the field. As an undergraduate, you should augment your studies with internships in urban planning offices and city planning commissions or departments. This on-the-job experience will make you more marketable.

On the graduate level, you can pursue a number of different degrees depending on the particular school: Master of Urban Planning; Master of Urban Planning and Urban Studies; Master of Arts in Architecture and Urban Planning; Master of Science in Environmental Planning; Master of Community Planning in Social Work; Master in Urban Transportation Planning; Master in Social Planning; Master of City and Regional Planning; Master of Business Administration or Real Estate and Urban Development. There are also many master-level joint degree programs which include planning; law; business; social work; urban design; architecture; landscape architecture (urban design); transportation engineering; public health; and civil engineering.

"Once in the job market, most planners find employment in public agencies where fifty or seventy percent of the jobs are. Others work at the federal level where national policies and programs are developed, or at the state level. Still others are consultants, serving either public agencies or private developers who are developing large subdivisions. The rest are teaching."

Whitley says the field can be lucrative: "It is a field where you can start out financially ahead of your peers but you will reach a ceiling very fast because most of you will work for public agencies. If you work in the private arena as a consultant, your salary can be very lucrative."

Juliet Blackburn-Beamon
Manager, Advertising and Promotion
MARTA
Atlanta, Georgia

Many people think narrowly of federal, state or local government careers. Most think of traditional jobs within the government. But government, like private industry has a wide variety of career opportunities. One such career area is advertising. Juliet Dobbs Blackburn-Beamon oversees the advertising operation for MARTA (Metropolitan Atlanta Rapid Transit Authority), the federal, state, city, and county subsidized transportation system. "It is my job to develop advertising programs that will encourage people in Atlanta to utilize the system," says Blackburn-Beamon. "Since we have been primarily a city that utilizes cars, we at MARTA must show the residents the benefits of using the train." She is responsible for MARTA's print and electronic media ads.

Blackburn-Beamon makes sure that the advertising and promotional needs of MARTA are met. The lengthy and complex creative process, which leads to completed advertising work, must be planned and created by Blackburn-Beamon and staff. She is responsible for coming up with the advertising concept; brainstorming sessions include input by staff. From these sessions evolve the advertisements' headline, visual (artwork) or copy (text).

Blackburn-Beamon's creative overseeing is multifaceted. She and her staff do most advertising and promotional work. "In print advertising, my responsibilities include getting the layouts completed and editing copy," she says. "I'm also involved in the marketing aspects. My job is to develop strategies, to recommend the best markets, vehicles to reach target populations, selling messages, and ways to get these messages across."

Blackburn-Beamon is responsible for MARTA's image building. "I help enhance MARTA's image by coordinating community programs and other good-will programs."

Blackburn-Beamon feels there are opportunities for Black women in the advertising end of government, but training and experience are prerequisites. She came to MARTA with a solid twenty-five-year background in retailing, training, and marketing. She has held buying positions at Alexander's and Lane Bryant, both New York department store chains, and a merchandise manager position at Sears, Roebuck and Company in Atlanta. She developed and taught a retailing and merchandising course for a manpower agency in New York, and later for a retail and wholesale company in the Bahamas. She worked as a marketing representative and public relations manager for Celanese but left New York to move to Atlanta. She was an independent marketing consultant for the U.S. government in West Africa, England, and this country and was senior marketing and research specialist for MARTA, Atlanta's transportation system before becoming advertising and public relations manager for M & M Products. She has since returned to MARTA.

Blackburn-Beamon's experience and expertise have landed her at the helm of MARTA's advertising department. Her creativity and administrative skills have contributed to MARTA's growing success.

Career Aids

Employment Information:

1. Federal Job Information Centers are located throughout the country and in Guam and Puerto Rico. For information, visit or call your local center. Many centers have toll-free numbers. For the nearest Federal Job Information Center in your state, see your local directory. If none is listed, call (800) 555-1212.

For information on city management careers, write to:
1. International City Management Association (ICMA)
   1120 G St., NW
   Suite 300
   Washington, D.C. 20005

For information on urban planning careers, contact:
1. American Planning Association
   1776 Massachusetts Ave., NW
   Suite 704
   Washington, D.C. 20036
   or
2. 1313 East 60th St.
   Chicago, Ill. 60637

All addresses are subject to change.

15

Not for Men Only

NONTRADITIONAL CAREERS

Traditionally, few women have worked in blue-collar positions such as construction laborers, carpenters, electricians, bricklayers, cement masons, insulation workers, painters and paperhangers, and plumbers and pipe fitters. Until recently, we had sidestepped these so-called "masculine" jobs for office jobs. Women soon realized that blue-collar positions are lucrative. Along with offering good union benefits, these jobs are among the higher-paying ones and pay considerably more than traditionally women's jobs like secretarial, clerical, and retail positions.

In the last decade, women have demanded inclusion in these high-paying fields. At the insistence of coalitions formed to ensure women's inclusion in the trades, there has been steady pressure to make the government uphold antidiscrimination laws and to make unions prohibit hiring discrimination practices. Blacks, too, have struggled for more work in the trades, and affirmative action guidelines and community activism have helped force our employment in these areas.

Still there are problems of racial and sexual discrimination. Women have testified that men at work sites have sexually harassed them by making lewd remarks, obscene gestures, and taking other derogatory actions. Blacks have felt unwelcomed and complained that bigoted remarks and overt racism are everyday occurrences.

As activist groups struggled to eliminate the sexism and racism in the trades, we are still asked to keep up the fight and seek employment in these areas.

There is, however, reluctance by some Black women to enter these occupations, which are often considered "dirty," "hard," and "unfeminine" work. But as more of us become heads of households, blue-collar work may be one of the options for better-paying jobs.

Our inclusion is crucial and needed. But many fear that these employment opportunities, like many of our gains, have been wiped away by the reversal of affirmative action programs and other factors have made job hunting in the blue-collar industry difficult.

Career Pathing in Nontraditional Careers

Most blue-collar training requires that you have a high school diploma or its equivalent. In many cases, to work in the trades and develop skills needed for employment, an apprenticeship or specified time of training is required. As an apprentice, you will receive on-the-job training, classroom instruction, and/or home study. Generally an apprenticeship can last from one to six years, but many are four years. During your apprenticeship, you will be paid and considered a full-time employee. After your apprenticeship, you will have full journeyman status.

You should spend considerable time selecting a trade. You should consider the nature, necessary educational and other requirements, and the employment outlook of the trade. You should also consider the physical requirements. Will you be lifting or climbing? Health hazards should also be examined. Will you be working in bad weather or working around material considered dangerous to your health?

Below is a selected list of trades and the apprenticeship requirements:

MACHINING OCCUPATIONS

All-around Machinist: Generally a four-year apprenticeship is the best preparation.[1] You should be mechanically oriented and adept at doing precision work. A high school diploma is highly recommended.

CONSTRUCTION OCCUPATIONS

Bricklayers, Stonemasons, and Marble Setters: On-the-job apprenticeship training for three to five years is usually required, as well as 144 hours of classroom training each year.[2] To enter apprenticeship programs, generally a high school diploma or its equivalent is preferred.

Carpenters: The best way to learn carpentry is to take the four-year apprenticeship program of on-the-job training and classroom instruction, but you can learn on the job.[3] Although the high school or vocational school diploma or its equivalent is not required, most employers prefer it.

Concrete Masons and Terrazzo Workers: Many learn on the job, but others participate in a two- or three-year apprenticeship program with classroom instruction.[4] A high school diploma is preferred by most employers and courses in shop mathematics and mechanical drawing are helpful.

Electricians (Construction): You should take a four-year apprenticeship. Some electricians, however, learn on the job.[5] Others learn skills in vocational school courses. In order to qualify for apprenticeship programs, you should have a high school diploma. Many employers prefer it. Course work in electricity, electronics, mechanical drawing, science, and shop are also helpful. In addition, in some cities, electricians are required to be licensed. Licensing requirements include passing a written test and demonstrating your skills.

Carpet Installers: Most learn their skills through on-the-job training, but others take formal apprenticeship programs.[6]

Painters and Paperhangers: A three-year apprenticeship program and classroom instruction is preferred, but such programs are limited.[7] Although preferred, the high school diploma is not required.

Plumbers and Pipe Fitters: Completing a four-year apprenticeship program and classroom instruction is highly desirable, but you may informally learn skills for this trade on the job.' A high school diploma is preferred and courses in mathematics, drafting, physics, and chemistry are helpful.

What Will You Earn in Nontraditional Careers?

All-around machinists averaged $12.45 per hour. Bricklayers and stonemasons in metropolitan areas earn about $380 per week; carpenters who aren't self-employed, about $325 a week; concrete masons and terrazzo workers earn approximately $365 a week. Electricians, $440; carpet installers, approximately $300; painters and paperhangers, $310; plumbers and pipe fitters, $400.

CAREER PROFILE

Martha Clanton is one of the growing number of Black women in the trades. She is an outspoken critic of the discriminatory hiring policies in the area and is working to help women and minorities overcome this problem.

Martha Clanton
Carpenter
New York, New York

Before becoming a carpenter, Martha Clanton took college course work and was an assistant teacher at the Henry Street Settlement in New York.

"When I was an assistant teacher at a day care center, I started looking for another job that paid well. Because I just needed a few credits to complete my college degree, every place where I interviewed said that I was either overqualified or underqualified. One day, I went to the library and read about women working in the blue-collar trades. I had always been interested in working with my hands and my father and grandfather are carpenters," she remembers. "I went to one of the Non-traditional Employment For Women [Formerly Women in Apprenticeship Project] Orientation Workshops. As a result, in 1979, I was among a group of twenty women who were indentured (put on the top of the list) as apprentice carpenters with the United Brotherhood of Carpenters and Joiners of America. To become indentured, I was required to fill out an application, take a physical examination, and prove that I had a high school diploma."

Prior work experience helped Clanton become indentured. "As a teenager, I had worked in an Arts for Living program and did some playground construction. My former teacher wrote an excellent letter of recommendation for me to the program's recruitment committee. This helped me get put on the list."

After Clanton was put on the apprentice list, she says, it was tough getting a job. "The way I got my first job was through an organization called 'Fight Back,' a community-based group founded by Jim Haughton and Gil Banks. Fight Back has a long history of organizing minorities to become included in the trades. To get employment, there is a cycle you must go through. You can't get a job without a union book and you can't get a union book without a job," she says. "There is also a great deal of resistance to letting women and minorities in the trades because of racism and sexism. The belief is that women and Blacks do not have the right to jobs that pay comparable salaries to our white counterparts."

Clanton was able to get employment on the Manhattan Sixty-third Street subway system that ran into problems and is now closed. "This job was forced to hire women and minorities because coalitions were complaining. These coalitions, like Fight Back, Black Economic Survival, East Tremont Trades, and South Brooklyn Construction Workers Association, have been instrumental in making contractors uphold affirmative action regulations," she says.

Clanton feels many people have false ideas of a carpenter's work. "When people think about carpentry, they usually imagine a person working with cabinets or around wood. Very few people do that type of work and it's an image that must be challenged," she stresses. "In New York, everyone is specialized. There may be a full journeyman who just puts up ceilings, walls, or, as in my case, concrete forms. A journeyman may be very good at her specialty, but can't put in a window or a door. In other parts of the country, the system is different. Because of New York's large skyscrapers and other buildings, there's more specialization."

Once in the trades, the work, as well as coexisting with fellow employees, may be hard. "When a woman or a minority person comes to the site, we are rarely taken under someone's wing and shown the ropes. Most of the men feel that we won't stick it out or we shouldn't be there," Clanton says. "At the sites, you can be isolated. Often I was the only Black woman at my site. From time to time, other women were hired, but soon fired. The company and men at the site said that the women couldn't handle it. Women are usually just placed on sites to satisfy quotas or because a coalition makes a demand."

There are other problems at the work site. "When you first start off, you must go through a phase doing 'gofer' work. It is the first test. This is where they try to break you. You either stay or quit. For example, one woman who had just come to the site was sent out for coffee for a crew of eight men. She was given the orders one at a time. This meant she had to climb innumerable steps, ladders, go get the coffee and return. The men watched the action like they were viewing a game. When you speak out, they say, 'Don't be so sensitive.' But on one job, I lost forty pounds walking back and forth. The important thing is not to take it to the point of breaking. There's also a great deal of racial name calling directed toward Blacks. It's not subtle, but very overt."

One major disadvantage of working in the trades is the continued resistance to affirmative action programs and health and safety regulations. Clanton says, "Many of us feel that the cutbacks in affirmative action programs have reversed the gains we've made. Just look at the statistics. They're even including clerical workers in the numbers of women and minorities in the trades."

Clanton has a history of fighting for our inclusion in the trades, and is a founding member of the United Tradeswomen. But many warriors get weary of battle. Clanton, who has found great difficulty in getting employment in the trades, is seriously considering giving up the battle, and getting more steady work in another field, though she applauds the sisters who have struggled and will continue to struggle for our right to work.

Career Aids

For general information about the following careers, contact:

BRICKLAYERS, STONEMASONS, AND MARBLE SETTERS

International Union of Bricklayers and Allied Craftsmen
International Masonry Apprenticeship Trust
815 15th St., NW
Washington, D.C. 20005

CARPENTERS

Associated Builders and Contractors, Inc.
729 15th St., NW
Washington, D.C. 20005

CONCRETE MASONS AND TERRAZZO WORKERS

International Union of Bricklayers and Allied Craftsmen
  Apprenticeship Training
815 15th St., NW
Washington, D.C. 20005

ELECTRICIANS

International Brotherhood of Electrical Workers
1125 15th St., NW
Washington, D.C. 20005

PAINTERS AND PAPERHANGERS

International Brotherhood of Painters and Allied Trades
1750 New York Ave., NW
Washington, D.C. 20006

PLUMBERS AND PIPE FITTERS

National Association of Plumbing-Heating-Cooling Contractors
180 S. Washington St.
Falls Church, Va. 22046

All addresses are subject to change.

Appendix A

SELECTED CAREER PLANNING/JOB RESEARCH BOOKS

1. Bear, John. *How to Get the Degree You Want: Bear's Guide to Non-Traditional College Degrees.* Berkeley, Cal.: Ten Speed Press, 1982.
2. Blanchard, Kenneth, and Spencer Johnson. *The One Minute Manager.* New York: William Morrow, 1982.
3. Blye, Robert W., and Gary Blake. *Dream Jobs.* New York: Wiley Press, 1983.
4. Bolles, Richard N. *The Three Boxes of Life.* Berkeley, Cal.: Ten Speed Press, 1981.
5. ———. *What Color Is Your Parachute?* Berkeley, Cal.: Ten Speed Press, 1984.
6. Catalyst. *Marketing Yourself: The Catalyst Guide to Successful Résumés and Interviews.* New York: Bantam Books, 1981.
7. ———. *Upward Mobility.* New York: Warner Books, 1982.
8. ———. *What to Do with the Rest of Your Life: The Catalyst Career Guide for Women in the 80s.* New York: Simon and Schuster, 1981.
9. Davidson, Peter. *Moonlighting.* New York: McGraw-Hill, 1983.
10. Davis, George, and Glegg Watson. *Black Life in Corporate America: Swimming in the Mainstream.* Garden City, N.Y.: Doubleday, 1985.
11. Denny, Jon S. *Careers in Cable TV.* New York: Barnes and Noble Books, 1984.
12. Douglas, Martha C. *Go for It! How to Get Your First Good Job.* Berkeley, Cal.: Ten Speed Press, 1983.

13. Gates, Anita. *90 Most Promising Careers for the 80s.* New York: Monarch Press, 1982.
14. Half, Robert. *Robert Half on Hiring.* New York: Crown Publishers, 1985.
15. Harragan, Betty Lehan. *Games Mother Never Taught You: Corporate Gamesmanship for Women.* New York: Warner Books, 1978.
16. Jackson, Tom. *The Perfect Résumé.* Garden City, N.Y.: Anchor Press/ Doubleday, 1981.
17. La Rouche, Janice, and Regina Ryan. *Janice La Rouche's Strategies for Women at Work.* New York: Avon Books, 1984.
18. Lathrop, Richard. *Who's Hiring Who.* Berkeley, Cal.: Ten Speed Press, 1977.
19. Medley, H. Anthony. *Sweaty Palms: The Neglected Art of Being Interviewed.* Berkeley, Cal.: Ten Speed Press, 1984.
20. Zimmerman, Caroline A. *How to Break into the Media Professions.* Garden City, N.Y.: Doubleday/Dolphin, 1981.

Appendix B

1. American Association of Black Women Entrepreneurs
   2300 South Elm/Eugene St.
   Greensboro, N.C. 27406
2. Alpha Kappa Alpha Sorority, Inc.
   5211 South Greenwood Ave.
   Chicago, Ill. 60615
3. Black Career Women
   2105 Madison Ave.
   Cincinnati, Ohio 45209
4. Black Women's Forum
   3834 Crenshaw Blvd.
   Los Angeles, Cal. 90008
5. Black Women in Publishing, Inc.
   P.O. Box 346
   Planetarium Station
   New York, N.Y. 10024
6. Chi Eta Phi Sorority, Inc.
   3029 13th St., NW
   Washington, D.C. 20009
7. Delta Sigma Theta Sorority, Inc.
   1707 New Hampshire Ave., NW
   Washington, D.C. 20009

8. General Federation of Women's Clubs
   1734 N St., NW
   Washington, D.C. 20036
9. Auxiliary to the National Dental Association
   6506 Connecticut Ave., NW
   Suite 25
   Washington, D.C. 20015
10. Links, Inc.
    1522 K St., NW, Suite 404
    Washington, D.C. 20036
√11. National Association of Black Women Entrepreneurs
    P.O. Box 1375
    Detroit, Mich. 48231
12. National Association of Colored Women's Clubs
    5808 16th St., NW
    Washington, D.C. 20011
√ 13. National Association of Negro Business and Professional Women's
    Clubs, Inc.
    1806 New Hampshire Ave., NW
    Washington, D.C. 20009
14. National Beauty Culturists League, Inc.
    25 Logan Circle, NW
    Washington, D.C. 20005
15. National Black Nurses Association, Inc.
    818 Harrison Ave.
    House Officers Bldg.
    Room 413
    Boston, Mass. 02118
16. National Council of Negro Women, Inc.
    701 North Fairfax St., no. 330,
    Alexandria, Va. 22314
17. National Coalition of 100 Black Women
    50 Rockefeller Plaza, Suite 46, Concourse Level,
    New York, N.Y. 10020
18. Women's Auxiliary, National Medical Association
    c/o National Medical Association
    1012 10th St., NW
    Washington, D.C. 20001
19. Zeta Phi Beta Sorority, Inc.
    1734 New Hampshire Ave., NW
    Washington, D.C. 20009

Notes

PLANNING YOUR CAREER

1. This method was developed by Richard Nelson Bolles, author of *What Color Is Your Parachute?* (Berkeley, Cal.: Ten Speed Press, 1984), and John C. Crystal, coauthor with Bolles on *Where Do I Go from Here with My Life?* (Berkeley, Cal.: Ten Speed Press, 1974).
2. Occupational daydreaming was first introduced by John L. Holland, Ph.D., author of *The Self-directed Search: A Guide to Educational and Vocational Planning* (Palo Alto, Cal.: Consulting Psychologists Press, 1970, 1977).
3. Catalyst, *Flexible Work Schedules* (New York: Catalyst, 1973), p. 8.
4. Ibid., p. 10.
5. Ibid., p. 12.
6. Ibid., p. 2–3.
7. Ibid., p. 4.

LAW

1. Alex Poinsett, "The Whys Behind the Black Lawyer Shortage," *Ebony,* 1974.
2. American Bar Association, *Law as a Career* (Chicago: American Bar Association, current edition), no page numbers.
3. Department of Labor, Bureau of Labor Statistics, Occupational Outlook Handbook (Washington, D.C.: Superintendent of Documents, 1986–87), p. 98.
4. Ibid.

HEALTH SERVICES

1. Department of Labor, Bureau of Labor Statistics, Occupational Outlook Handbook (Washington, D.C.: Superintendent of Documents, 1986–87), p. 152.
2. Ibid., p. 149.
3. Ibid., p. 150.
4. Department of Labor, Bureau of Labor Statistics, Occupational Outlook Handbook, op. cit., p. 150.
5. Ibid., p. 152.
6. Ibid., p. 146.
7. Ibid., p. 147.
8. Ibid., p. 153.
9. Ibid., p. 148.
10. Ibid., p. 149.
11. Ibid., pp. 155–56.
12. Lois Decker O'Neill, editor, *The Women's Book of World Records and Achievements* (Garden City, N.Y.: Anchor Press/Doubleday, 1979), p. 232.
13. Department of Labor, Bureau of Labor Statistics, Occupational Outlook Handbook, op. cit., p. 185.
14. Ibid., p. 168.
15. Ibid., p. 162.
16. Ibid., p. 196.

PSYCHOLOGY

1. American Psychological Association, *Careers in Psychology* (Washington, D.C.: American Psychological Association, 1978), p. 20.
2. Ibid.
3. Department of Labor, Bureau of Labor Statistics, Occupational Outlook Handbook (Washington, D.C.: Superintendent of Documents, 1980), p. 430.
4. American Psychological Association, *Careers in Psychology,* op. cit., p. 21.

ENGINEERING

1. College Placement Council, *CPC Salary Survey Final Report* (Bethlehem, Pa.: College Placement Council, 1986).
2. Department of Labor, Bureau of Labor Statistics, Occupational Outlook Handbook (Washington, D.C.: Superintendent of Documents, 1980), p. 285.
3. Bell System, *Minorities in Engineering* (Bell System), p. 12.
4. Ibid., p. 13.
5. Department of Labor, Bureau of Labor Statistics, Occupational Outlook

Handbook (Washington, D.C.: Superintendent of Documents, 1986–87), p. 67.
6. Ibid.
7. Ibid., p. 62.

SCIENCE

1. Lois Decker O'Neill, editor, *The Women's Book of World Records and Achievements* (Garden City, N.Y.: Anchor Press/Doubleday, 1979), pp. 152–81.
2. Ibid., p. 187.
3. Ibid., p. 407.
4. U.S. Department of Energy, Office of Public Affairs, *Black Contributors to Science and Energy Technology* (Washington, D.C., no date), pp. 11, 19.
5. Department of Labor, Bureau of Labor Statistics, Occupational Outlook Handbook (Washington, D.C.: Superintendent of Documents, 1986–87), p. 82.
6. Ibid.
7. Ibid., p. 83.
8. Ibid.
9. Ibid., p. 82.
10. Ibid.
11. Ibid., p. 89.
12. Ibid.
13. Ibid.
14. Ibid.
15. Ibid., p. 87.
16. Ibid.
17. Ibid., p. 89.
18. Ibid., p. 87.
19. Ibid., p. 302.
20. Department of Labor, Bureau of Labor Statistics, Occupational Outlook Handbook (Washington, D.C.: Superintendent of Documents, 1980), p. 302.
21. Department of Labor, Bureau of Labor Statistics, Occupational Outlook Handbook (Washington, D.C.: Superintendent of Documents, 1986–87), pp. 84, 85.
22. Ibid., p. 80.
23. Ibid., pp. 84, 85.

COMPUTERS

1. American Federation of Information Processing Societies, Inc., and the Council of Better Business Bureaus, Inc. (Arlington, Va.: 1977), p. 9.
2. Ibid.
3. Ibid., p. 11.
4. Ibid., p. 10.

ADVERTISING

1. Parts of this chapter first appeared in the author's article "The Ad World," *Élan,* February 1982.
2. American Association of Advertising Agencies, *Advertising, a Guide to a Career in Advertising* (New York, 1975), p. 1.
3. *The Gallagher Report,* "1980 Average Salaries for Key Jobs in Marketing, Advertising, Media, Public Relations," March 23, 1981, p. 3.

BANKING

1. National Association of Bank Women, *Careers for Women in Banking— Commercial Banking* (Chicago).
2. Ibid.
3. Ibid.
4. Ibid.
5. National Association of Bank Women, *Careers for Women in Banking— Trust Administration* (Chicago).
6. National Association of Bank Women, *Careers for Women in Banking— Marketing* (Chicago).
7. National Association of Bank Women, *Careers for Women in Banking— Operations* (Chicago).
8. National Association of Bank Women, *Careers for Women in Banking— Personnel Administration* (Chicago).

SALES

1. Department of Labor, Bureau of Labor Statistics, Occupational Outlook Handbook (Washington, D.C.: Superintendent of Documents, 1986–87), p. 257.
2. Ibid., p. 267.
3. Ibid., p. 258.
4. Ibid., p. 208.
5. Ibid., p. 259.
6. Ibid., p. 268.

INSURANCE

1. Insurance Information Institute, *Careers in Property and Liability Insurance* (New York, 1978), p. 14.
2. Department of Labor, Bureau of Labor Statistics, Occupational Outlook Handbook (Washington, D.C.: Superintendent of Documents, 1986–87), p. 51.
3. Ibid., p. 255.
4. Ibid.
5. Ibid.
6. Ibid., p. 52.
7. Ibid., p. 257.

REAL ESTATE

1. National Association of Realtors, *Careers in Real Estate* (Chicago), pp. 2–3, 10–16, 18–19.
2. Ibid.
3. Ibid.
4. Ibid.
5. Department of Labor, Bureau of Labor Statistics, Occupational Outlook Handbook (Washington, D.C.: Superintendent of Documents, 1986–87), p. 261.

RETAILING

1. The Council on Economic Priorities, *Help Wanted: Minorities and Women in the Retail Industry* (New York, 1974).
2. National Retail Merchants Association, *Your Opportunities in Retailing* (New York), p. 5.
3. Ibid., p. 7.
4. Ibid.
5. Ibid.
6. Ibid.
7. Ibid., p. 6.
8. Department of Labor, Bureau of Labor Statistics, Occupational Outlook Handbook (Washington, D.C.: Superintendent of Documents, 1986–87), p. 54.

PERSONNEL

1. American Society for Personnel Administration, *Careers in Personnel and Industrial Relations* (Berea, Ohio: American Society for Personnel Administration), p. 3.

2. Ibid.
3. Ibid.
4. Ibid.
5. Ibid.
6. Ibid.
7. Ibid.
8. Ibid.
9. Department of Labor, Bureau of Labor Statistics, Occupational Outlook Handbook (Washington, D.C.: Superintendent of Documents, 1986–87), p. 48.
10. Ibid.
11. Ibid.

NONTRADITIONAL CAREERS

1. Department of Labor, Bureau of Labor Statistics, Occupational Outlook Handbook (Washington, D.C.: Superintendent of Documents, 1986–87), p. 423.
2. Ibid., p. 380.
3. Ibid., p. 381.
4. Ibid., p. 385.
5. Ibid., p. 388.
6. Ibid., p. 383.
7. Ibid., p. 393.
8. Ibid., pp. 396, 397.

Index